ENDO

KENDO
Elements, Rules, and Philosophy

Jinichi Tokeshi

A Latitude 20 Book
University of Hawai'i Press
Honolulu

Printed in the United States of America

08 07 06 05 04 03   6 5 4 3 2 1

Library of Congress Cataloging-in-Publication Data

Tokeshi, Jinichi.
      Kendo : elements, rules, and philosophy / Jinichi Tokeshi.
            p. cm.
      Includes bibliographical references and index.
      ISBN 0-8248-2598-5 (paper : alk. paper)
      1. Kendo. I. Title.

GV1142.T76 2003
796.—dc21   2002034772

University of Hawai'i Press books are printed on acid-free paper and meet the
guidelines for permanence and durability of the Council on Library Resources.

Designed by Argosy

Printed by Versa Press, Inc.

To Dr. Noboru Akagi, who has helped to preserve and nurture kendo in Hawai'i

The Precepts of Kendo
Kendo is a way to discipline the human character through the application of the principles of the sword.

The Aims of Kendo Practice
One should learn kendo properly and diligently; mold the mind and body; cultivate a vigorous spirit through correct and rigorous training; strive for improvement in the art of kendo; hold others in esteem and behave with courtesy, honor, and sincerity; and forever pursue the cultivation of oneself. Thus will one be able to love one's country and society, contribute to one's culture, and promote peace and prosperity among all people.

—All Japan Kendo Federation, 1975

Contents

Preface

This book is a revised, enlarged edition of my earlier publication, *Aiea Taiheiji Kendo Manual* (1995). It includes additional illustrations, a discussion of the new rules and regulations, and the Nihon Kendo Kata. I have taken apart some of my equipment to see how it was constructed. I have placed uniforms and equipment on the floor of my study and have drawn numerous sketches. Over the years I have read many references and periodicals written mostly in Japanese and talked to many kendo instructors to learn about the art of kendo, its history, and its philosophy. I have also used tea ceremony *(chado)* books for the history of *reiho,* a book on knots, and history books. It became quite obvious to me why kendo and *bushido* (the way of the samurai) played a significant part in Japanese culture.

I have also included in this volume a glossary of kendo and kendo-related terms. As one might expect, it is sometimes quite difficult to translate certain Japanese terms related to kendo and its philosophy into practical English. I consulted dictionaries and other reference materials for accuracy, but some definitions are my own interpretations, while others are literal translations.

More experienced students of kendo may find some of the material too elementary. My intention is neither to insult experts nor to write extensively about the art, techniques, and philosophy of kendo. This book is an introduction to the fundamentals. I will be honored if some readers find kendo interesting and decide to pursue the art.

Acknowledgments

In writing this book I owe a great deal to the teachings of Dr. Noboru Akagi, the founder of the Aiea Taiheiji Kendo Dōjō and chairman emeritus of the Hawaii Kendo Federation Board of Directors. Some of the discussion on the technical aspects of kendo and its philosophy are taken directly from his seminars. I appreciate and acknowledge Dick Teshima's contribution to the chapters on Nihon Kendo Kata and the Rules and Regulations of *shiai* and *shinpan*. He also gave me useful suggestions in all phases of this book. Mr. Teshima has been a good role model for many kendo students, including myself, and is also responsible for conducting fundamental *keiko* in our joint sessions of all *dōjō* in Hawai'i. Mr. Rick Warrington created the beautiful cover diesign as well as the drawings in Nihon Kendo Kata. I would also like to thank Mr. Arnold Fukutomi, seventh dan, chief instructor at the Aiea Taiheiji Kendo Dōjō and current Chairman of the Board of Directors of Hawaii Kendo Federation. He demonstrated many difficult techniques for me and made them look easy. His input was invaluable. I extend my heart-felt appreciation to Dr. Edward Seidensticker for his many constructive criticisms. Finally, I thank my wife and my family for their patience while I stayed up late into the night pounding my keyboard.

PART I

Evolution

The History of Kendo

Kendo, from *ken* "sword" and *dō* "the way," is the highly ritualized practice and formal art of Japanese swordsmanship that emerged over a thousand years ago. Although its exact origin remains uncertain, kendo probably evolved gradually from combat experience. Stories of mythological gods and goddesses show that the ancient Japanese saw the use of swords in terms of rebirth and peace. For example, Amaterasu Ōmikami (the sun goddess) broke a sword given her by her brother, Susanoo no Mikoto, into three pieces to produce three more gods. A famous legend tells how Susanoo no Mikoto, who was banished from Takama no Hara (the Plains of High Heavens), descended to Izumo and destroyed Yamata no Orochi (the eight-headed, eight-tailed giant snake), and discovered a sword in its belly.

The swords mentioned in *Kojiki* (the *Records of Ancient Matters*) were *chokken* (the straight swords) made in Korea or China. Weak material and lack of a *shinogi* (the ridge along the back of the blade) made the *chokken* impractical for cutting, so it was used in combat only for thrusting.

The *chokken* improved from double-edged to single-edged ones made of iron. By the beginning of Heian Period curved swords, which were much stronger and more useful in cutting, emerged. This clearly marks the shift of technique from thrusting to cutting.

The Heian Period (794–1185)

During the Heian Period (eighth to twelfth centuries) annual contests of martial skill were held in Heian, the capital. Warriors must have practiced kendo and other martial arts diligently for these events. This same period saw a shift of power from the aristocrat to the warrior class, beginning with the Taira (Heike), Minamoto (Genji), and Hōjō clans. Art, literature, religion, and culture in general flourished during the Heian period, but complacency and corruption in the capital created anarchy in the land when the conflicts between the powerful Taira and Minamoto marked the end of the period. Taira no Kyōmori overpowered the Minamoto to control the government, but they lived like aristocrats and eventually lost their martial skills. On the other hand, the Genji, who fled to an eastern province, led a frugal life and trained in the martial skills, preparing to overcome the Taira.

The Kamakura, Muromachi, and Azuchi-Momoyama Periods (1185–1600)

The Taira clan briefly controlled the government until a two-year conflict that ended with the famous Dan no Ura campaign in 1185, in which the Genji prevailed. Minamoto no Yoritomo started his military government *(bakufu)* in Kamakura (near present-day Yokohama). The Minamoto clan declined with the death of Yoritomo in 1199, but Hōjō Tokimasa and his family rose to power through marriages, politics, assassinations, and military strength.

During the Hōjō's reign (1205–1333), Japanese military skills were tested twice by the mighty armies of Kublai Khan, which consisted of an armada of large ships. After bloody sea and land battles, a typhoon, which the Japanese called *kamikaze* (divine wind), sank and damaged most of the armada on the night of November 19, 1274, and eventually the Japanese turned away the Mongols in a major defeat with great loss of life. A much larger expeditionary force was similarly decimated by the *kamikaze* in 1281, and the Mongols never returned. Japanese samurai proved to be quite formidable in combat. Their spectacular victories no doubt heightened their confidence and interest in the martial skills.

However, the tremendous costs of the Mongol wars and government corruption weakened the *bakufu,* which met almost complete annihilation at the hands of the Ashikaga clan, backed by Emperor Godaigo. The government moved back to Muromachi, Kyoto. Ashikaga Takauji overthrew Godaigo and took control of the government. The aristocratic life in Kyoto weakened the Ashikaga *bakufu* and the country grew unstable. Constant civil wars threw Japan into turmoil, and ultimately cost the Ashikaga their ruling position. Historians call the latter part of the Ashikaga period, which was particularly bloody, Sengoku jidai (Age of the Warring States).

Zen Influence

During the Kamakura, Muromachi, and Azuchi-Momoyama periods, kendo gained a spiritual and religious quality through the incorporation of Zen Buddhism. Zen Buddhism originated in the tenth century in China at the mouth of Yangtze River. The form of Buddhism called *Ch'an,* derived from the Sanskrit *dhyana,* meaning "meditation," was adopted by the Chinese government and prospered. A Japanese Rinzai priest named Eisai (1141–1215) visited China and brought back *Ch'an,* known as Zen in Japan.

Zen emphasized simple but very effective concentration and self-discipline over memorizing the sutras. It is easy to imagine that samurai sought spiritual solace in Zen, since martial art training required concentration and death in combat was common. The simple Zen philosophy also promised the masses salvation as they endured constant warfare, earthquakes, and famine. Thus Zen influenced not only the martial arts but also other arts, architecture, and even the tea ceremony. It is interesting to note that Eisai also introduced quality tea and the tea ceremony to Japan; kendo terms such as *chakin shibori* often come from the tea ceremony.

Time of Warlords

This period (1490–1590) was a time of famous warlords, such as Takeda Shingen, Uesugi Kenshin, Date Masamune, Hōjō Sōun, Shimazu Yoshihisa, Imagawa Yoshimoto, Mōri Motonari, Oda Nobunaga, Toyotomi Hideyoshi, and Tokugawa Ieyasu. Brothers fought brothers and sons fought fathers in order to survive and take power. A time of turmoil and warfare continued until Oda Nobunaga, Toyotomi Hideyoshi, and ultimately Tokugawa Ieyasu unified Japan.

Muskets, introduced by the Portuguese through Tanegashima island in 1543, improved in quality and were mass-produced by skillful Japanese craftsmen within a few decades. Oda Nobunaga was the first warlord to use this new weapon on a massive scale when he defeated Takeda's cavalry during the Nagashino campaign in 1575. The introduction of muskets changed the tactics of warfare forever in a large battlefield, but in a close combat they proved to be useless and soldiers still depended on their lighter and shorter swords.

Swordsmanship
The style of kendo must have been very simple in the beginning and probably was limited to wielding *tachi* (long swords), stabbing or piercing one's enemy through openings in armor, or simply swinging the sword from horseback. However, it soon became apparent that a samurai who excelled in using the *katana* (Japanese sword) tended to succeed in close combat, which ultimately helped him get promoted more rapidly than other soldiers. It is not difficult to imagine that the demand for skills in kendo eventually created a need for kendo schools, where younger samurai could practice close combat skills.

Hayashizaki Jinsuke Shigenobu (1545–?) founded the Musōshinden ryū school, where students practiced the art of rapid drawing, called *iaido*. Many prominent swordsmen succeeded him, and his school continues to flourish today, although some swordsmen founded their own schools of *iaido*.

In *iaido* the opponent fight quite close to each other, so training does not require a large space. One slays the opponent with an initial strike in a single motion of drawing and cutting. This method of swordsmanship became popular because it was very practical. Other schools of *iaido* include Musōjikiden Eishin ryū, Hokki ryū, Shintō ryū, Seikiguchi ryū, Tamiya ryū, and Mugai ryū.

In the mid-sixteenth century, with the establishment of many different schools, kendo became more organized. The major schools were Kashima ryū from Hitachi (Ibaragi prefecture), Kage ryū (Shadow School) in Iga (Mie prefecture), Ittō ryū (One-sword-technique) on Izu Ōshima Island, and Jigen ryū, established by Tōgō Shigetaka (1561–1643) in Satsuma (Kagoshima prefecture). The practitioners of Jigen ryū emit a peculiar *kiai* (cry), which has been compared to a monkey's scream, which intimidates opponents. Their exercises with wooden swords against a standing pole are so vigorous that the pole actually smokes. Yakumaru Gyōbuzaemon (1607–1689), a student of Tōgō Shigetaka, further improved Jigen ryū, now known as Yakumaru Jigen ryū. Jigen ryū and Satsuma samurai played an important role during the Meiji Restoration and Seinan War.

Tsukahara Bokuden (1490–1571), the second son of a Kashima Shrine priest, was adopted by Tsukahara Tosa no Kami. He was trained under his father in Kashima no Hitachi (Secret Sword of Kashima), which was transmitted by the priests of the Kashima Shrine for many generations. His father also learned under Iizasa Chōisai (1387–1488), a priest of the neighboring Katori Shrine and founder of the Tenshin Shōden Katori Shintō ryū. Bokuden eventually established Kashima ryū, which he called Shintō ryū. The young

Ashikaga ShōgunYoshiteru and the famous lord Takeda Shingen both trained under Tsukahara Bokuden.

The founder of Kage ryū was Aisuhyūga no Kami Ikosai (1452–1538). Kamiizumi (Kōzumi) Ise no Kami Nobutsuna (1508? –1577), who learned his skills from Aisuhyūga no Kami, eventually named his school Shinkage ryū (New School of Shadow). When Kamiizumi (Kōzumi) Nobutsuna visited the territory of Yagyū, he instructed Yagyū Sekishūsai Muneyoshi (1529–1606), and thus was born the Yagyū Shinkage ryū (New Shadow School of Yagyū). A son of Yagyū Muneyoshi, Yagyū Tajina no Kami Munenori (1571–1646) eventually inherited Yagyū Shinkage ryū and became a chief kendo instructor of the Tokugawa shōgunate. This Yagyū Shinkage ryū is called Edo Yagyū to distinguish it from Owari Yagyū, which was established by Munenori's brother, Yagyū Hyōgonosuke Toshiyoshi (1579–1650). Toshiyoshi served as a kendo instructor to the lord of Owari (Aichi prefecture), Tokugawa Yoshinao.

Itō Ittōsai Kagehisa was born in 1550 on the island of Izu Ōshima. Itō left the island of his birth and trained himself by traveling the land. He eventually established Ittō ryū, and his followers included Oda Nobunaga. Ono Tadaaki (1565–1628), who became kendo instructor for the Tokugawa bakufu, along with Yagyū Munenori, inherited the Ittō ryū School. It was later called Onoha Ittō ryū (Ono-style one-sword-technique).

Oda Nobunaga (1542–1582) was attempting to unify Japan when he was assassinated by one of his generals, Akechi Mitsuhide, at Honnōji Temple. Nobunaga had already subjugated about half of Japan and placed his headquarters in Kyoto when he sent Toyotomi Hideyoshi (1536–1598), one of his loyal commanders, to the west to capture the mighty Mōri territory (Bitchū, present-day Okayama). Nobunaga was entertaining Tokugawa Ieyasu in the beautiful Azuchi castle when he received an urgent messenge from Hideyoshi requesting assistance. Nobunaga ordered Mitsuhide and other generals to head west to support Hideyoshi's army. Mitsuhide gathered over ten thousand men for this purpose, but instead he attacked unsuspecting Nobunaga, who was only guarded by a hundred men in Honnōji temple. Nobunaga committed suicide and was engulfed by a fire in the early morning of June 1, 1582. Hideyoshi returned rapidly, after securing a truce with Mōri, to hunt down Akechi Mitsuhide. Mitsuhide failed to anticipate the speed at which Hideyoshi's army would return and, unprepared, was completely defeated. Hideyoshi moved from the Azuchi castle to Osaka to establish his headquarters in a newly constructed magnificent Osaka castle and continued the work of unification Nobunaga had begun. He emerged as the strongest lord in Japan and renewed his alliance with Ieyasu. Hideyoshi almost succeeded in uniting the country, but he died before his job was completed. Within two years of Hideyoshi's death Japan was divided into two camps, consisting of the largest armies ever assembled in the history of Japan. They fought at Sekigahara in Mino Province (Gifu prefecture) in the fall of 1600. The western camp was composed of Ishida Mitsunari and other Toyotomi Hideyori (son of Hideyoshi) followers based in Osaka castle, and the eastern camp was composed of Tokugawa Ieyasu (1542–1616) and his followers, based in Edo castle. Tokugawa Ieyasu won and the period of unrest in Japan came to an end.

The Edo Period (1603–1867)

Peace that prevailed much of the Edo period meant that many samurai lost their jobs as warriors. These samurai were called *rōnin* (lordless or out-of-work samurai). During the Edo period the schools of kendo numbered more than three hundred. This offered *rōnin* who excelled in kendo a chance to work, and the Edo period produced numerous legendary kendo masters, such as Miyamoto Musashi, Tsukahara Bokuden, Kamiizumi Nobutsuna, Yagyū Sekishūsai Mitsuyoshi, Yagyū Tajima no Kami Munenori, Tōgō Shigetaka, Nakanishi Chūzō, Chiba Shūsaku, and Yamaoka Tesshū. The philosophy of those kendo masters changed the emphasis from courage, skill, and individual potential to loyalty to the lords or masters, as emphasized by Confucianism. This philosophy was an important backbone of the feudal system under the Tokugawa government.

The latter half of the eighteenth century also saw the evolution of modern kendo, with its use of protective kendo armor, similar to what is worn today, and the use of bamboo swords *(shinai),* now standard equipment. Before the use of these protective devices, kendo was practiced only as *kata* (form), since actual, freeform sparring was dangerous.

The Meiji, Taishō, and Pre-WWII Periods (1868–1941)

During the Meiji period the influx of Western culture as well as the prohibition of wearing swords in public greatly lessened public interest in the traditional Japanese martial arts, including kendo. The Meiji government issued an edict prohibiting the wearing of the swords in

public and of topknots in 1870. However, because of the entrench-
ment of the sword in Japanese culture, it was many years before former samurai gave up their swords. There are many photographs from
this period of awkward-looking samurai with topknots in Western-
style uniforms with two swords in their belt and of samurai without
topknots but wearing traditional *haori* (coat) and *hakama* (skirt) with
Western-style shoes. Floods of samurai, estimated to number two mil-
lion, lost their jobs after the Meiji Restoration. Sakakibara Kenkichi
took to the streets with fellow kendo practitioners, demonstrating
kendo skills for money. Such demonstrations are said to have been
popular for a while. The Seinan War of 1877, between Satsuma
(Kagoshima) samurai headed by Saigō Takamori and the conscripted
former civilian (farmers and merchant) and low-ranking samurai
government troops, led people to renew their interest in kendo.
When the Metropolitan Police Department adopted kendo, it
became popular among students and the public. The Sino-Japanese
War (1894–1895) stimulated interest in kendo, and the Dai Nippon
Butoku Kai, a national organization to popularize kendo, was
established in 1895.

In the early twentieth century, interest in kendo grew with its
inclusion in the high school physical education curriculum. The victory in the Russo-Japanese War (1904–1905) brought international
recognition of Japanese military power. In 1906, Butoku Kai established the three-form *kata* to promote kendo in grade schools.
Watanabe Noboru assisted in establishing the first college kendo federation in Tokyo Imperial University and popularized kendo among
college students. The educational reform of 1911 mandated the incorporation of kendo into the Japanese school curriculum. The Dai
Nippon Teikoku Kendo Kata was formed in 1912 by a group of
prominent kendo practitioners of different schools, including Negishi
Shingorō, Tsuji Shinpei, Naitō Takaharu, Monna Tadashi, and Takano
Sasaburō, to teach kendo fundamentals to high school students. In
1928, the Zen Nihon Kendo Renmei (All Japan Kendo Federation)
was established. It held annual examinations for promotion. The
kendo masters of this period included Nakayama Hakudō, Sasamori
Junzō, Mochida Moriji, Saimura Gorō, Ogawa Kinnosuke, and
Nakakura Kiyoshi.

The Japanese imperial government promoted all forms of martial
arts, especially kendo, during the conflict in Manchuria (1931), the
invasion of China (1937), and eventually World War II (1941–1945).

The Post-WWII Period (1945–Present)

After World War II the practice of kendo was temporarily prohibited by the order of General Douglas MacArthur of the occupying Allied Forces. The Dai Nippon Butoku Kai was disbanded and kendo instruction in the schools was suspended. However, the Zen Nihon Kendo Renmei (AJKF) was reestablished in October 1952. In 1955 kendo was recognized as one of the events in Japanese National Athletic Competition. Gradually kendo began to earn international recognition. In 1970 the International Kendo Federation (IKF) was established, and it held its first world tournament in Japan.

Zen Nihon Kendo Renmei

The Zen Nihon Kendo Renmei has been very active in the promotion of kendo and the kendo spirit. We see technical changes in Kendo Kata, and several major changes in the rules and regulations governing the promotion of ranking and honor titles as well as *shiai* (matches) and *shinpan* (judging). The AJKF holds seminars to train instructors and sanctions tournaments.

The Purpose of Kendo Training

In kendo training, young children learn the kendo fundamentals. The main objective of long-term kendo training is to develop a youngster into an adult who will be an asset to the community. The requirements for becoming a good citizen are to have a strong, healthy body, a sound and good character, mental fortitude, understanding of the meaning of *wa* (compassion and cooperation), and an ability to cope with the rigors and adversities of life. Proper and diligent kendo training will nurture these qualities.

The overall goal of kendo, according to the Zen Nihon Kendo Renmei, is to "mold the mind and body, cultivate a vigorous spirit through correct and a rigorous training, strive for an improvement in the art of kendo, hold others in esteem courtesy and honor, associate with others with sincerity, and forever pursue the cultivation of the self," as well as to develop the ability to observe, analyze, understand, and promptly cope with any situation without fear, doubt, or surprise.

Shinai (Bamboo Sword)

Bamboo for *Shinai*

In the past skilled artisans in Japan produced the *shinai,* but due to the shortage of craftsmen as well as raw material, today Japan depends on foreign countries to provide substantial quantities of *shinai* and other kendo *bōgu* (equipment). Countries such as Taiwan, Korea, and China supply an estimated 85 percent of *shinai* and other equipment. As the quantity of non-Japanese products increases, it becomes more and more urgent to set general standards for *shinai* and equipment. Recently, at the request of the Zen Nihon Kendo Renmei, the Japanese manufacturer has set a strict standard for such equipment.

Bamboo is native to many Southeast Asian countries. There are over 600 different species of bamboo. In Japan, varieties include: *madake, mōsō chiku, hachiku, kurochiku,* and others. They grow very well in the south, but have some difficulty in the north. *Madake* is the most suitable in making *shinai* because of its thickness, hardness, malleability, and flexibility. The circumference of the bamboo for a *shinai* should be approximately 18 cm. Only about 150 cm of the bamboo growing above ground should be used for a *shinai*. The bamboo does not have annual rings like trees, but with each passing winter it will harden its grain. This improves the flexibility of bamboo.

In Kyoto, bamboo is harvested at three years. In Kyushu, it is harvested at five to seven years. The most appropriate month to harvest bamboo is October or November, because the bamboo absorbs less water during these months. For a *shinai,* the ideal thickness of bamboo is twice as thick at the trunk as at the tip *(kensen).*

History of the *Shinai*

According to one theory, Kamiizumi Nobutsuna was the first to make *shinai* from bamboo. He repeatedly split the end of a length of bamboo, then wrapped it with leather. He called this a *fukuro shinai* (wrapped bamboo sword). Some people think this type of *shinai* was used during the match between Kamiizumi (Kōzumi) Nobutsuna and Yagyū Muneyoshi. Even today in Yagyū Shinkage ryū, this *fukuro shinai* is used for practice.

Bōgu consisting of *men, dō, kote,* and *tare* was improved and widely used by the Jikishinkage ryū expert Naganuma Shirōzaemon in the mid–Tokugawa period.

Nakanishi Chūzō was the first person to make the *shinai* in its present form, four pieces of bamboo: *tsuru, sakigawa, tsukagawa,* and *tsuba.* The length originally varied, but around 1856, the Kōbusho (Tokugawa military office) forbade the use of a *shinai* longer than 3 *shaku* 8 *sun* (117 cm).

Parts of the *Shinai*

The parts of the *shinai* are shown in Fig. 1. The *monouchi* (striking zone), Fig. 1b, is defined as one fourth of the entire *shinai* located between the *nakayui* (Fig. 1h) and the *kensen* (sword tip, Fig. 1e). The *tsuka* (Fig. 1c) is covered by the *tsukagawa* (handle sheath, Fig. 1k), which is made of leather. The *sakigawa* (leather cap, Fig. 1f) keeps all four pieces of bamboo tightly bound at the *kensen* with the small metal fasteners, *tomegane* or *chigiri,* shown in Fig. 1o. The *nakayui* (middle tie, Fig. 1h), which is a small leather strap, secures the *tsuru* to the *shinai* at one end of the *monouchi.* The *komono* (Fig. 1i) is used to hook the *tsuru* as it goes through the *tsukahimo.* The *tsuka himo* (Fig. 1j) ties the open end of the *tsukagawa* and fastens to the *tsuru* (Fig. 1l), which is usually made of nylon or *koto* (a Japanese musical instrument) strings. The *tsuba* (Fig. 1m) is made of leather or plastic, and the *tsubadome* (Fig. 1n) is made of rubber.

The term *shinai* derives from *"shinau,"* meaning to flex. This is in contrast to the real sword and *bokken* (wooden sword), both of which are rigid.

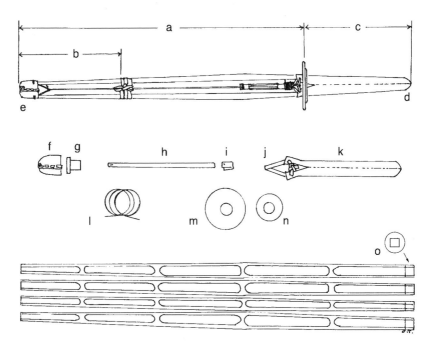

Fig. 1. Parts of the *shinai*: (a) *jinbu* (blade area); (b) *monouchi* (striking zone); (c) *tsuka* (handle); (d) *tsukagashira* (handle butt); (e) *kensen* (sword tip); (f) *sakigawa* (leather cap); (g) *sakigomu* (rubber stopper); (h) *nakayui* (middle strap); (i) *komono* (leather hook); (j) *tsukahimo* (leather handle strap); (k) *tsukagawa* (leather handle sheath); (l) *tsuru* (string); (m) *tsuba* (hand guard); (n) *tsubadome* (hand guard stopper); (o) small metal fastener, *tomegane* or *chigiri*.

Manufacture of the *Shinai*

The art of *shinai*-making requires splitting the bamboo along the grain, correcting the curvature, and shaving the bamboo into an appropriate thickness. It takes about ten years to master these skills. The most proficient craftsmen can make only thirty to forty *shinai* a day. The bamboo harvested in the autumn and winter months are split roughly and dried in the shade for approximately six months while being exposed to the dry winter air. Craftsmen avoid drying bamboo in direct sunlight because sunlight robs the bamboo of resin and flexibility of grain.

It takes approximately twenty steps to make a *shinai*. When splitting the bamboo, craftsmen prefer to use a machete that cleaves bamboo along the natural grain. In contrast, a machine will cut straight regardless of the natural grain, thus severing the fibers. Where the bamboo curves, craftsmen straighten it with a *tamegi* (straightening instrument). In the final shaping of individual pieces of bamboo, they use several different planes.

Purchasing a *Shinai*

When you purchase a *shinai,* you must pay close attention to the following characteristics.

Thick wood and relatively light weight indicate that the bamboo was young. Slightly reddish coloration is preferable over light coloration. Dark stains near the knots are thought to indicate stronger bamboo. Also, a clear and prominent grain over the cut surface is thought to indicate durability in bamboo. If a fine powder spills from the *shinai* when it is swung, it may be worm-infested. Examine it carefully for evidence of worm infestation, such as the presence of tiny holes.

When buying a completed *shinai,* make sure that the *sakigawa* (leather cap) is not too thick, that the *tsukagawa* (handle sheath) is firm, and that the *tsuru* (string) is taut. A *nakayui* (middle tie) should be in the correct position and tightly bound. A loose *tsuru* or loose *nakayui* can cause the *sakigawa* to come off the *shinai.* The danger is that when you strike the *men* (headgear), the *sakigawa* can come off and the tips of bamboo can pass between the *mengane* (*men* bars) to pierce your opponent's eyes.

Make sure that the bamboo piece does not cave in and slide between adjacent bamboo pieces when you press it with your fingers. This happens when the individual pieces are not well balanced. You can check this by looking at the neat and even grooves between the individual pieces. A good *shinai* has greater tensile strength. If you bend the *shinai* by pressing the tip on the floor, it should spring strongly.

It is common to have four knots in a *shinai.* The *ichiban bushi* (first knot) is at the largest diameter of the *shinai.* There are two knots located above and one knot located below the *ichiban bushi.* It is prudent to buy two or three *shinai* with the knots in similar locations so that when one *shinai* is damaged, you can salvage the undamaged parts to make a new *shinai.* When assembling the different pieces of bamboo into a new *shinai* you must make a saw mark at the same level on each piece so that the *tomegane* or *chigiri* (small metal fastener) fits into all pieces at the same level. Another way to alter a *shinai* to your taste is to shave off bamboo near the *tsukagashira* (butt end) to form an oval called a *koban* (an old Japanese oval-shaped gold coin). It is relatively simple to shave about 10 cm of *tsuka* (handle) near the *tsukagashira* with a plane to form an oval. Some people like the feel of an oval-shaped *tsuka* in their hands because the *tsuka* of a real sword is shaped like a *koban.* The four pieces of bamboo should be of equal thickness.

It is preferable to buy a *shinai* made from a single bamboo. However, *shinai* are often made from different bamboos, because south-facing knots are slightly higher than those facing north, due to the differential growth rates between the north and the south sides of the bamboo. Inspect your *shinai* carefully to make sure it is free of any damage or physical defects.

Size of the *Shinai*

The most appropriate length of a *shinai* for an individual kendo practitioner is from ground to about the height of the chest (see Fig. 2a). The weight of the *shinai* should be such that one can freely swing it without strain. It is easier to swing the *shinai* when the center of

Fig. 2. Proper length of the (a) *shinai* and (b) *tsuka*.

a

gravity is closer to the *tsuka*. The diameter of *shinai* varies and depends on individual preferences. However, the *shinai* must fall within the minimum and maximum standard range of weight and length set by the Zen Nihon Kendo Renmei. To get the proper length of a *tsuka*, grab the *shinai* at the *tsuba* with your right hand and bend your right elbow. The *tsuka* end should touch the inner portion of your right elbow (see Fig. 2b). The following tables show *shinai* length and weight regulation (1999 revision).

Table 1: *Shinai* Dimensions for *Ittō*

	Gender	Middle School	High School or Equivalent Age	University and Adult
Length	Both	≤114 cm (37)	≤117 cm (38)	≤120 cm (39)
Weight*	Male	≥440 g	≥480 g	≥510 g
	Female	≥400 g	≥420 g	≥440 g
Diameter	Male	≥25 mm	≥26 mm	≥26 mm
	Female	≥24 mm	≥25 mm	≥25 mm

Table 2: *Shinai* Dimensions for *Nitō*

		University and Adult (18 years and older)	
	Gender	Daitō (long sword)	Shotō (shorter sword)
Length	Both	≤114 cm (37)	≤62 cm (20)
Weight*	Male	≥440 g	280 g ~ 300 g
	Female	≥400 g	250 g ~ 280 g
Diameter	Male	≥25 mm	≥24 mm
	Female	≥24 mm	≥24 mm

*The weight of the *shinai* without the *tsuba*. The diameter of the *tsuba* should be about 9 cm.

Shinai are customarily measured by *sun* (39 *sun* is *sanku;* 38 *sun* is *sanpachi;* 37 *sun* is *san nana;* and 36 *sun* is *saburoku*).

    1 *shaku* = 10 *sun* = 100 *bu* = 30.22 cm = 11.9 in.
    1 *sun* = 10 *bu* = 3.03 cm = 1.19 in.
    1 in. = 2.54 cm = 0.84 *sun*
    1 oz = 28.6 g; 100 g = 3.5 oz

Types of *Shinai*

Shinai come in different lengths and weights but the shapes also vary (see Fig. 3). The *dō* area (first knot above the *tsuba*) of the *shinai* determines the type. The *dōbari shinai* (Fig. 3a) is the thickest. Its center of gravity is near the handle, making it effective in *suriage waza* (sliding

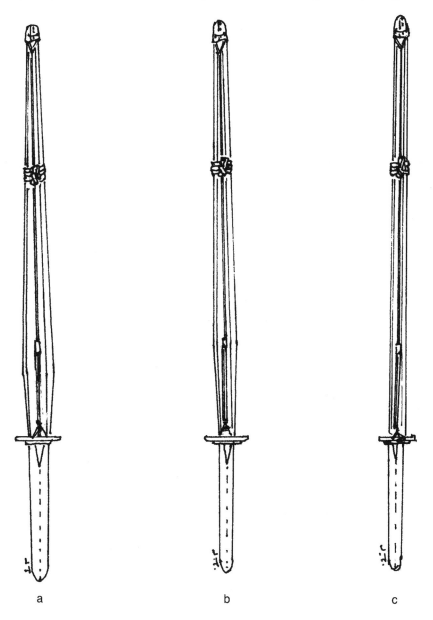

a   b   c

Fig. 3. Types of *shinai:* (a) *dōbari* (round); (b) *chūbuto* (medium); (c) *hosomi* (slim).

up technique). The *chūbuto shinai* (Fig. 3b) is thicker than the *hosomi* and thinner than the *dōbari*. The *hosomi* (Fig. 3c) is the thinnest.

Care of the *Shinai*

As is true with any kendo equipment, the *shinai* should be used with great care. *Shinai* represents a Japanese sword that was considered to be a spirit of the samurai and as such it should be handled with respect. Never step on or step over a *shinai*. If you have to go to the other side of a *shinai*, remove it first or go around it. Never use a *shinai* as a cane or lean on it. Young kendo practitioners should be taught not to play around with the *shinai* before and after practice. When practice is finished store the *shinai* in a *shinaibukuro* (*shinai* sack) and keep it in a cool place.

Depending on how often and intensely you practice, your *shinai* may last anywhere from a few days to many months. The durability also depends on the material the *shinai* is made of. The synthetic carbon *shinai* lasts longest but it does break eventually. A heat- and smoke-treated *shinai* is fairly hard and durable. This type of *shinai* is treated to retain the natural resin of the bamboo longer and is more brownish than natural bamboo. The natural bamboo *shinai* is weakest of the three but with proper care it can last longer.

Probably the most detrimental element to the life of *shinai* is drying of the bamboo. A *shinai* should be disassembled and oiled thoroughly before use. It is ideal to oil after each practice but if this is not practical, you should take it apart and oil it at least periodically. Use a soft cloth saturated with light oil to wipe the bamboo. If the *shinai* splinters you should immediately take it apart and repair it so it does not split completely and injure your opponent. You can repair the splinters by shaving off the splintered area with a knife or plane. Also it is important to shave off the sharp edges of the length of *shinai* with a knife or plane to keep the bamboo from splintering. You should use a rubber bottle opener or something of similar, resistant material to remove the *tsukagawa* to avoid excessive stretching of the leather. If the *tsukagawa* is too loose, moisten it, then dry it in a cool area, allowing it to tighten over the *tsuka* as it dries.

How to Tie the *Shinaibukuro*

The *shinaibukuro* comes in many different styles. The modern *shinaibukuro* comes with zippers and snaps, and the use of it is self-explanatory. But the traditional *shinaibukuro* must be tied, as shown in Fig. 4.

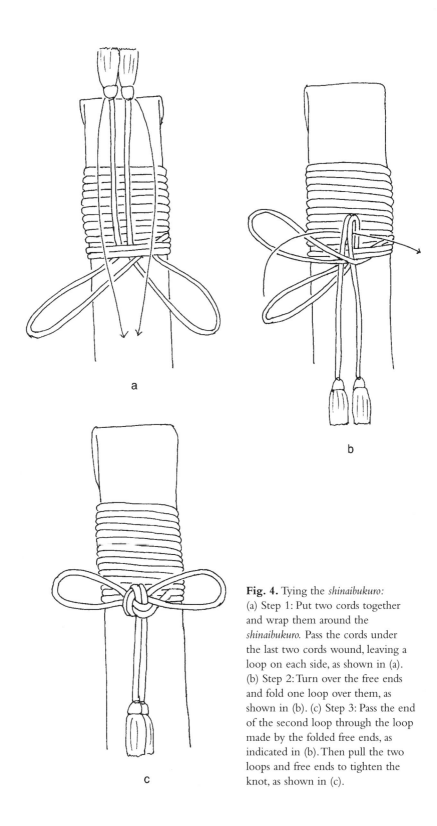

a

b

c

Fig. 4. Tying the *shinaibukuro:*
(a) Step 1: Put two cords together
and wrap them around the
shinaibukuro. Pass the cords under
the last two cords wound, leaving a
loop on each side, as shown in (a).
(b) Step 2: Turn over the free ends
and fold one loop over them, as
shown in (b). (c) Step 3: Pass the end
of the second loop through the loop
made by the folded free ends, as
indicated in (b). Then pull the two
loops and free ends to tighten the
knot, as shown in (c).

The *Chigiri* or *Tomegane* (metal fastener)

A small square metal fastener fits into the grooves to secure the four pieces of bamboo. When different pieces from different *shinai* are put together, new grooves are cut evenly to fit the new *shinai,* as illustrated in Fig. 5.

How to Tie the *Tsuru* (String) and *Nakayui* (Middle Strap)

The *Sakigawa* (Leather Cap)

The *sakigawa* (Fig. 6) plays an important part in making the *shinai* safe. The thickness of the *sakigawa* is 2 mm and with the 22 mm thickness of the *shinai,* the diameter of *shinai* over 37 sun is 26 mm (22 mm + 2 mm + 2 mm) and 25 mm (1 mm less) measured at 1 cm from the tip for high school students and adult women, respectively. In *nitō ryū* (the two-sword school), the *daitō* (long sword) is 25 mm for men and 24 mm for women. The *shōtō* (short sword) is 24 mm for both men and women. This is considered a safe diameter because the *mengane* are up to 15 mm apart at the widest opening (*monomi* or *mushamado*). All *sakigawa* are 5 cm in length. If your *sakigawa* becomes damaged, you should replace it with a new one. You should not attempt to mend it. The damaged *sakigawa* could expose the tip of *shinai* and endanger your opponent. One end of the *tsuru* is tied

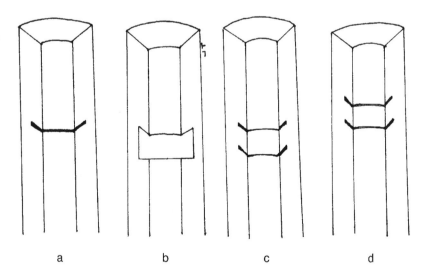

a   b   c   d

Fig. 5. Grooves cut to fit the new *shinai:* (a) original groove; (b) with *chigiri;* (c) new groove cut evenly with original groove; (d) new groove cut evenly with original groove.

a

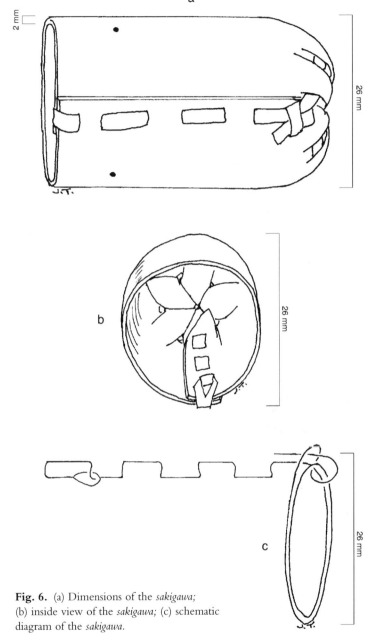

Fig. 6. (a) Dimensions of the *sakigawa;*
(b) inside view of the *sakigawa;* (c) schematic
diagram of the *sakigawa.*

securely to the *sakigawa* using a *moyai musubi* (bowline knot). The *sakigawa* wraps around the tip of the *shinai* with the *sakigomu* in it.

The three types of *sakigomu* (rubber stopper) are shown in Fig. 7. Fig. 8 illustrates how to tie the *tsuru* to the *sakigawa* in a *moyai musubi* (bowline knot). Fig. 9 shows how to tie the *tsukahimo*. Fig. 10 demonstrates how to tie the *tsuru* to the *tsukahimo*. See Fig. 11 for tying of the *tsuru*.

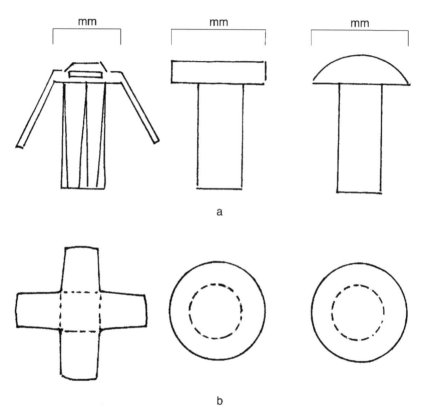

Fig. 7. Three types of *sakigomu:* (a) side views (17–24 mm); (b) top views.

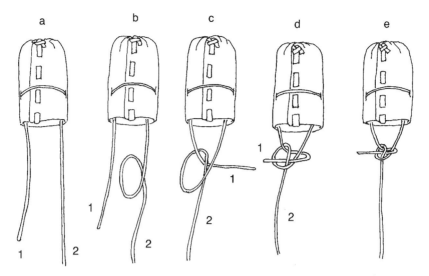

Fig. 8. Tying the *tsuru* to the *sakigawa:* (a) Insert the *tsuru* into the tiny hole in the *sakigawa* from the inside, bring it halfway around the outside of the *sakigawa*, and reinsert it from the outside. (b) Make a loop in string 2. (c) Insert string 1 through loop 2. (d) Bring string 1 behind and around string 2, and back through the loop. (e) Tighten the knot by pulling strings 1 and 2.

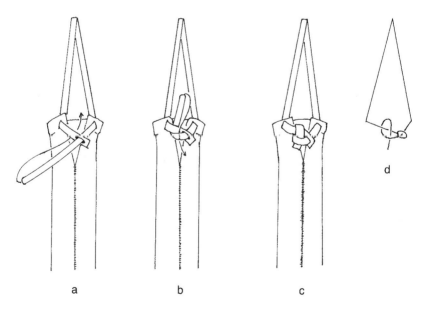

Fig. 9. Tying the *tsukahimo:* (a) Thread the *tsukahimo* through the slit in the cuff of the *tsukagawa* and reinsert it into a slit at the opposite side of *tsukagawa*. Insert one end of the *tsukahimo* into a slit in the opposite end of *tsukahimo*. (b) Pass the free end of the *tsukahimo* under and over the joined ends to form a loop. Insert the free end into this loop. (c) Tighten by pulling the loose end. (d) Schematic diagram of the knot.

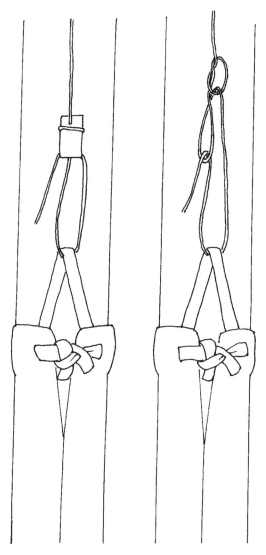

a   b

Fig. 10. Tying the *tsuru* to the *tsukahimo:* (a) If you are using a *komono,* the *tsuru* goes through the lower portion of it. (b) If you are not using a *komono,* thread the *tsuru* through the *tsukahimo,* then thread the *tsuru* through its own loop, as illustrated.

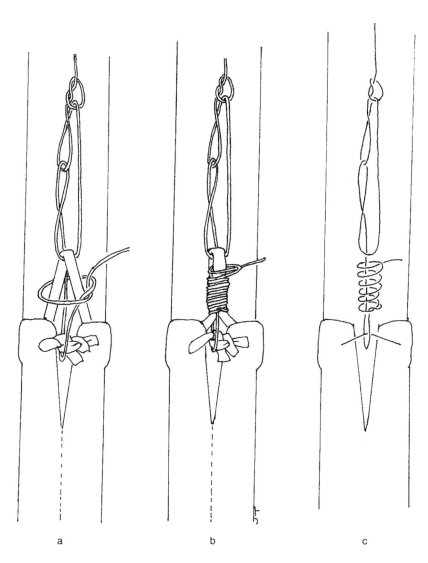

a   b   c

Fig. 11. Tying the *tsuru:* (a) Pass the *tsuru* under the knot of the *tsukahimo,* then tie the *tsuru* in an overhand knot around the *tsukahimo* and itself. (b) Wrap the *tsuru* tightly around the *tsukahimo* several times, then tie it off with another overhand knot. (c) Schematic diagram of the tied *tsuru.*

How to Use the *Komono* (Leather Hook)

Komono literally means "small piece." It is a small piece of leather that can be cut off the *nakayui* (middle strap). You can make a hole or a slit in the middle as illustrated in Fig. 12. The *komono* serves as an anchor to the *tsuru,* as it loops around the *tsukahimo.*

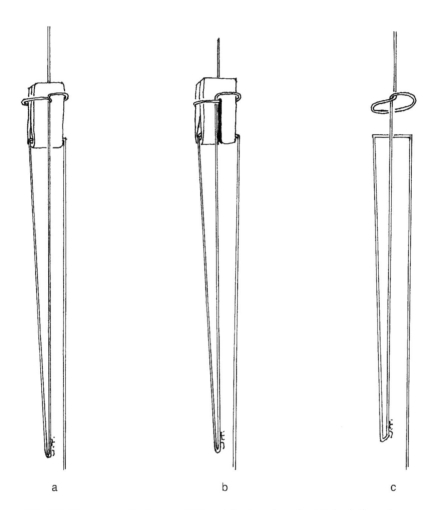

a   b   c

Fig. 12. How to use the *komono:* (a) Insert the *tsuru* from front to back through a small hole in the *komono* and loop it around the *komono* once. Hook the *tsuru* into the loop, wrap it once around the *tsukahimo,* and make another loop around the end of *komono.* (b) The slit in the middle of *komono* works the same way as the hole. (c) Schematic diagram of (a) and (b).

The *Nakayui* (Middle Strap)

The purpose of the *nakayui* is to secure the *tsuru* (string) to the *shinai* to prevent the *sakigawa* from coming off on impact, as the *shinai* bends and the distance between the *tsuba* (hand guard) and *kensen* (sword tip) shortens. The *nakayui* is tied at a quarter of the length of the *shinai* (including the *tsuka*) from the *kensen.* To prevent the *nakayui* from moving around during practice some instructors recommend a knot in the *tsuru.* The *nakayui* is tied securely to the *shinai,* as shown in Fig. 13.

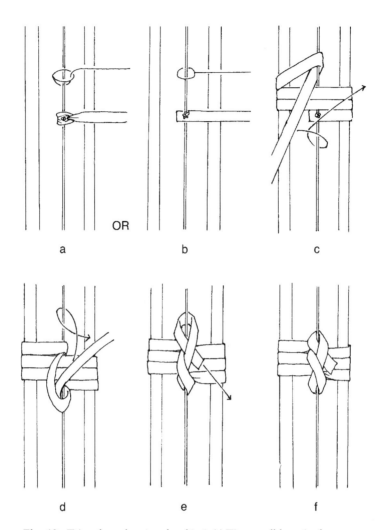

Fig. 13. Tying the *nakayui* to the *shinai:* (a) Tie a small knot in the *tsuru* to secure the *nakayui*. Insert the free end of the *nakayui* into the hole at the other end of it. (b) Alternatively, the *tsuru* can go through the opening of *nakayui*. (c) Wrap the *nakayui* around the *shinai* three times. Hook the free end around the *tsuru*. (d) Loop the free end of the *nakayui* around the *tsuru* on the other side of the wrap. (e) Bring the free end back up and around the *tsuru* once again. Then tuck the free end under the loop. (f) Tighten the *nakayui* by pulling the free end.

How to Trim the *Tsukagawa* (Leather Handle Sheath)

Occasionally it is necessary to trim the *tsukagawa* to fit different *shinai*. See Fig. 14.

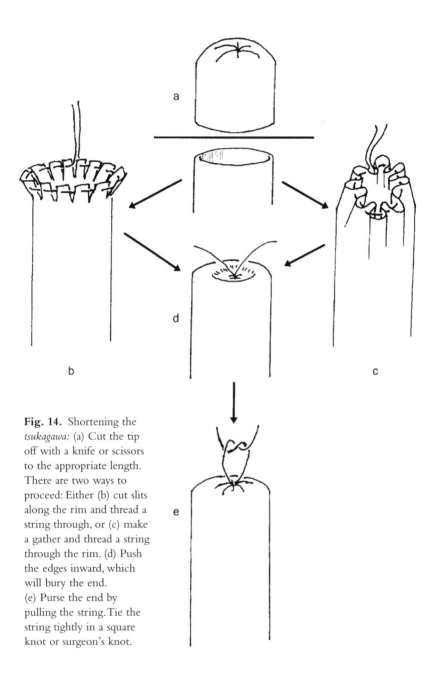

Fig. 14. Shortening the *tsukagawa:* (a) Cut the tip off with a knife or scissors to the appropriate length. There are two ways to proceed: Either (b) cut slits along the rim and thread a string through, or (c) make a gather and thread a string through the rim. (d) Push the edges inward, which will bury the end. (e) Purse the end by pulling the string. Tie the string tightly in a square knot or surgeon's knot.

The *Bokken* or *Bokutō* (Wooden Sword)

Bokken or *bokutō* means "wooden sword." The *bokken* is made from a variety of woods such as oak, cherry, loquat, and ebony. The *bokken* is often used during Nihon Kendo Kata practice. The parts of the *bokken* are shown in Fig. 15.

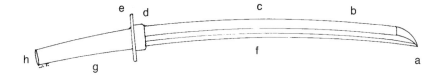

Fig. 15. Parts of the *bokken:* (a) *kissaki* (cutting tip); (b) *monouchi* (striking zone); (c) *jinbu* (blade area); (d) *tsubadōme* (hand guard stopper); (e) *tsuba* (hand guard); (f) *mine* or *mune* (back of sword); (g) *tsuka* (handle); (h) *tsukagashira* (handle butt).

The Japanese Sword

Japanese swords are used for Nihon Kendo Kata or *iai* practice and performance. It is important to be familiar with all the parts of the sword so that you can handle it with safety and respect. The parts of the Japanese sword are shown in Figs. 16, 17, 18, and 19.

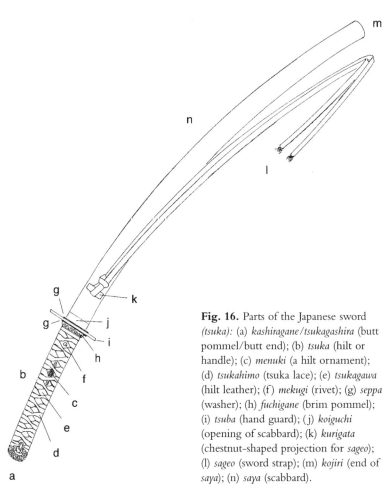

Fig. 16. Parts of the Japanese sword *(tsuka):* (a) *kashiragane/tsukagashira* (butt pommel/butt end); (b) *tsuka* (hilt or handle); (c) *menuki* (a hilt ornament); (d) *tsukahimo* (tsuka lace); (e) *tsukagawa* (hilt leather); (f) *mekugi* (rivet); (g) *seppa* (washer); (h) *fuchigane* (brim pommel); (i) *tsuba* (hand guard); (j) *koiguchi* (opening of scabbard); (k) *kurigata* (chestnut-shaped projection for *sageo*); (l) *sageo* (sword strap); (m) *kojiri* (end of *saya*); (n) *saya* (scabbard).

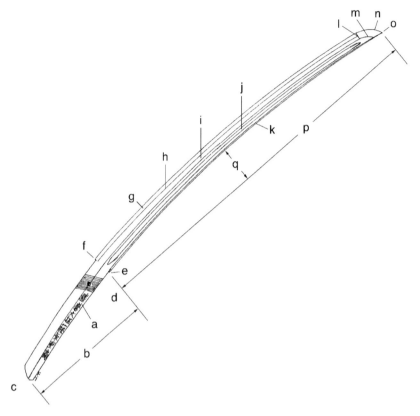

Fig. 17. Parts of the Japanese sword (blade): (a) *omote mei* (face emblem); (b) *nakago* (tang); (c) *nakagojiri* (end of tang); (d) *yasurime* (file marks); (e) *munamachi* (end of *mune*); (f) *hamachi* (end of blade); (g) *ha* (blade, an area between the tempered line and the cutting edge of the blade); (h) *hamon* (temper line pattern); (i) *shinogi* (ridge of sword); (j) *hi* (groove); (k) *mune/mine* (roof of sword); (l) *yokote* (straight, small ridge at right angles to the *shinogi* before the *kissaki*); (m) *koshinogi* (small ridge/ *shinogi* in the *bōshi* area); (n) *bōshi* (outline of the blade on the *kissaki* beyond *yokote*); (o) *kissaki* (sword tip); (p) *nagasa* (length of the sword); (q) *sori* (curvature).

How to Hold the *Shinai*

It is important to hold the *shinai* correctly. The left hand grasps the *tsuka* with the base of the little finger wrapping the *tsukagashira* (Fig. 20a). The ring and middle fingers snugly grasp the *tsuka*, but the index finger and thumb grasp it loosely. The right hand is about one fist width above and has a grip like the left (Fig. 20b). Grasp the *tsuka* tightly with the little and ring fingers, but less tightly with the middle finger. The index finger and thumb should hold the *tsuka* very lightly. Both thumbs point toward the floor, and the web of each thumb and index finger form a V over the midline of the *tsuka* (Fig. 20c).

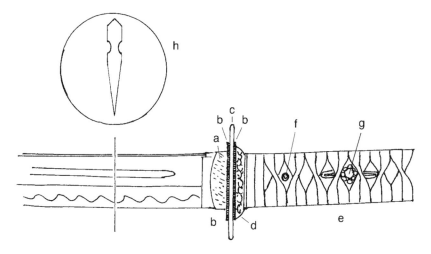

Fig. 18. Parts of the Japanese sword (handle, hand guard, and blade): (a) *habaki* (metal collar or sleeve); (b) *seppa* (washer/spacer); (c) *tsuba* (hand guard); (d) *fuchigane* (brim pommel); (e) *tsuka* (hilt); (f) *mekugi* (rivet); (g) *menuki* (hilt ornament); (h) cross section of the blade.

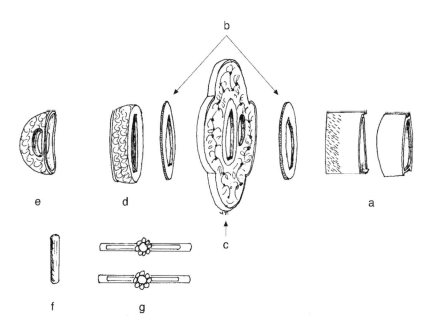

Fig. 19. Parts of the Japanese sword (schematic of hand guard): (a) *habaki* (metal collar or sleeve); (b) *seppa* (washers/spacers); (c) *tsuba* (handguard); (d) *fuchigane* (brim pommel); (e) *kashiragane* (butt pommel); (f) *mekugi* (rivet); (g) *menuki* (hilt ornament).

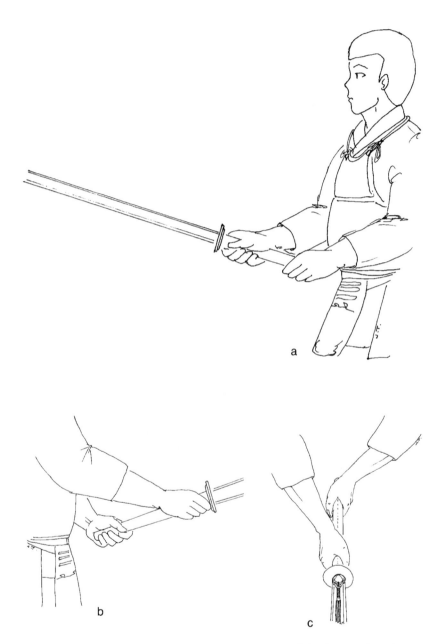

Fig. 20. Holding the *shinai*: (a) View from the left. The left hand grasps the *tsuka* with the right hand placed one fist length ahead. (b) View from the right. The base of the little finger of the left hand wraps the *tsukagashira*. (c) View from front. The web of each thumb and index finger form a V over the midline of the *tsuka*.

Kendōgi
(Kendo Uniform)

The *Dōgi* (Jacket)

The *dōgi* may be black, white, or indigo *(ai)* and is usually made of cotton but may be nylon or another synthetic fabric. The indigo-dyed *dōgi* must be washed with care in cold water with a small amount of vinegar and no detergent to avoid excessive bleaching of the dye. If the *dōgi* becomes faded, it is possible to restore the color by dying it with a commercially available dying agent.

Two pairs of *munehimo* (straps), one on the inside and the other on the outside, are used to tie the *dōgi* closed. In the case of woman's *dōgi,* another pair of straps or Velcro may be added to prevent the front of the *dōgi* from opening inadvertently.

Hakama (Trousers)

The *hakama* is a pair of skirt-like trousers worn by both men and women. Traditionally, the *hakama* is worn during practice. A *koshiita* (backplate) in the rear of the *hakama* straightens the posture. There are five pleats in front and one pleat in the rear. The five pleats in front indicated mercy *(jin)*, justice *(gi)*, courtesy *(rei)*, wisdom *(chi)*, and faith *(shin)*; and the one in the rear stands for truth *(makoto)*.

The *hakama* should be hand-washed with great care so the pleats remain in place. If the *hakama* is washed by machine the pleats are often lost. The *hakama* should be hung upside down from a line with the pleats pinned in place to dry.

Chakusō

The term *chakusō* refers to putting on the kendo uniform—the *dōgi* and the *hakama*—and the *bōgu* (protective gear).

How to Don the *Dōgi*

When you put on the *dōgi*, tie the inner and outer *munehimo* tightly (Fig. 21). Pull the front of the *dōgi* downward, bringing the collar close to the back of your neck to assure correct posture. Women may want to add an extra pair of *himo* (straps) or Velcro to prevent the *dōgi* from opening inadvertently. When the *dōgi* is worn properly, the collar in front forms a V. Make sure both sides are equally tight and that the *dōgi* does not puff out in back. Students should check each other after donning the *keikogi* (practice uniform).

Fig. 21. Putting on the *dōgi*.

How to Don the *Hakama*

To put on the *hakama*, always place your left leg in first, then your right leg. When you remove the *hakama*, step out with the right leg first. Figs. 22 and 23 show how to tie the *maehimo* (front belt) and *ushiro himo* (back belt) of the *hakama*.

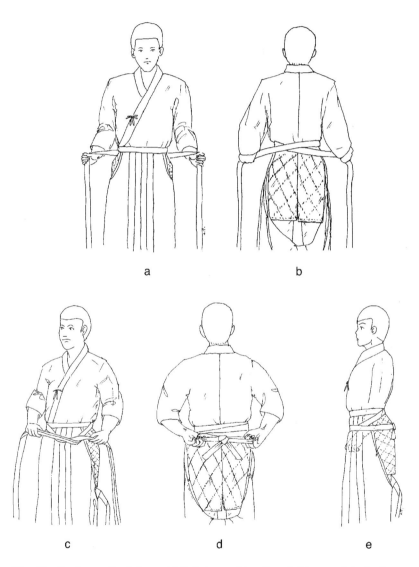

Fig. 22. Putting on the *hakama*: (a) Pull the *maehimo* (front belt) around the back, cross them, and bring them to the front. (b) Cross the *maehimo* at the back.
(c) Holding the *maehimo* at the side, bring them to the lower abdomen and cross one over the other by twisting the top one around. (d) Tie the *maehimo* behind in a *hanamusubi*. (e) Side view of the tied *maehimo*.

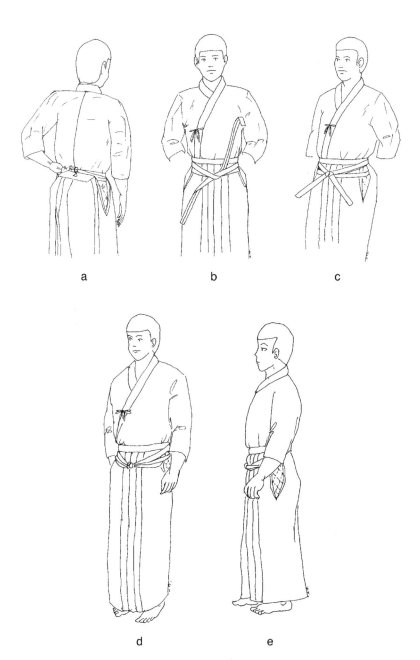

a   b   c

d   e

Fig. 23. Putting on the *hakama* (cont.): (a) Tuck the *hera* or *koshibasami* (fastening plate) into the *maehimo* or *obi* (sash). (b) Take the *ushiro himo* (back belt) and bring both ends to the front. Cross one end over the other. Loop one under the front *obi* and pull. (c) Tie the ends of the *ushiro himo* in a square knot. During *iaidō* practice this is tied in a cross. (d) Take the remaining ends of the *ushiro obi* and tuck them under the *obi* on both sides. (e) The front of the *hakama* is lower than the back when properly worn. The front touches the top of the foot slightly and the back of the *hakama* is at ankle level. Reach inside the slits of the *hakama* and pull down the *dōgi* to set the collar and tighten the back of the *dōgi*.

How to Fold the *Dōgi* and the *Hakama*

Figs. 24, 25, and 26 show how to fold the *dōgi* and the *hakama*. To fold the *dōgi* properly not only keeps it free of wrinkles but also shows respect to the tradition of kendo.

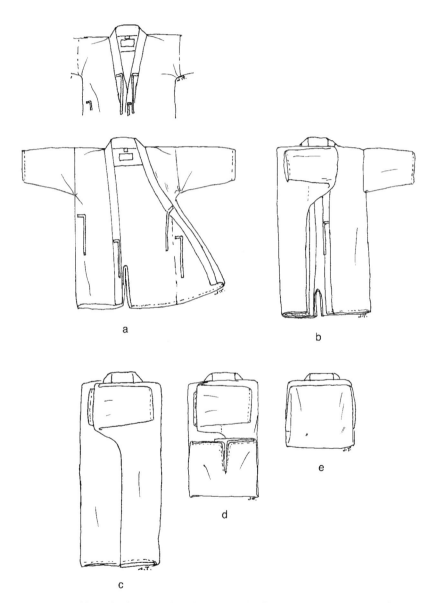

Fig. 24. Folding the *dōgi:* (a) Place the *dōgi* on the floor. Note the extra pair of straps. (b) Fold a sleeve. (c) Fold the other sleeve. (d) Fold up the lower portion. (e) Fold again to complete.

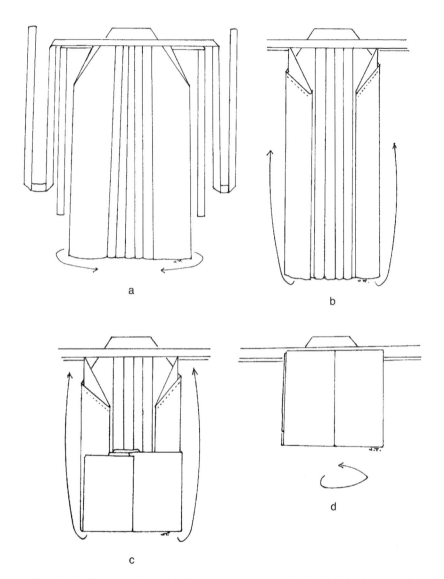

Fig. 25. Folding the *hakama*: (a) Place the *hakama* on its back. (b) Fold the sides of *hakama* about 10 cm toward the center. (c) Fold the hem end upward once. (d) Fold again. Flip the *hakama* to face front side back.

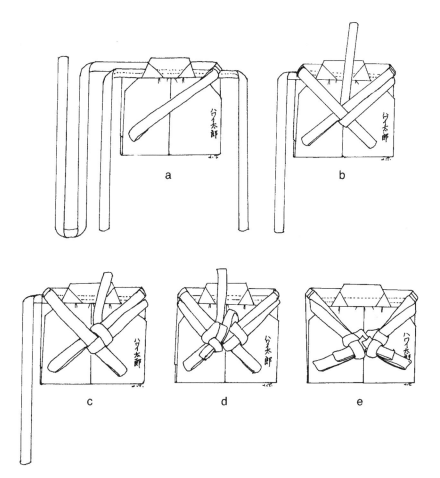

Fig. 26. Folding the *hakama* (cont.): (a) Take the *maehimo* and fold it in half, then fold it in half again. Do the same on the other *maehimo* and cross them over each other. (b) Take the *ushiro himo,* wrap it around the cross, and come out from the top of the cross. (c) Go around the *maehimo* and *ushiro himo* of the same side and come out from the top. (d) Do the same on the other *ushiro himo*. Fold the end of the *ushiro himo* and tuck it into the loop previously made by the opposite *ushiro himo*. (e) Tighten all the sides. The *hakama* is ready to be stored.

Bōgu (Protective Gear)

The *Men*

The purpose of the *men* (headgear) is to protect the head, eyes, ears, neck, and shoulders from the opponent's *shinai*. When choosing your *men,* make sure the *menbuton* (headgear cushion) is of good quality and that it is wide enough to cover the back of your head. If it is too narrow, it may not provide enough protection from head injury during a backward fall. It is best to try on the *men* for fit and comfort, but if you must order equipment through the mail or online, be sure to take proper measurements. You should check the level of the *monomi* or *mushamado* (viewing window) as well, because this differs for each individual.

Because the *men* is heavy, neck exercise is important before wearing it. You should wipe the *men* clean after each practice because perspiration may cause mildew and bacterial growth. It is a good idea to dry the *men* in direct sunlight for thirty minutes or wipe it with a towel soaked in hot water. When you store the *men,* spread the *menbuton* on the floor.

The Parts of the *Men*

The *menbuton* (headgear cushion, Fig. 27a) is the fabric covering the *men*. The *sashiko* (Japanese-style quilting) thickens the top *(menbōshi)* for added cushioning. The portion below the *mimizuri* (ear guard, Fig. 27k) is called the *mendare* (headgear apron, Fig. 27p) and measures approximately 30 cm. It protects the neck and shoulders from *shinai* strikes. When you place the *men* on a flat surface, the *mendare* should bend at an angle.

The *mengane* (headgear bars, Fig. 27b) are the metal bars of the *men*. The *mengane* are made up of one vertical bar (*nakagane, tategane,* or *nakahigo,* Fig. 27n) and fourteen (thirteen for children) horizontal bars (*yokogane, yokohigo,* or *sen,* Fig. 27o) that are made of duralumin (a strong alloy of aluminum, copper, magnesium, and manganese), stainless steel, or titanium. The space between the eighth and ninth bars from the bottom (between the ninth and tenth for children) is slightly wider to give the wearer an unimpeded view. This space is called the *monomi* or *mushamado* (viewing window, Fig. 27j). Because of an injury caused by the tip of a *shinai* several years ago, the *monomi* has been narrowed to 15 mm. The top five horizontal bars of the *men* are slightly thicker and stronger than the rest because of their close proximity to *datotsubui* (target areas). Their inner surface is painted red to brighten the view and to reduce the after-image of the inner side of the *men*.

The *maedare, tsukidare,* or *ago* (front apron or shield, Fig. 27c) is made of deerskin over layers of cloth, paper, and leather for durability. A standard embroidered design is an X with two or three horizontal bars beneath it. The *maedare* receives *tsuki* (thrusts) and plays an important part in protecting the throat and neck. The *uchidare, yōjin dare,* or *nijūago* (inner apron, Fig. 27d), as the inside cover of the *maedare,* reduces the impact of *tsuki.*

The *menhimo* (men cord, Fig. 27e) is fastened to the fourth *yokogane* (horizontal bar) and goes behind the *nakagane* (vertical bar) at the top *yokogane*. The *menhimo* are tied behind in a *hanamusubi* and the ends (without counting the ruffled parts) measure 40 cm from the knot. If the *menhimo* is too long it is cut to the proper length and the loose ends knotted to prevent fraying. The *men chichigawa* (men leather loop, Fig. 27f), a small leather strap wrapped around the fourth *yokogane* from the bottom, has slits at both ends for the *menhimo.*

The top and bottom cushions inside the *men* (Fig. 27l and 27m) for the forehead and chin are called *ten* and *chi* (heaven and earth). The cushions tend to get wet with perspiration. A sweat guard is available for the chin cushion. Always wipe the guard clean after use.

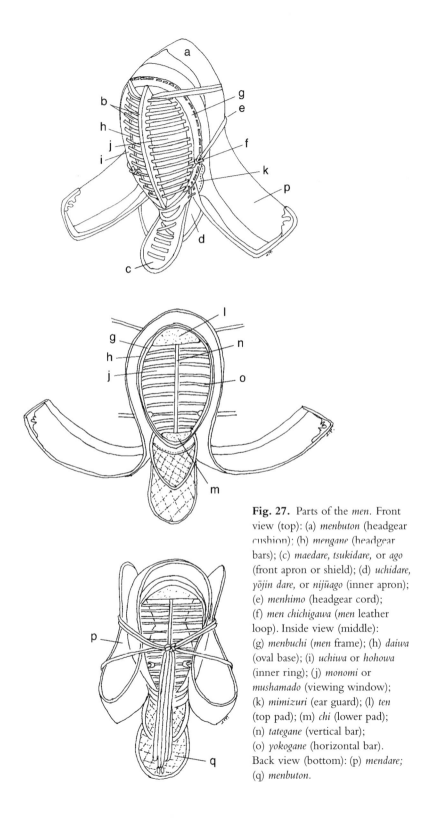

Fig. 27. Parts of the *men*. Front view (top): (a) *menbuton* (headgear cushion); (h) *mengane* (headgear bars); (c) *maedare, tsukidare,* or *ago* (front apron or shield); (d) *uchidare, yōjin dare,* or *nijūago* (inner apron); (e) *menhimo* (headgear cord); (f) *men chichigawa* (*men* leather loop). Inside view (middle): (g) *menbuchi* (*men* frame); (h) *daiwa* (oval base); (i) *uchiwa* or *hohowa* (inner ring); (j) *monomi* or *mushamado* (viewing window); (k) *mimizuri* (ear guard); (l) *ten* (top pad); (m) *chi* (lower pad); (n) *tategane* (vertical bar); (o) *yokogane* (horizontal bar). Back view (bottom): (p) *mendare*; (q) *menbuton*.

The *menbuchi* (*men* frame, Fig. 27g) is a leather strap around the face of the *men,* stitched with leather string. The oval base where the *tategane* and *yokogane* are fastened is called the *daiwa* (Fig. 27h). It is straw or cotton wrapped with tape. The inner ring, which makes contact with the face, chin, and forehead, is called the *uchiwa* or *hohowa* (Fig. 27i) and is made of cotton wrapped with a cloth for comfort.

How to Shape the *Menbuton*
To shape the *menbuton* turn it up with a large, open fold at the bottom where neck meets the shoulder and tie it in place with the *menhimo* (Fig. 27q). Leave the *men* stored this way until your next practice. This will lift the *menbuton* from both shoulders and reduce the impact to the shoulders if they are hit inadvertently.

Fitting the *Men*
It is important that your *men* fit properly, both so that it will offer maximum protection and so that you can see through the *monomi* (Fig. 28a and 28b). To ensure a correct fit, measure the circumference of your head starting at mid forehead and from chin to crown (Fig. 28c). Fig. 28d shows how to tie the *menhimo* to the *men.*

How to Trim and Tie the *Menhimo* and *Dōhimo*
The *menhimo* and *dōhimo* (plastron cords) are made from bundles of strings braided together. It is important that they be properly trimmed and tied. An unraveled *himo* can be dangerous and distracting as well as unsightly. As shown in Fig. 29, you should cut the *himo* to the proper length, unravel the end of it, and separate out two pairs of string. Wrap the two pairs around the unraveled portion of the *himo* twice and tie them off in square knots. This should prevent any further unraveling of the *himo.*

The *Kote*
In general the *kote* (arm guard) wears out more rapidly than either the *men* or *dō.* As a general rule, the ratio of wear is one *dō,* two *men,* and three *kote.* You should choose proper fitting *kote* or a slightly smaller size, as the leather can stretch. The price of a *kote* depends on the number of *kera* (ornaments), type of leather, and complexity of design.

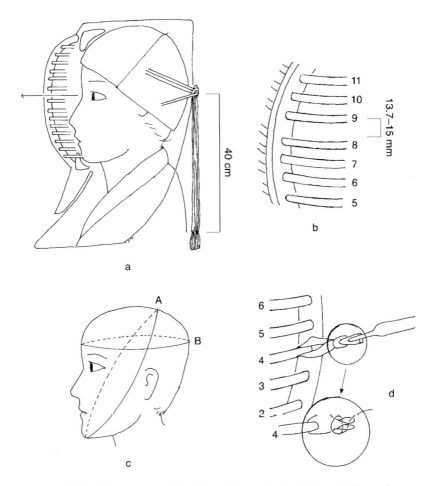

Fig. 28. (a) Side view of *monomi/menhimo:* Eyes are level with the window and the knot of the *menhimo* is 40 cm from the knot to the end of the cord (above the ruffle). (b) Regulation width of the *monomi* (13.7–15 mm). (c) Measurement of *men* size at A, the circumference of the chin to the top of the head, and B, the circumference of the head around the forehead. (d) Tying the *menhimo* to *yokogane,* with schematic drawing. Numbers in (b) and (d) indicate *yokogane* (horizontal bars).

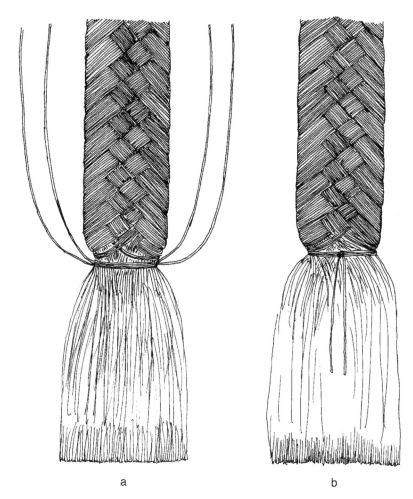

a   b

Fig. 29. Trimming and tying the *menhimo* and *dōhimo:* (a) Unravel the end of the *himo* and separate out two pairs of string. Wrap these around the *himo.* (b) Tie the *himo* strings in a separate knot to prevent further unraveling.

The Parts of the *Kote*

The parts of the *kote* are listed in Fig. 30.

1. The *kotegashira* (*nigiri,* Fig. 30a) is the fist portion of the *kote.* This is the most difficult part of *kote* to make. It is made of leather or cloth with *sashiko*-style needlework and has deer hair padding.

2. The *kera* (*namako* or joint, Fig. 30b) is the wrist portion of the *kote.* A pair of *kote* may have no *kera* or as many as three *kera.* It is easier to move the wrist in the counterattack when there are more *kera.* The cushioning material is cotton or deer hair.

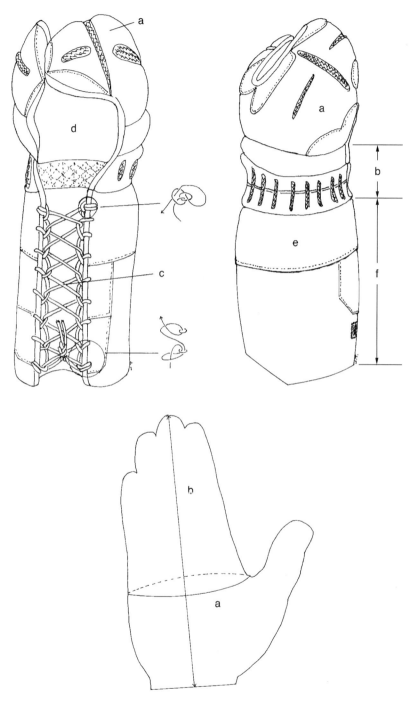

Fig. 30. Top, parts of the *kote* (left is front and right is back): (a) *kotegashira (nigiri);* (b) *kera (namako);* (c) *kotehimo;* (d) *tenouchikawa;* (e) *kotebuton;* (f) *tsutsu* or *kotetsutsu.* Bottom, measurement of *kote* size: (a) Circumference across the hand at the web of the thumb; (b) length between the tip of the middle finger to the wrist.

3. The *kotehimo,* the string or lace used to tighten the fit of the *kote,* is strung through the holes and tied as illustrated in Fig. 30c.

4. The palm portion of the *kote,* called the *tenouchikawa,* is made of specially treated deerskin or synthetic leather. It wears out easily because it comes into contact with the *shinai tsuka.*

5. The *kotebuton* (cuff, Fig. 30e) covers two-thirds of the forearm. The cushioning material is cotton.

6. The *tsutsu* or *kotetsutsu* is the cylinder-like portion of the *kote* between the *kera* and the *kotebuton.*

How to Tie the *Kotehimo*

The *kotehimo* is a lace used to tie the opening of the *kote* together, much like shoelaces. It is tied in a way that maximizes flexibility, as shown in Fig. 31.

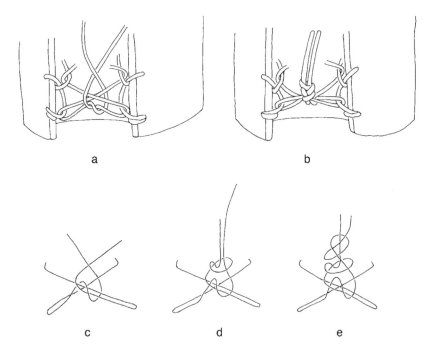

Fig. 31. Tying the *kotehimo:* (a) Begin tying. (b) Finish tying. Schematics: (c) Take both free ends and bring them up. (d) Take one *kotehimo* around the other and make a simple overhand knot. (e) Tie another overhand knot with the other *kotehimo.*

The *Dō*

The *dō* (plastron, Fig. 32) protects your chest and torso from the impact of the *shinai*. It comes in many different materials and with decorations that can increase the cost considerably. In general, the more bamboo strips, the greater the cost. The covering material of the bamboo strip also determines the cost. The more exotic and elaborate the design the more expensive. The decoration on the *dō* is probably the only part of the *bōgu* where one can express individual taste.

The size of the *dō* should be such that there is an approximately 5 cm space between the *dō* and your chest. You cannot erase the scratch marks on the *dō,* but you can easily wipe off the dirt or wax marks with wet towels and buff the *dō* with a dry cloth. Clean the *mune* portion with a regular brush or toothbrush.

The Parts of the *Dō*

1. The *dōmune* (chest, Fig. 32a) is covered with leather and rendered with elaborate embroidery. The *dōmune* consists of the *shokkō* (background design, Fig. 32b), *kumo kazari* (cloud design, Fig. 32c), and *komune* (small chest piece, Fig. 32d). The *kumo kazari* prevents the tip of the *shinai* from sliding under the *maedare* (front apron) of the *men* and injuring the neck.

2. The *mune chichigawa* (chest leather strap, Fig. 32e) are leather rings through which the *munehimo* passes. Figs. 33 and 34 show two methods for tying the *mune chichigawa* to the *dō*.

3. The *dō, dōdai,* or *taiko* (torso, torso cover, or drum, Fig. 32f) consists of 43, 50, 60, or 70 shaved, curved bamboo strips (*uradake,* Fig. 32k) strung together through holes on both ends with *koto* string. The front part of the *dō* is covered with buffalo skin, although sometimes sharkskin or turtle shell is used. Both the outside and inside are lacquered to protect the *dō* from moisture. The *dō* may come in black, red, brown, or other colors. The *dō* receives the brunt of the *datotsu* (strikes), so it was traditionally made of very durable natural material, though synthetic fiber or plastic now prevail.

4. The *dōhimo* is attached at the *yotsukata chichi* or *yotsu chichigawa* (four-corner straps, Fig. 32g). The leather straps are secured through four holes in the corners of the *dō* in a special way.

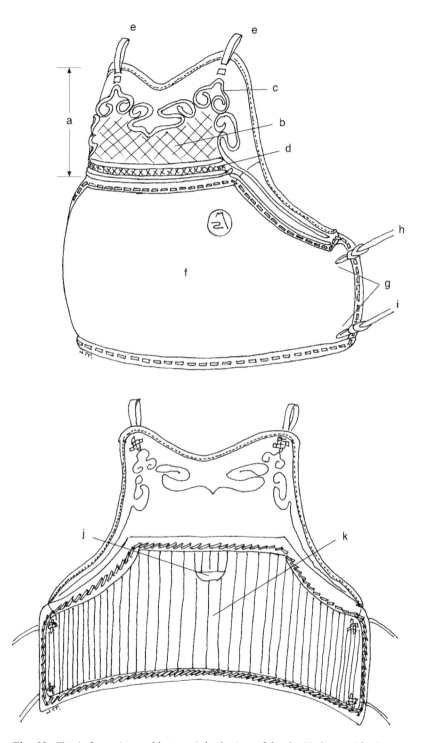

Fig. 32. Top is front view and bottom is back view of the *dō:* (a) *dōmune* (chest); (b) *shokkō* (background design); (c) *kumo kazari* (cloud-like design); (d) *komune* (small chest piece); (e) *mune chichigawa* (chest leather strap); (f) *dō, dōdai,* or *taiko* (torso, torso cover, or drum); (g) *yotsukata chichi* or *yotsu chichigawa* (four-corner straps); (h) *munehimo* (chest cords); (i) *koshihimo;* (j) *wa* (ring); (k) *uradake.*

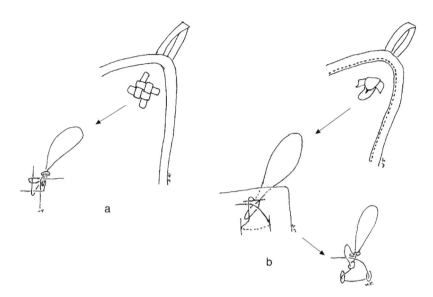

Fig. 33. Fastening the *mune chichigawa* to the *dō:* (a) Method 1. Make a loop and insert the end of the adjacent piece. Insert the next one into the loop just made and continue until the four pieces interlock. Tighten the four pieces. (b) Method 2. Insert two ends of the *mune chichigawa* into the hole. Take one end through the slit on the other. Pull the free end through two holes and insert into its own loop. Tighten the loose ends.

5. The *munehimo* (chest cords, Fig. 32h) are permanently secured at one end to the top *yotsukata chichi,* and the free ends are tied to the *mune chichigawa* on the opposite side. (See Fig. 33 for different ways to tie the *munehimo* to the *mune chichigawa*.)

6. The *koshihimo* (back cord, Fig. 32i) is tied in a *hanamusubi* in the back. The free ends are permanently tied to the bottom *yotsukata chichi.*

7. The *wa* (ring-shaped leather strap, Fig. 32j), sewn on the back of the *dō* between the *mune* and the *dō dai* is used for hanging it on the wall by the *menhimo* after the *bōgu* has been tied together.

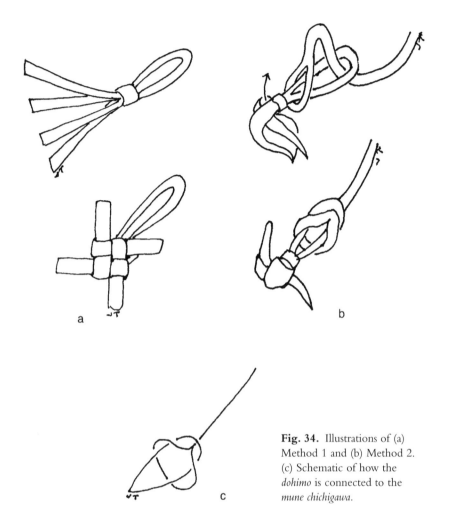

Fig. 34. Illustrations of (a) Method 1 and (b) Method 2. (c) Schematic of how the *dohimo* is connected to the *mune chichigawa.*

The *Tare*

The *tare* (apron plate, Fig. 35) offers protection from a *shinai* that has missed its target. The *tare* should gently curve outward to be effective. To maintain balance with the other *bōgu*, the *tare* should be of equal quality.

The *tare* is worn so that the top half of the *tare obi* (apron belt, Fig. 35c) is covered by the *dō*. The *tare* can be cleaned with a regular brush. The *wakihimo* (hip strap, Fig. 35d) should be stretched to remove wrinkles and ironed occasionally to remove the creases that could cause it to break. The *zekken* or *nafuda* (name tag, Fig. 35e) identifies the person behind the *bōgu*, with the last name of the kendo practitioner in the center, vertically (Fig. 35g), and his organization on the top horizontally in white letters (Fig. 35f). The *zekken* used to be embroidered but today is usually white, with artificial leather cut-outs. The background of the *zekken* is either black or navy. The style of writing usually is *kaisho* (formal writing).

Parts of the *Tare*

1. The *ōtare* or *maedare* (large apron plate or front apron, Fig. 35a) consists of three thick plates in front, partly covered by leather around the edges. The *zekken* is placed in the center of the *ōtare*.

2. The *kotare* or *ushirodare* (small apron plate or back apron plate, Fig. 35b) consists of two plates located behind and between the *ōtare*.

3. The *tare obi* is thick in front and the ends are attached to the *wakihimo.*

4. The *wakihimo* loops around the back and is tied in front and behind the center *ōtare* in a *hanamusubi.*

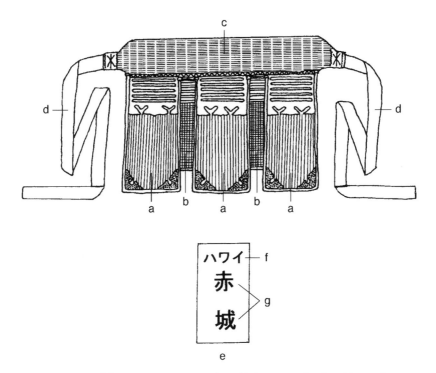

Fig. 35. Parts of the *tare:* (a) *ōtare* or *maedare;* (b) *kotare* or *ushirodare;* (c) *tare obi;* (d) *wakihimo;* (e) *zekken;* (f) team name; (g) family name.

How to Don the *Bōgu*

5

Seated in the traditional position, *seiza,* you don the *bōgu* in the following order: *tare, dō, men,* left *kote,* and right *kote.* Figs. 36 through 40 illustrate this in detail.

Putting on the *Tenugui* or *Hachimaki*

The *tenugui* (towel), also called the *hachimaki,* is basically a towel made of cotton. In Japan, people use it in the kitchen and the bathroom.

    The primary purpose of the *tenugui* in kendo is to absorb perspiration, cushion impacts to the head, and keep the hair neat. Often the *tenugui* display words of wisdom that are important in the training of kendo or words related to Zen. Japanese, by tradition, feel the head is one of the most sacred parts of the body, so wrapping the *tenugui* around the head has a special meaning in kendo. It is important to place it correctly and wash it after every use. Make sure it is dry and clean when you use it. It is strongly frowned upon to just crumple the *tenugui* and pack it in the *bōgu* bag, because the *tenugui* will be damp and smell musty at the next practice. The instructors should teach these lessons to beginners.

Fig. 36. Putting on the *bōgu:* (a) Place the center portion of the *tare* over your lower abdomen. (b) Take the *wakihimo* and cross it behind your back, past the lower portion of the *koshiita* (back plate). (c) Bring the *wakihimo* to the front. Tie it in a *hanamusubi* behind the center *ōtare* (shown flipped up here).

Fig. 37. Putting on the *dō:* (a) Put the *munehimo* over your chest and abdomen so that it covers approximately the upper half of the *tare obi* (apron belt). (b) Pull the left *munehimo* across your back, over your right shoulder, to the right *mune chichigawa,* and tie it. Repeat with the right *munehimo.* (c) Tie the *koshihimo* (hip cord) behind your back in a horizontal *hanamusubi.* (d) Properly fitted *dō.*

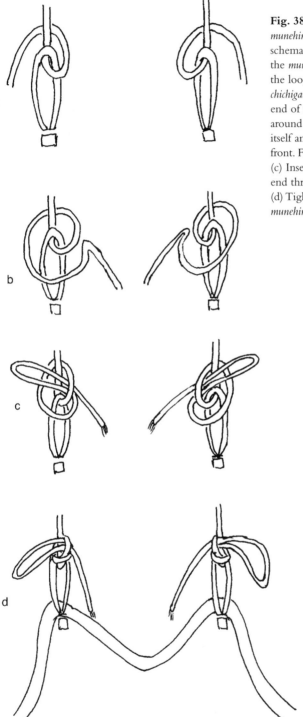

Fig. 38. Tying the *munehimo* (Method 1 schematic): (a) Thread the *munehimo* through the loop of the *mune chichigawa*. (b) Take the end of the *munehimo* around the back of itself and come out in front. Fold the free end. (c) Insert the folded end through the loop. (d) Tighten the *munehimo*.

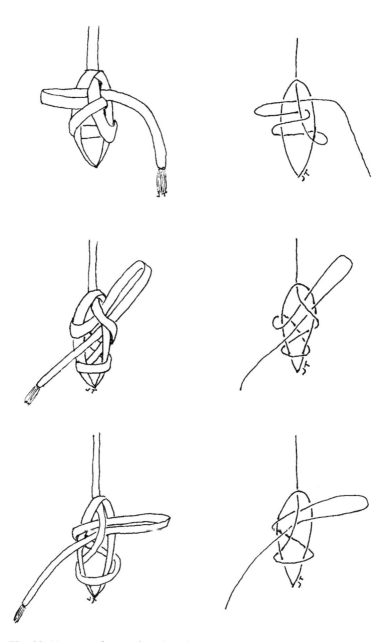

Fig. 39-40. Tying the *menehimo* (cont.):
Method 2 schematic *(top):* Thread the *munehimo* through the loop of the *mune chichigawa* and take the free end around the *mune chichigawa* to come out from the opposite side. Fold the *munehimo* to make a loop and push the loop into the space between the *munehimo* and *mune chichigawa*. Tighten the *munehimo*. Method 3 schematic *(middle):* Thread the *munehimo* through the loop of the *mune chichigawa* once and go around a second time. Fold the *munehimo* and make a loop. Insert the loop into the space between the *munehimo* and *mune chichigawa*. Tighten the *munehimo*. Method 4 schematic *(bottom):* Wrap the *munehimo* around the loop of the *mune chichigawa*. Fold the *munehimo* to make a loop. Insert the loop into the space between the *mune chichigawa* and the *munehimo*. Tighten the *munehimo*.

You must put on a *tenugui* before putting on the *men*. There are three ways to do this. Whichever way you prefer, start by grasping the upper corners in both hands and looking at the words written on the towel. The words should face you so you can read them. When worn properly, the *tenugui* should cover the back of the head so the *menhimo* is over the *tenugui* and not the hair.

The first method for putting on the *tenugui*, illustrated in Fig. 41, results in a tight fit, with both ears outside the *tenugui*. The second method, illustrated in Fig. 42, is a somewhat loose way to wrap the *tenugui,* and requires that you pull it down to cover both ears. The third method (Fig. 43) is ideal for children. In this method, you must learn where to fold the *tenugui* to get a perfect fit. This method results in both ears being hidden, with the thick end of the *tenugui* in front.

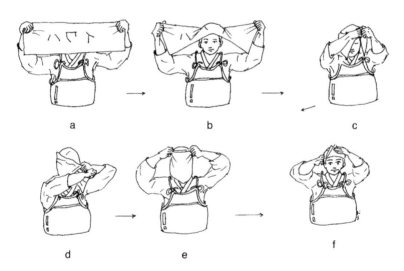

Fig. 41. Putting on the *tenugui*, Method 1: (a) Hold the *tenugui* with the right side facing yourself. (b) Put it over the head. (c) Bring one end across your forehead. (d) Do the same with the other end. (e) Tighten both ends. (f) Push the *tenugui* up to expose your face and ears.

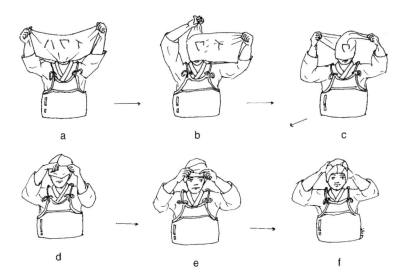

Fig. 42. Putting on the *tenugui*, Method 2: (a) Holding the edge with your mouth, bring the *tenugui* over your head. (b) Wrap one end behind your head. (c) Wrap the other end in the opposite direction and tie in front. (d) Fold the *tenugui* upward to expose your face. (e) Do not expose your ears. (f) Tighten neatly.

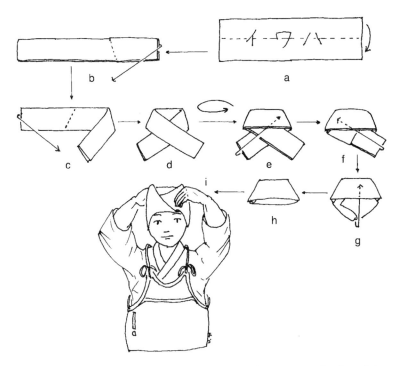

Fig. 43. Putting on the *tenugui*, Method 3: (a) Place the *tenugui* on the floor facing you. (b) Fold it in half. (c) Fold one end diagonally down. (d) Fold the other end diagonally over the first end. (e) Turn the *tenugui* around. (f) Tuck in one end into the main portion of *tenugui*. (g) Tuck in the other end. (h) Take the bottom portion and tuck it into the main portion to create a cap. (i) Place the *tenugui* on your head.

Putting on the *Men* and the *Kote*

Men

Fig. 44 shows how to put on the *men*. Once you have tied the *menhimo* in a *hanamusubi* at eye level, the loops of the *hanamusubi* should be of equal length measuring approximately 40 cm or 15.5 in. (without counting ruffled ends). The loops and the free ends of the *menhimo* should also be of equal length, and the two *menhimo* should be parallel to each other and lie flat at the sides of the *men*. After tying the *menhimo*, leave a space between the *men* and your ears; this will prevent damage to your eardrums if you are hit over the ears.

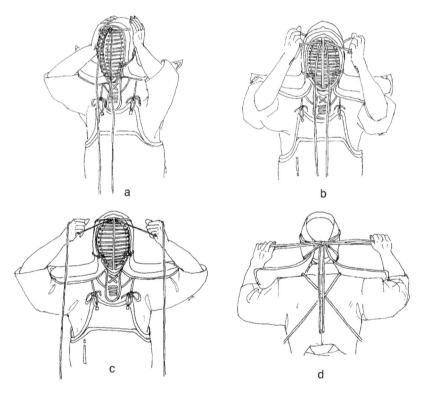

Fig. 44. Putting on the *men*: (a) Put your chin in the *men* first. (b) Pull the *menhimo*. (c) Pull the *menhimo* to further tighten the fit. (d) Tie the *menhimo* in a *hanamusubi* in the back, leaving 40 cm hanging from the knot.

Kote

You should always put on the left *kote* first, then the right (Fig. 45). This keeps your right hand ready for an unexpected enemy attack.

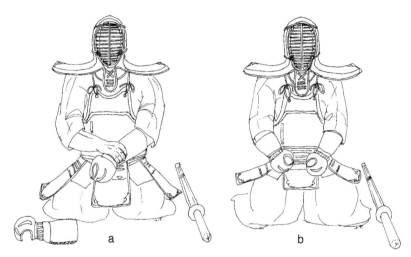

Fig. 45. Putting on the *kote:* (a) Put on the left *kote* first. (b) Put on the right *kote* last, so that the right hand remains ready for combat up to the last second.

How to Put Away
the *Bōgu*

6

Seated in the *seiza* position, remove the *bōgu* in the reverse order of donning. Take off the right *kote* first, then the left. Do not pull the *kote* by the *kera* or the fist portion, as this may damage the *kote*. After you remove the *kote*, place them in front of you diagonally to the right, palm down with the thumbs pointing toward each other. To take off the *men*, wrap the *menhimo* around your left hand in front of your face (Fig. 46a). Support the *men* with your right hand, over the *mengane* and push the *men* forward with your left hand (Fig. 46b). Place the *menhimo* inside the *men* and the *men* face down on the *kote* (Fig. 47a). Wipe the inner portion of the *men* with the *tenugui*. Fold the *tenugui*. Then you may wipe your face with the folded *tenugui*. Place the folded *tenugui* neatly into the *men* (Fig. 47b).

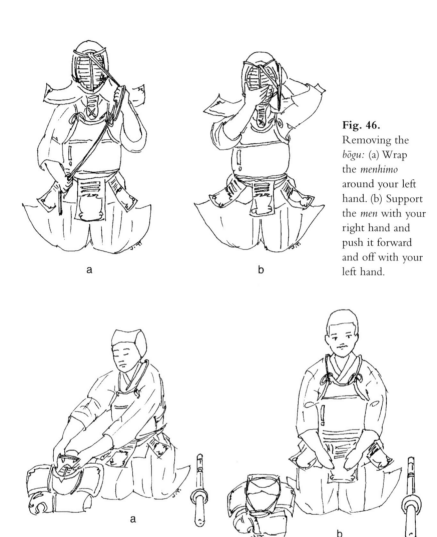

Fig. 46. Removing the *bōgu:* (a) Wrap the *menhimo* around your left hand. (b) Support the *men* with your right hand and push it forward and off with your left hand.

a   b

a   b

Fig. 47. Removing the *kote* and *men:* (a) Place the *menhimo* inside the *men*. Place the *men* over the *kote*. Take off the *tenugui* and fold it. Wipe the inner portion of *men* and place it inside. (b) Finished taking off the *kote* and *men*.

Next take off the *dō* and place it in front of you face up. Do not place the *taiko* on the floor, as this may damage the lacquer.

Take the *tare* and tie it to the *dō,* as illustrated in Fig. 48. Place the *men* and *kote* inside the *dō* and tie it with the *koshihimo* (Fig. 49). Alternatively, you may tie the *menhimo* as illustrated in Fig. 50 and hang it on a hook on a wall.

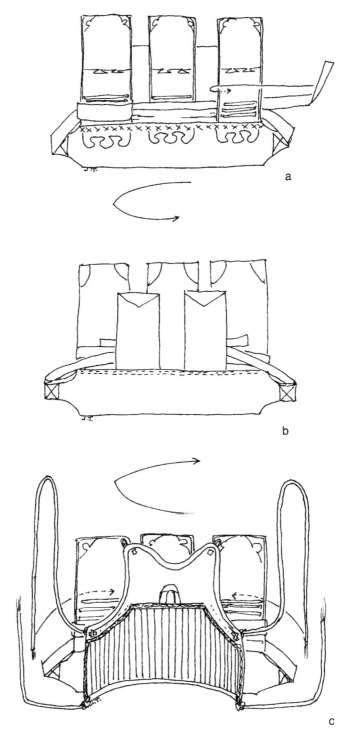

Fig. 48. Putting away the *tāre* and *dō:* (a) Wrap the *koshihimo* around the *ōtare*. (b) Flip the *tare*. (c) Place the *dō* over the *tare*.

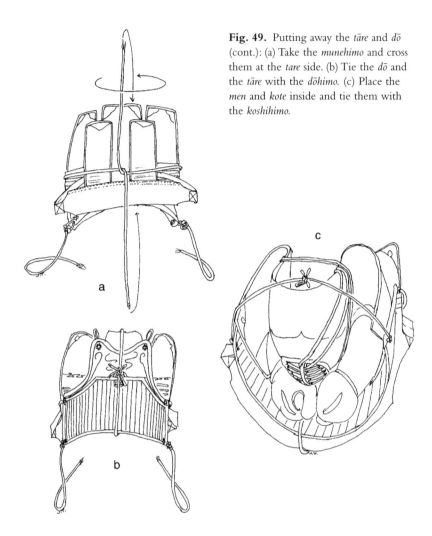

Fig. 49. Putting away the *tāre* and *dō* (cont.): (a) Take the *munehimo* and cross them at the *tare* side. (b) Tie the *dō* and the *tāre* with the *dōhimo*. (c) Place the *men* and *kote* inside and tie them with the *koshihimo*.

After returning home from the *dōjō*, immediately unpack the *bōgu* and air each article before the next practice. This will reduce odor and prevent mildew. You may use a warm wet towel to clean the *bōgu* if necessary.

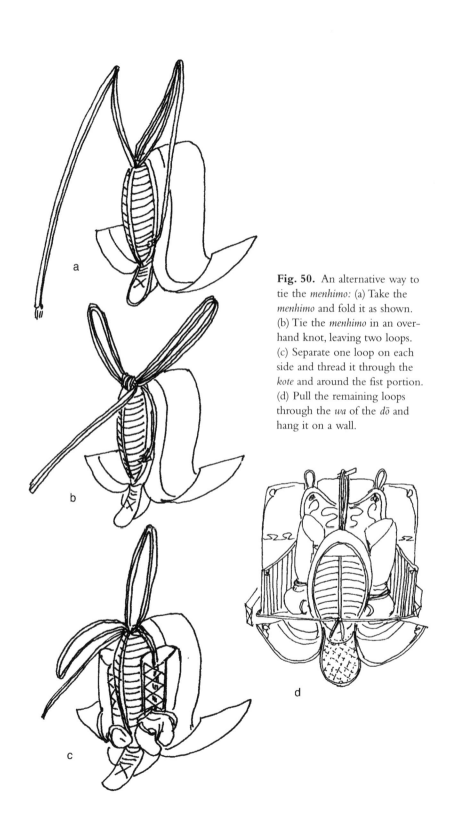

Fig. 50. An alternative way to tie the *menhimo:* (a) Take the *menhimo* and fold it as shown. (b) Tie the *menhimo* in an overhand knot, leaving two loops. (c) Separate one loop on each side and thread it through the *kote* and around the fist portion. (d) Pull the remaining loops through the *wa* of the *dō* and hang it on a wall.

PART II

Basic Elements

Dōjō (Place of Practice)

The *dōjō,* the training hall or school, is a sacred place where physical and spiritual disciplines are taught. The word *dōjō* is from the Sanskrit and refers to the place where Buddha was enlightened or a place where he taught. Since the Meiji period, *dōjō* has commonly meant a place where martial arts are practiced. Therefore, a *dōjō* may be a formal training hall, gym, park pavilion, or even an open-air location, so long as it is where practice takes place.

The entrance to the *dōjō* is usually in the *shimoza* (lower seat), the side opposite from the *kamiza* (higher seat). The *kamiza* is also called *shinzen.* The word *shinzen* literally means "in front of the god" and in traditional Japanese this meant a Shintō god. In old Japanese *dōjō* it was common to see a Shintō altar located at the north end, although today altars are rare, especially in schools, and this area is simply designated as *shōmen* (front). The highest-ranking kendo practitioners and any honored guests are usually are seated in front at the center or in front of the *shinzen,* if there is one, and the national flag of the country of the *dōjō* is also placed here.

According to the old Japanese custom, the *kamiza* is to the east where the sun rises, and the *shimoza* is to the west where the sun sets. Therefore, the *sensei* (teachers) sit at the east or *kamiza,* and the students sit at the west or *shimoza.* On either side, the order of seating is based on rank, with the kendo practitioners of higher ranks sitting closer to the *shōmen.*

It is easy to orient yourself in an unfamiliar *dōjō* if you remember that the *shōmen* or *shinzen* is where the national flag or altar is located. The *kamiza* is an L-shaped configuration of the *dōjō* that includes the *shōmen* as well as the east side seats where the *sensei* or higher-ranking kendo practitioners sit. The *shimoza* is the complementary L-shaped configuration that includes the west side seats where students sit, opposite the *shōmen.*

At times the traditional order of seating may vary, depending on the structure of the *dōjō.* The location of the entrance or the bathrooms (or locker room) may determine the seating in a *dōjō.* It is important to respect the customs of the individual *dōjō* and to ask politely when in doubt.

On entering the *dōjō,* you should remove all earthly things, including footwear (shoes, slippers, and socks), headwear (caps, hats, or hair ornaments), sunglasses, watches, necklaces, bracelets, earrings, and other jewelry. When you remove your shoes, you should place them neatly pointing outward without blocking the entrance or into the shoebox if one is available. Smoking, drinking, or chewing gum in a *dōjō* is strictly prohibited. Whistling, singing, or making annoying remarks or noise and unruly, disruptive, or disorderly behavior are also absolutely prohibited.

It is proper etiquette to bow from standing *(ritsurei)* toward the *shōmen* (front), *kamiza* (upper seat), or *shinzen* (altar) on entering and leaving the *dōjō.* You should take the *bōgu* bag off your shoulder before bowing. The *ritsurei* shows respect and appreciation for the teachers, fellow kendo practitioners, the place of practice, and implies a solemn promise to do your best in a fair way in the *dōjō.*

A *dōjō* should be kept neat and clean at all times. Before kendo practice begins, the *dōjō* should be swept and mopped, sharp foreign objects removed, and any slippery areas on the floor wiped dry. The objects sometimes picked up from the floor include nails, pins, splinters, honeybees, and pieces of rocks: anything that could injure the feet. Traditionally, the newest members and beginners should clean the floor, but anyone who comes in early may do it. Cleaning the *dōjō* can be a part of the warm-up exercises. We should clean the *dōjō* with feelings of pride and respect.

The ideal *dōjō* floor is a wooden surface over springs or cush-ioned beams. Probably the least ideal is a concrete surface, which is hard on the feet, the joints of the lower extremities, and the spine. When the floor and space are not ideal, the style of practice may be changed to accommodate the deficiencies. When space is limited due to the number of people practicing, injuries from collisions and other partners' swinging *shinai* can be a problem. In the old days a *dōjō* had high windows, called *mushamado,* to prevent people (usually students from other schools) from observing the practice. In the modern *dōjō* it is more important to have good ventilation and lighting than *mushamado.*

Reihō (Etiquette)

It is often said among the students of Japanese martial arts that *"rei ni hajimari rei ni owaru":* "practice begins with etiquette and ends with etiquette." This saying means that we should be mindful of respect and humility from the start to the end of the martial art practice. This concept is also important in the practice of kendo. Etiquette is a basic requirement for a civilized person and one of the essential virtues of a samurai. It is also the mark of a person with grace *(kihin),* who will be respected by others. *Rei* (etiquette or bow) is an outward expression of inner humility and respect. At the same time, the act of *rei* teaches young people inner humility and respect. In kendo as in our daily life we must not boast of victory or success, or scorn the defeated. When we are defeated we must not feel resentment, shame, or disappointment. We should instead be thankful for the experience and respectful of others.

In kendo, we strike another person with a weapon and often inflict pain and discomfort. It requires a discipline to hold back our emotions when this happens. The practice of *reihō* (etiquette) helps us to control our raw emotions and cultivate respect and humility.

It is improper etiquette to walk in front of the *sensei* or another student who is putting the *bōgu* on. If you must walk in front of a sitting student for any reason, extend your right hand and bow as you pass. If you must cross in front of a *sensei*, stop in front of him and bow before passing. No one should walk behind the examiners during an examination.

The *Rei*

The *rei* (bow) indicates courtesy, honor, respect, humility, and sincerity. *Rei* without true humility is an empty body motion. According to Sasamori Junzō, a renowned kendo instructor, one must bow to pay respect to the founder of the school *(ryūso)*, teacher *(shi)*, senior students *(senpai)*, colleagues *(dōryō)*, junior students *(kōhai)*, and oneself *(jiko)*. The act and idea of bowing to everyone, including yourself, is a fundamental part of personal training. You must bow to the *shinzen* (altar) and *shōmen* or *kamiza* (front) on entering and exiting the *dōjō*. It is also proper to thank an opponent who delivers a clean strike because he has shown you where your weakness is. Between entering and leaving the *dōjō*, you may bow as many as sixty or eighty times. You should bow before and after each *keiko* (training) session with each partner. When practice is finished, you should bow in front of all the *sensei*, starting with the highest-ranking one. It is proper to raise your head after each *sensei* raises his head, either in a *ritsurei* (standing bow) or a *zarei* (sitting bow).

On special occasions, such as a tournament or performance, everyone present stands at the opening and end of the event to bow to the *shōmen* or the national flag. At the opening, it is customary to play the national anthem of the hosting country. The players of the first and the last match will bow to the *shinpanchō* (chairman of the tournament) or invited dignitaries before they bow to each other. The audience must also follow the rules and show respect for the competitors and other audience. The audience should refrain from making loud or impolite remarks.

Seiza and *Mokusō*

The terms *seiza* and *mokusō* (meditation) are used interchangeably. *Seiza* may mean either kneeling in tranquility or sitting in a formal fashion (Fig. 51a). In this book we use *seiza* to mean kneeling in tranquility, which is essentially a state of *mokusō*. In this state the eyes are partially closed *(hangan)*. At some *dōjō*, *mokusō* is done before and after practice.

Fig. 51. *Seiza* (kneeling in tranquility)
or *mokusō* (meditation): (a) Kneeling.
(b) To perform the *ritsurei*, begin by
standing straight.

a   b

When you hear the command *"shisei o tadashite . . . seiza!"* you
should straighten your posture and place your right hand in front of
your lower abdomen with the palm up, place your left hand palm up
on your right hand, then lightly bring the tips of your thumbs
together to make an oval, with the center of the oval in front of your
lower abdomen. Then close your eyes halfway *(hangan);* breathe in
quickly from the nose and breathe out slowly and completely from
the mouth with pursed lips using abdominal breathing *(fukushiki
kokyū).* The length of the *seiza* should be about three deep breaths
(about 45 seconds). You should feel as though you are putting all your
spiritual energy in your lower abdominal area.

The *Ritsurei* (Standing Bow)

To perform the *ritsurei,* tuck your chin in, straighten your spine, thrust your chest forward gently, and lower both your shoulders naturally (Fig 51b). Look squarely into your opponent's eyes. Exchanging bows with your opponent, bend forward at the waist at 15 degrees while maintaining eye contact (Fig. 52a). Alternatively, you may focus your eyes on your opponent's knees. You should focus your eyes on your opponent, but try not to be preoccupied with details. This is a form of *otagaini rei* or "bow to each other."

When you bow to the *shōmen (shōmen ni mukatte rei)* you bow forward 30 degrees while casting your eyes on the floor (Fig. 52b). Keep your arms at your sides with your fingers together. Do not dangle your arms. Keep your back straight (do not hunch).

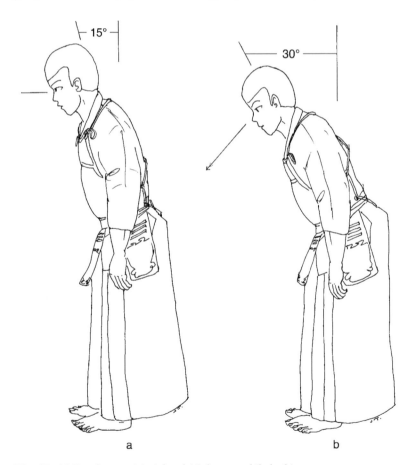

a   b

Fig. 52. (a) For the *otagaini rei,* bend 15 degrees while looking at your opponent. (b) For the *shomen ni mukatte rei,* bend 30 degrees while casting your eyes to the floor.

Chakuza and the *Zarei* (Kneeling Bow)

Chakuza

When you hear the command to kneel down from a standing position, *"chakuza!"* bend your left knee and place it on the floor as you sweep the inner part of the left leg of your *hakama* (trousers) backward (Fig. 53a and 53b). Then repeat this with your right leg and right hand *(hakama sabaki)*. Your toes should be extended to touch the floor and your back should be straight (Fig. 53c). Then lower your hips to rest on your legs. The distance between your knees should be about one fist wide if you are a woman and one to two fists wide if you are a man. You may place one big toe over the other to make this position more comfortable. As you kneel, your hands should fall naturally from your side to rest on your thighs. Keep your spine straight. The nose to navel should be in a vertical line for most people. Your fingers should be close together, as spread fingers are unsightly as well as vulnerable to an opponent's attack. Your elbows should be close to your torso to make it difficult for an opponent to attack by grabbing your arm (Fig. 53d).

When standing back up *(tachiagari),* place your right foot forward about half a step and lift your body up without bending forward. Bring your left foot to rest beside your right foot. This sequence of sitting and standing is called *sa-za u-ki* (left to kneel and right to stand). Your upper body should remain unchanged as you stand up and your hands should fall naturally from your lap to your sides.

Zarei

Always look your opponent or *sensei* squarely in the eyes before bowing (Fig. 54a). Bend your elbows naturally and place both hands on the floor in front of your knees, forming a triangle with the thumbs and index fingers touching each other (Fig. 54b). Your thumbs should be in one straight line, forming an inverted V or isosceles triangle. Bow gently and solemnly until your elbows almost touch the floor and cast your eyes to the floor in a formal *shin-zarei* (Fig. 54c). You should not raise your hips, show the nape of your neck, or have your elbows in the air.

In a semi-formal *gyō-zarei,* place your fingers up to the second joint on the floor and do not bend your back as much. In an informal *sō-zarei* only the fingertips touch the floor and the back is bent slightly.

When you change direction while sitting in *seiza,* keep your hands on your thighs and your upper body steady (without leaning forward). Lift your hips over your heels and place your toes on the

Fig. 53. The *chakuza:* (a) To kneel down, begin with *hakama sabaki.* (b) Place your left knee on the floor. (c) Place both knees on the floor, keeping your back straight. (d) Lower your hips and straighten your toes, then place both hands over your thighs neatly.

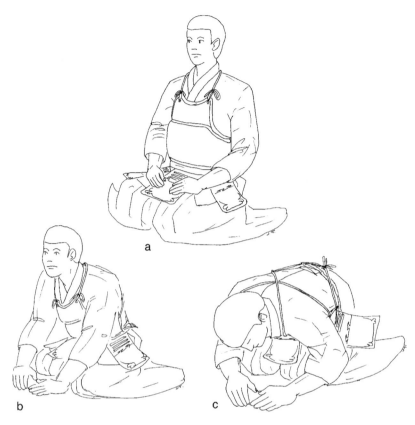

Fig. 54. Beginning the *zarei:* (a) Sitting in *seiza* requires straight posture and looking the opponent in the eyes. (b) To bow from a kneeling position *(zarei),* place both hands on the floor. (c) *Zarei,* the kneeling bow.

floor. Point one knee to the direction of change and let the other knee follow. Then shift to the desired direction, straighten your toes, and sit in *seiza*.

Sonkyo no Rei (Bow from *Sonkyo*)

Squatting on the balls of your feet (*sonkyo* stance), lower your right hand and your head while looking at your opponent. This is not usually done in modern kendo but is done in old-style kendo practice and in sumo wrestling.

Rei During Practice

You should perform *ritsurei* with your *shinai* in your left hand before starting practice. During practice you may bow by lowering your *shinai* and pointing it slightly to right as you would in *kamae o toku* (disarming). Kendo practitioners should recognize each other's *datotsu* (a strike) honestly and humbly by saying, *"Mairimashita!"* (I surrendered), *"Chōdai shimashita!"* (I have received your strike), or *"Arigatō gozaimashita!"* (thank you). It is also good etiquette to reply *"Fujūbun deshita!"* (it was quite an inadequate strike). It is not proper to act as if you have delivered a clear *datotsu* when you have not. It is equally improper to say *"Mada mada"* (not quite adequate) when you have received a good *datotsu*.

Kamae (Stance) and *Datotsubui* (Target Areas)

Gogyō no Kamae (Five Basic Stances)

Gogyō refers to the five elements (fire, wood, earth, gold/metal, and water) that constitute the universe, thus the five basic stances.

1. *Chūdan no kamae* (middle stance), also known as *mizu no kurai* (rank of water) or *hito no kamae* (stance of person) (Fig. 55a)

2. *Jōdan no kamae* (above stance), also called *hi no kurai* (rank of fire) or *ten no kamae* (stance of heaven) (Fig. 55b)

3. *Hassō no kamae* (eight-faceted stance), also called *moku no kurai* (rank of wood) or *in no kamae* (stance of *yin*) (Fig. 55c)

4. *Gedan no kamae* (lower stance), also called *tsuchi no kurai* (rank of earth) or *chi no kamae* (stance of earth) (Fig. 56a)

5. *Wakigamae* (hip stance), also known as *kin no kurai* (rank of gold) or *yō no kamae* (stance of *yang*) (Fig. 56b)

Fig. 55. Five basic stances: (a) *chūdan no kamae* (middle stance); (b) *jōdan no kamae* (above stance); (c) *hassō no kama* (eight-faceted stance).

Fig. 56. Five basic stances (cont.):
(a) *gedan no kamae* (lower stance);
(b) *wakigamae* (side stance), showing
left foot extended in the *migi wakigami*,
or right side.

Chūdan no Kamae

Chūdan no kamae is the most practical and useful stance. It can be
applied in defense and in offense, and can be changed instantaneously
into the next move.

From the *shizentai* (natural body stance), place your left toes
slightly behind your right heel about a foot width apart. Lift your left
heel slightly. In actual practice or a match you must put your right
foot forward from *shizentai* to assume the same foot position. Balance
your weight over both feet. Your left fist should be a distance of one

fist from your lower abdomen, below the navel, and always positioned in the midline as you hold the *shinai*.

When using a *bokken* or sword your left fist will be much farther from your navel because the *tsuka* in both weapons are shorter than the *shinai tsuka*. However, your right fist should be at about the same location whether you are holding a *shinai, bokken*, or sword.

The *kensen* (sword tip) should generally be at the level of your opponent's throat, pointing at the face or left eye. It is important to be flexible and relaxed enough to meet the needs of a changing situation. You should be looking into the eyes of your opponent in a manner called *enzan no metsuke* (gazing at a far mountain), but you must also pay attention to your opponent's whole body, especially the fists and the tip of the *shinai*, where you can detect the first movement of an attack. It is essential to maintain the *seichu sen* (center line) or *seimei sen* (life line), which is an invisible line between you and your opponent. It may be easier to understand the concept if you imagine that this line is only big enough for one *shinai* and that a person who takes this line has an advantage over an opponent.

Jōdan no Kamae

Jōdan no kamae is a very aggressive, offensive stance in which you strike down from above upon finding a *suki* (opening) in your opponent. If your opponent makes a move, you strike before he can execute an attack. In this stance, you are exposed to your opponent's strike; therefore strength, aggressiveness, and determination are essential.

Because of the nature of this *kamae,* you say *"Gomen"* (pardon me) or more appropriately *"Shitsurei shimasu"* or *"Goburei shimasu"* (a more polite form of "pardon me") if your opponent is a kendo practitioner of higher rank.

The most common *jōdan* is *hidari morote jōdan*. For this stance, you move your left foot forward from *chūdan* and lift your right heel slightly with both hands over your head. You must be careful to keep your feet parallel and pointed forward because the right foot tends to become *shumoku ashi* (T-shape stance). Your left hand should be directly above your left foot, at a distance of one fist from your forehead. Your *kensen* should be slightly to the right of the midline.

In *migi morote jōdan*, your right foot is forward and the *kensen* is almost at the midline.

Hassō no Kamae

Hassō no kamae is a variation of *jōdan*, but is not as offensive a stance. From a *hidari morote jōdan* or from a *chūdan*, place your right hand at the level of your chin (*tsuba* at the level of your lips) and your left fist in front at the midline. The blade should face forward. In the Onoha ittō ryū, the *shinai* stands straight up. In the Shinkage ryū the *shinai* is almost horizontal, or *yoko ichimonji*. In the Nihon Kendo Kata, the *shinai* is tilted to the back and to the right, a compromise between the stances of the other two schools. You should be able to adapt to any change in your opponent's movement from this stance. This stance was used originally when one was wearing *kabuto* (helmet) and not able to assume *jōdan no kamae* (above stance) or in a room where ceiling made it impossible to raise a sword in *jōdan*.

Gedan no Kamae

Gedan no kamae is the opposite of *jōdan no kamae* and is a very effective defensive stance. Flexibility and readiness are important so that one can strike upon seeing a *suki* (opening) in the opponent. Lower the *kensen* to the level of your opponent's knee without lowering your eyes or head.

Wakigamae

Wakigamae is a variation of *gedan* (lower stance). It enables you to shield your *shinai* or sword from your opponent. It is difficult for the opponent to foresee the striking technique in this stance.

Strike quickly on finding a *suki* (opening). From *chūdan,* pull back your right foot and turn your body in *hanmi* (half-body stance). Place your right hand around your hip and your left hand at your navel, while pointing your *shinai* diagonally downward so that your opponent cannot see the entire *shinai*. This is the *migi wakigamae* (right side stance). The *hidari wakigamae* (left side stance) is the opposite of this, with the right foot forward.

Metsuke

A focal point is crucial for a kendo practitioner. The best focal point is called *enzan no metsuke* (gazing at a far mountain), in which you can see the entire opponent and not be preoccupied by small details. Another technique is called *obi no nori* (rule of the *obi*), in which you look at your opponent's belt to feel out his next move. It is not recommended to focus on one spot, such as *kote*, even if you are intending to strike the *kote*, as this will give away your next move.

Datotsubui (Target Areas)

Datotsubui are target areas or strike zones. A hit in a proper manner in these areas counts as a point *(ippon)*. Fig. 57 shows the *datotsubui* for the middle stance (Fig. 57a) and the above stance (Fig. 57b).

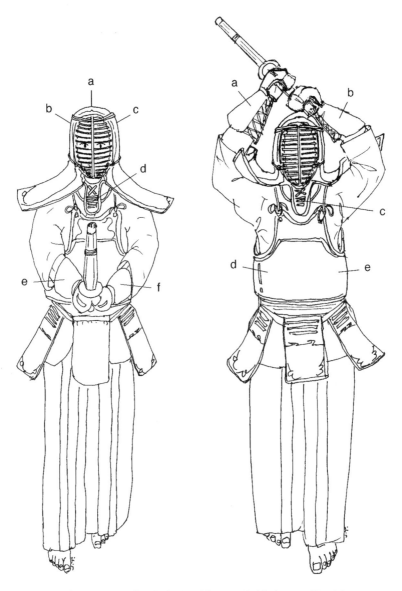

Fig. 57. Left, target areas for *chūdan* (middle stance): (a) *shomen;* (b) *migimen;* (c) *hidarimen;* (d) *tsuki;* (e) *migikote;* (f) *hidarikot.* Right, target areas for *jōdan* (above stance): (a) *migikote;* (b) *hidarikot;* (c) *tsuki;* (d) *migidō;* (e) *hidaridō.*

Nitō Ryū
(Two-Sword School)

C
H
A
P
T
E
R

1
0

Though the Nitō ryū (two-sword school) was quite widespread early in the Shōwa period (1926–1988), it has declined in popularity and has been forbidden in tournaments since the end of World War II. Recently, there has been a resurgence of Nitō ryū among Japanese college students.

The origin of Nitō ryū, or more precisely Niten ichi ryū or Nitō ichi ryū, is credited to Miyamoto Musashi. In his self-portrait, Musashi reveals himself as an old samurai with wrinkles between his eyebrows and half-closed eyes staring at his opponent. He is holding a pair of swords, a long one in his right hand and a short one in his left hand. Both are pointing toward the ground in a unique stance called *mugamae* or "stance of void," which is not one of the modern kendo stances.

Musashi explains the Nitō ryū in the "Book of the Earth" in his *Gorin no Sho*. In the section titled "I name my way of strategy Nitō ryū," he begins, "Samurai bears two swords. Whether one understands the meaning of it or not, that is the way we do it in this country. When one dies in combat, one should have wielded all the weapons at his disposal, and it is shame to die with one's *wakizashi* (short sword) still in his belt." He continues, "It is especially useful when one is fighting many opponents or in combat within an enclosed area. I will not further elaborate [on] this matter. One will appreciate it when he achieves this method by practicing arduously." He also states that even though it is awkward to use a sword with one hand at the beginning, it will get easier as one gets used to it.

Shinai Size in Nitō Ryū

The long *shinai* for men has a maximum length of 114 cm with a minimum weight of 440 g. For women it has a maximum length of 114 cm with a minimum weight of 400 g. The short *shinai* for men has a maximum length of 62 cm with a weight range between 280 g and 300 g. For women, it has maximum length of 42 cm with a weight range between 250 g and 280 g. The relatively heavy weight of the short *shinai* is quite useful in blocking the full force of the opponent's strike or in making it easier to slap or press the opponent's *shinai*.

Tachiai in Nitō Ryū
(Preparation for a Match in the
Two-Sword School)

The short and long *shinai* are both held in the left hand. The *shinai* are easier to hold when the long *shinai* is on the outside and the short *shinai* is inside. With your right hand, draw the *shinai* that you hold in your left hand and regrasp it with your left hand. Then draw the other *shinai* and hold it with your right hand. Assume the *sonkyo* (squatting) stance, and cross both *shinai*.

Insert the sword *(nōtō)* by placing your right-hand *shinai* in your left hand. Then transfer the other *shinai* to your right hand and regrasp it with your left hand. When you are sitting in *seiza,* place the long *shinai* outside (away from you) and the short *shinai* inside (closest to you) on the floor beside you.

Kamae in Nitō Ryū
(Stances in the Two-Sword School)

The Basic Stance

Place your left hand (or right hand if you are left-handed) with the short *shinai* forward and raise your right hand (or left if you are left-handed) with the long *shinai* at the level of your right ear. Use the short *shinai* as a decoy or for feinting purposes as well as for blocking, pressing, or sometimes striking. Use the long *shinai* for striking the *datotsubui* (target areas) and sometimes for blocking. Place the foot forward on the side of the forward hand. It is easier to synchronize the forward foot and the forward hand. The *kensen* (sword tip) of the short *shinai* is usually pointed toward your opponent's chest, for better defense and offense. The forward foot should be about twelve inches in front of the back foot, shoulder length apart. Lift the heel of your back foot slightly.

Specific Stances

1. *Jōdan no kamae* (above stance): Hold the long *shinai* over your head and the short *shinai* in the *chūdan no kamae* (middle stance) position, in front of your chest (Fig. 58a and b). Either the right or left foot can be in front (Fig. 58c). You can also hold both *shinai* in *jōdan no kamae* (Fig. 58d). This is an offensive stance. Make a strong *seme* (spirit of offense) and strike with both *shinai* at the same time when your opponent begins to attack. Alternatively, you can make a *kamae* with the short *shinai*, letting your elbows touch the *dō* gently so it is easier to defend your *kote* and *dō*.

2. *Chūdan no kamae* (middle stance): When your opponent assumes *jōdan no kamae*, point the *kensen* (sword tip) of both *shinai* at your opponent's nose (Fig. 59a). When your opponent attacks from *jōdan*, block the attack with your *shinai* in *jūji* (crossed) and hit your opponent's *dō* with your long *shinai*. If your opponent attempts to strike your *men* from *chūdan*, block with your short *shinai* and *tsuki* (thrust) with your long *shinai* to strike your opponent's *dō*. You can close the *ma'ai* and *osaeru* (press) your opponent's *shinai* with your short *shinai* and hit your opponent's *men* with your long *shinai*, or *harau* (slap) with your short *shinai* and hit your opponent's *dō* with your long *shinai*.

3. *Jūji no kamae* (cross stance): When your opponent assumes *jōdan*, cross both of your *shinai* in front (Fig. 59b). Then strike your opponent's *kote* with your long *shinai* as you block your *men* or hit your opponent's *dō* with your short *shinai*. When your opponent tries to hit your *dō*, block with your short *shinai* and *tsuki* (thrust) with your long *shinai*.

4. *Zangetsu no kamae* (crescent moon stance): Raise your long *shinai* above your head and point it diagonally at the floor to cover your *men* (Fig. 59c). When your opponent tries to hit your *men*, *ukenagashi* (deflect) his *shinai* or slide it down as you step forward diagonally and hit your opponent's *men*.

Fig. 58. Stances in the two-sword school: (a) long *shinai jōdan* and short *shinai chū-dan* with right foot forward; (b) side view of (a); (c) long *shinai jōdan* and short *shinai chūdan* with left foot forward; (d) both *shinai jōdan no kamae,* an offensive stance.

5. *Kasumi* (mist stance): Grasp your long *shinai* near the *tsuba* and place it horizontally *(yoko ichimonji)* in front of your *men* (Fig. 59d). Place your short *shinai* in the *chūdan no kamae* position in front of your chest. This stance protects all your *datotsubui* (point areas).

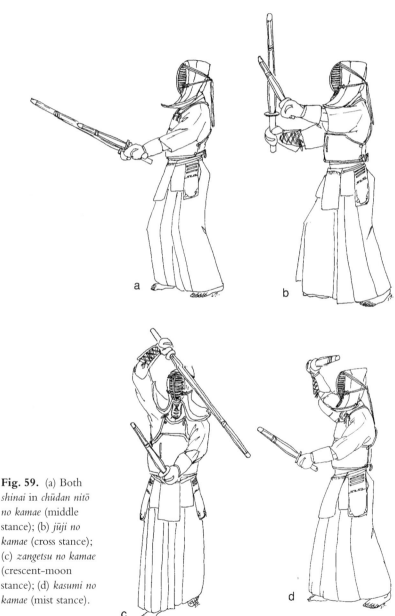

Fig. 59. (a) Both *shinai* in *chūdan nitō no kamae* (middle stance); (b) *jūji no kamae* (cross stance); (c) *zangetsu no kamae* (crescent-moon stance); (d) *kasumi no kamae* (mist stance).

Gyaku Nitō (Reverse Two-Sword School)

The Basic Stance
Place your right foot forward with the short *shinai* in your right hand. Hold your long *shinai* in your left hand as you would in *hidari jōdan*. Bend your right knee slightly and slightly lift your left heel. This indicates readiness to leap forward.

Tachiai in the Gyaku Nitō
Hold both *shinai* in your left hand in the *taitō* position (at the waist) and take three steps. Draw your long *shinai* with your right hand and transfer it to your left hand, then draw your short *shinai*. Assume the *sonkyo* (squatting) position. Hold both *shinai* in a cross in front of you. In the case of *tachiai* with Nitō ryū, draw your short *shinai* and transfer it to your left hand before transferring your long *shinai* to your right hand.

Ma'ai (Distance)

Ma'ai is the distance between opponents, not just the physical distance but also the spiritual and the temporal distance. Purely physical distances are *chikama, issoku ittō no ma,* and *tōma.* With *chikama* (a short distance, Fig. 60a), there is no time to hesitate in either offensive or defensive movement. *Issoku ittō no ma* (one-foot-one-sword distance, Fig. 60b), also called *chūma* (middle distance), is measured as one step from striking distance and one step from warding off an opponent's strike. *Tōma* (long distance, Fig. 60c) is a distance from which it is safer to defend than to attack. *Ma'ai* is a crucial concept in kendo.

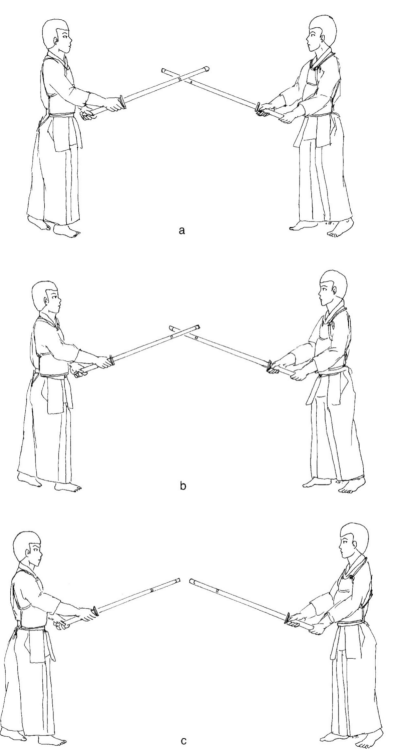

Fig. 60. (a) *Chikama* (short distance); (b) *issoku ittō no ma'ai* (one-foot one-sword distance); (c) *tōma* (long distance).

C
H
A
P
T
E
R

1
2

Ashisabaki (Footwork)

Ashisabaki (footwork) is one of the most important skills in kendo for a stable defense as well as an aggressive offense. From *shizentai* (natural stance), place your left foot one foot-width to the left and one foot-length to the back. Lift your left heel gently. All *ashisabaki* starts from this basic stance.

- *Ayumiashi* (walking footwork, Fig. 61a): Step alternately right and left as you would normally walk, but use a *suriashi* (gliding foot) technique; that is, glide on the balls of your feet. Use this technique to close in from afar or to retreat a long distance.

- *Tsugiashi* (connecting footwork, Fig. 61b): In a manner unnoticeable to the opponent, bring your left foot forward and close to the right foot, then take a step with your right foot in *suriashi*.

- *Hirakiashi* (open footwork, Fig. 61c): Step left or right diagonally with the foot facing the direction of the movement and quickly draw your other foot close. This step is used to fend off attacks and to strike back immediately.

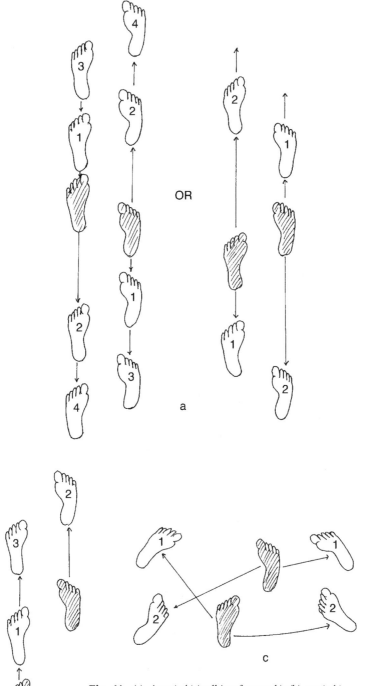

Fig. 61. (a) *Ayumiashi* (walking footwork); (b) *tsugiashi* (connecting footwork); (c) *hirakiashi* (open footwork). Here and in the following footwork sequences, the numbers refer to sequence of steps. The dark shading indicates the starting point.

OR

a

b

c

- *Okuriashi* (sending footwork, Fig. 62a, 62b, and 62c): Step with the foot facing the direction of movement first, then quickly draw the other foot in close. This technique is used to take one or two steps forward, backward, from side to side, or diagonally.

- *Fumikomiashi* (thrusting footwork): This is a type of *okuriashi* used in *uchikomi* (striking in proper form). Lift your forward foot and take one step forward quickly, pulling the back foot in close.

- *Nusumiashi* (stealthy footwork): Inconspicuously move the left foot toward the right foot so your opponent will not notice the movement below the lower edge of the *hakama*. *Nusumiashi* can change to *fumikomiashi* quickly so you can strike from *tōma*.

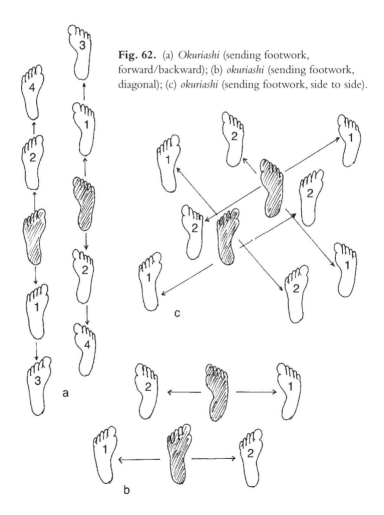

Fig. 62. (a) *Okuriashi* (sending footwork, forward/backward); (b) *okuriashi* (sending footwork, diagonal); (c) *okuriashi* (sending footwork, side to side).

Keiko (Training)

Keiko (training) in kendo is a lifelong activity. The dictionary definition of *keiko* is "to reflect and learn from the old." In kendo *keiko*, you practice and learn what many kendo practitioners in the past found important in their training. You should faithfully follow training examples set by your predecessors.

As a beginner it is crucial to find a good teacher who can watch and correct you before bad habits become permanent. If you find practice enjoyable and look forward to it, improvement is inevitable. It may be difficult to get used to the *bōgu* (protective gear) at the beginning, but the feeling of claustrophobia soon will disappear.

There are sets of kendo *keiko* that should be a part of every *keiko*, more than can be included here. Ask your instructor which *keiko* would be most appropriate for you.

In all technique *(waza)* practice it is important to make a big movement from good posture rather than a small one from a rigid stance. You must master one technique at a time and try to acquire as many techniques and variations as you can. If you are a beginner practicing with an expert, do not concern yourself with delivering a strike or being hit. You should do your best and concentrate as hard as you can, take a break when you can no longer keep up, and resume when you feel refreshed. You should practice as many times as possible; practice makes perfect and there is no expert who has not practiced. After the practice, listen humbly to your instructor, colleagues, or observers, and try to improve at the next practice.

Warm-up Exercises

As in any physical training, the warm-up exercises are an important part of kendo training and injury prevention. The basic warm-up exercises are described in this chapter. Remember, "Prevention is the most important strategy for all injury and illness."

Purpose

Warm-up exercises will acclimatize the muscles and tendons. The range-of-motion exercise will stretch the muscles and tendons so that they can withstand vigorous use during the practice. Remember to stretch the Achilles tendons because the sudden stretching required in *fumikomiashi* (thrusting) and other footwork can result in injury if you are not already limber. The range-of-motion exercise of the neck is also valuable because of the weight of the *men* and the impact of strikes to the *men*. In thrusting technique *(tsuki waza),* the front of the neck is struck with a sudden impact, and strong neck muscles are essential in withstanding such blows. The wrist exercises help prevent wrist sprains in such maneuvers as returning technique *(kaeshi waza).* Exercise of the fingers, elbows, knees, shoulders, and hips are just as important. Warm-up exercises are usually conducted from the peripheral (outer) parts of the body to the more central parts, and from the less strenuous to the more strenuous.

The examination of the *shinai* at the onset of practice and frequently during the practice is important to prevent injuries from a faulty weapon. Make sure that there are no splinters on the *shinai,* and that the *sakigawa* (leather cap) is intact. If the *sakigawa* loosens during practice, the *shinai* may split at the end. The sharp ends of the *shinai* may cause severe injuries if they pass between the *mengane* (headgear grid).

Procedure

Warm-up exercises start with stretching the smaller and peripheral muscles, followed by the central and larger muscles. By convention, the left side of the body or movement to the left starts first.

Warm-up Exercises without the *Shinai*

1. Fingers, hands, wrists, and knees: Bend the fingers of both hands. Shake and rotate the wrists and ankles. Interlace your fingers and raise them over your head, stretching to tiptoe. Cross one leg before the other, bend at the waist, and touch the floor.

2. Ankles: Stretching the Achilles tendons is very important. Extend one foot backward and stretch your Achilles tendon, then repeat with the other leg.

3. Feet, ankles, and knees: Jump up and down and loosen up.

4. Neck: Stretch forward and back, left to right, side to side, and in a circular motion.

5. Arms, elbows, and shoulders: Cross your arms in front of your chest and then raise them over your head.

6. Legs and thighs: Squat on one leg while stretching the other leg to the side.

7. Hip and torso: Stretch forward and back, from side to side, and in a circular motion of the torso.

Warm-up Exercises with the *Shinai*

Begin by inspecting your *shinai,* because a defective *shinai* can be dangerous. See Figs. 63–65 for the sequence.

1. *Taitō:* Bring the *shinai* to your left hip.

2. *Nuketō:* Draw the *shinai* and assume the *sonkyo* (squatting) position.

3. *Suburi* (empty swing): Without wearing your *men* and *kote,* practice swinging your *shinai,* paying attention to grip, form, and footwork. This is important for both beginners and experts.

4. *San kyodō* (three movements) *suburi:* Starting from *chūdan no kamae* (middle stance), raise your *shinai* and step forward with your right foot. Strike while drawing your left foot forward in *okuriashi* (sending footwork), then step back into *chūdan no kamae.*

5. *Ni kyodō* (two movements) *suburi:* Raise your *shinai* and simultaneously take a step and strike. Do all the following six *suburi.*

    a. *Zenshin shōmen uchi* (forward advance straight *men* strike): Take a step forward with your right foot and strike your opponent's *shōmen.*

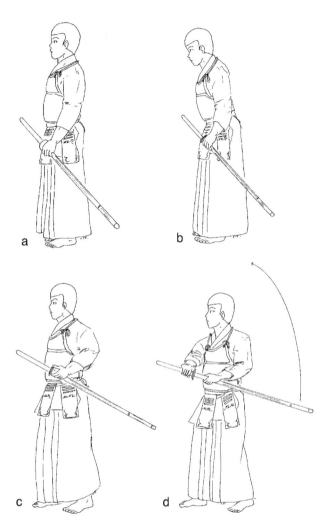

Fig. 63. Preparation *(tachiai)* for practice *(keiko)*: (a) Stand straight. (b) Bow. (c) *Taitō* and take three large steps. (d) Take the *shinai* with your right hand.

b. *Kōtai shōmen uchi* (retreat front *men* strike): Take a step back with your left foot and strike your opponent's *shōmen*.

c. *Zenshin kōtai shōmen uchi* (combination of a and b). Strike your opponent's *shōmen* while advancing and again while retreating.

d. *Sayū men uchi* (left and right *men* strike) with *hirakiashi* (open footwork): Strike your opponent's left and right *men* with *hirakiashi*. Strike the right *men* with a step to the right, and strike the left *men* with a step to the left.

e. *Sayūdōuchi* (left and right *dō* strike) with *hirakiashi:* Strike your opponent's left and right *dō* with *hirakiashi.*

f. Combinations with L shape: Strike your opponent's *shōmen* with a forward advance. Strike the *shōmen* again while in retreat. Strike your opponent's right and left *men* with *hirakiashi* to the right and left.

6. *Ikkyodō* (one movement) *hayasuburi:* Rapidly swing the *shinai* while jumping forward and back. Strike your opponent's *men* on the forward jump.

7. *Chōyaku suburi:* Swinging your *shinai* as you jump backward and forward on alternating feet.

8. *Sonkyo chōyaku jōge suburi:* Jump from a *sonkyo* stance and swing your *shinai* up as you jump up and swing it down as you land.

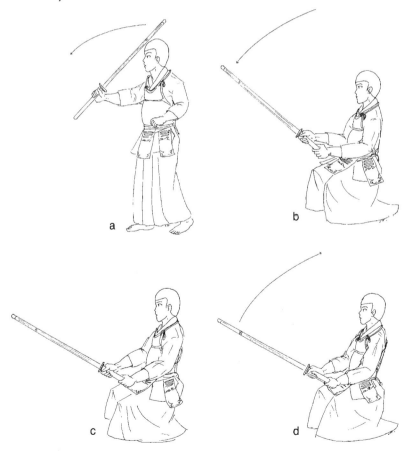

Fig. 64. (a) Draw the *shinai* (b) while assuming *sonkyo.* (c) Assume *sonkyo,* then (d) take the *shinai* back to the left hip *(osametō).*

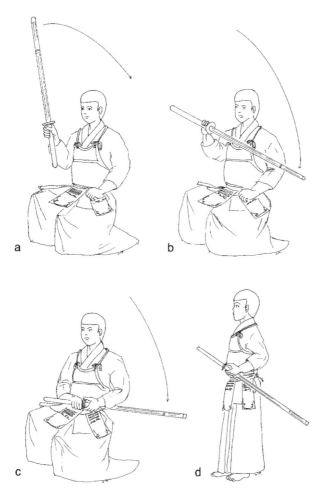

Fig. 65. (a) Take the *shinai* with your right hand. (b) Swing it back. (c) Grab the *shinai* with your left hand at your left hip. (d) Stand up and take five small steps backward.

9. Squat-jump *suburi:* Jump up and swing your *shinai* up. Swing your *shinai* down as you jump forward.

10. *Shinkokyū:* Take a deep breath through your nose while raising your *shinai* in *hidari morote jōdan* (above stance with left foot forward), then exhale slowly through pursed lips as you lower your *shinai* to resume *chūdan no kamae.* Repeat this several times until you have settled down from your warm-up exercises.

11. *Osametō:* Bring your *shinai* back to the *taitō* position (place *shinai* into the sash).

Keiko

Seating Arrangements
Prior to the start of *keiko* it is customary in most *dōjō* (practice hall) to have the *sensei* and students line up. The seating arrangements before the beginning of *keiko* are as follows: Facing the front *(shōmen)*, the *sensei* line up on the right side *(kamiza)* and students line up on the left side *(shimoza)* of the *dōjō;* this may be modified according to the *dōjō* design.

A few minutes prior to the start of *keiko* (after stretching and warm-up exercises), students promptly line up according to rank (higher rank toward the *shōmen*), sit down *(chakuza),* quietly assume the *seiza* position, and wait for the *sensei* to line up. Late arrivals sit at the lower end of the line regardless of rank. The highest-ranking student directs everyone *"Seiza!"* (sit in *mokusō*) for about 45 seconds (three deep breaths). The same student then stops it by directing *"Yame!"* (stop) and directs *"Shōmen ni rei!"* (bow to the front) and *"Sensei ni rei!"* (bow to the teachers). When bowing to the *sensei,* start before the *sensei* and raise your head after the *sensei* raise theirs.

Holding and Placing the Equipment
While standing, hold your *shinai* on your left side at rest stance *(teitō* or *sagetō)* and your *men* (headgear) and *kote* (arm guard) under your right arm. Hold your *men* face down and chin to the front, *kote* in the *men* with fists pointing down. After seating in *seiza,* place your *shinai* on your left [one fist away from your left knee, *tsuka* (hilt) in the front, *tsuba* (hand guard) at knee level, *tsuru* (string) facing the outside]. Then place your *kote* to the right and about 20 cm in front of your right knee with the fists to the right and palms down. Gently place your *men* on them. Fold your *tenugui* (towel) neatly and place it over the chin support of your *men.*

Donning Equipment and Beginning *Keiko*
When the highest-ranking student directs *"Men o tsuke!"* (put on your *men*) all the students must promptly and properly don their *men* and *kote* (left one first). The students should be ready for *keiko* before the *sensei* are ready.

The students should check each other for loose strings or other improper *chakusō (menhimo, koshihimo, tenugui, zekken, hakama,* and *dōgi).* The students will then stand in front of the practice instructor *(motodachi)* in full alert so as not to make him wait. At the start and end of *keiko,* each student bows *(ritsurei)* before the instructor to express appreciation. Students come to *sonkyo* or stand from *sonkyo* slightly after the instructor. If a student is unable to make an effective *datotsu* (strike) against the instructor in practice, or when a match is over, students are encouraged to ask for charging practice *(kakari geiko)* or striking practice *(uchikomi geiko)*.

Tachiai (Preparation)

At the beginning of the *keiko* you stand facing your opponent, nine steps apart, and bow to each other in the *teitō* or *sagetō* (at rest stance) position. Bring your *shinai* to your left hip and assume the *taitō* (sword-in-sash) position. Starting on your right foot, advance three large steps in *ayumiashi* (walking footwork), and take your *shinai* in your right hand to draw as you assume the *sonkyo* position. Stand up with full of *ki* (spirit) and start the practice.

To finish the practice, bow with your *shinai* lowered, or assume the *sonkyo* position, then bring your *shinai* back to your left hip *(osametō)* and stand up. Take five small steps to the starting position. Lower your *shinai* to the *teitō* or *sagetō* position and bow to your opponent.

Kirikaeshi Keiko (Repeat Cutting Practice)

Practice with a partner typically begins with *kirikaeshi,* performed twice in succession before the partners move on to other drills. *Kirikaeshi keiko* is probably the most important exercise for everyone from beginners to the high-ranking kendo practitioner *(kōdansha)*. *Kirikaeshi keiko* teaches the most important aspects of kendo, including *ki ken tai ittchi* (spirit, sword, and body in harmony), *ma'ai* (distance), *shisei* (posture), *kiai* (exclamation), *kokyū* (breathing), *ashisabaki* (footwork), *tenouchi* (holding the *shinai*), accurate *datotsu* (strike), *zanshin* (alertness), and developing endurance.

From *issoku ittō no ma'ai* (one-step-one-sword distance), when the *ki* (spirit) is full, the *shidachi* (striker/student) steps forward to strike the *shōmen* in a large and fast movement, followed by *taiatari* (body crush), then steps back to create a proper *ma'ai* (distance). If you are a *shidachi,* take a quick deep breath, then without hesitation, raise your left fist over your *men,* following the centerline until you can see the *motodachi*'s (receiver's) *men.* Relax your shoulders and step forward to strike the *sayū men* (left and right *men*) boldly, in big movements, four (or any even number of) times. Then step backward to strike the *sayū men* five (or any odd number of) times.

Start with the *hidari* (left) *men* and finish with the *hidari men.* All the *sayū men* should be struck at a 45-degree angle. Once again from *issoku ittō no ma'ai,* strike the *shōmen* and follow with the *taiatari.* Repeat striking the *sayū men* forward and backward, followed by striking the *shōmen* one last time, all in a single breath, and pass the *motodachi.* Again strike the *shōmen* and return to your original position. Maintain *zanshin* to finish this movement. Produce the loud *kiai* (exclamation) *"Men!"* deep from within your abdomen when striking the *shōmen.* Also, your left fist should go up and down along the centerline and it should be your right hand that changes the direction of the *shinai.* Footwork for *shidachi* is *okuriashi* (sending footwork).

The *motodachi* should receive the *shōmen* strikes and *taiatari* correctly while full of *ki* (spirit) (Fig. 66). To receive *sayū men* strikes as the *motodachi,* raise your *shinai* straight up from *chūdan no kamae.* Your right fist should be at chest level and your left fist is at waist level. As the *motodachi,* let the *shidachi* (student/striker) strike your *shinai* near your left or right *men* by pulling your *shinai* closer. As the *motodachi,* the footwork is *ayumiashi* (walking footwork). After the *taiatari* draw your left foot back to receive the *hidari men.* Measure the timing so that it matches the tempo of the *shidachi* with *ki ken tai ittchi* (spirit, sword, and body in harmony).

Variation: There is *aiuchi kirikaeshi keiko* (dual striking and receiving practice) where both partners hit and receive strikes simultaneously instead of alternating.

Kihon Keiko (Fundamental Practice)

Kihon keiko encourages you to develop a, bold, individual striking technique and correct footwork. Footwork is done in *suriashi* and *okuriashi.* Initially, beginners should practice with slow and big motions. Most fundamental technique is *shōmen uchi* (Figs. 67 and 68). *Hidari men, migimen, dō, kote,* and *tsuki* techniques are practiced in a similar manner.

Uchikomi Keiko (Striking Practice)

Uchikomi keiko is a fundamental exercise that can be performed with other students or the *sensei,* or by using instruments or *uchikomi-bō* (a stick used for striking practice). Use all of the basic techniques with good footwork and *ma'ai.* Strike with correct form and spirit when the *sensei* shows a *suki* (an opening to strike). It is essential to follow through correctly and return to a *zanshin* (state of readiness).

Renzoku Waza Keiko (Sequence Practice)

Commonly, *renzoku waza keiko* is performed twice in succession toward the end of paired drills or instruction. You should exercise designated skills in sequence—for example, *men, kote-men, kote-men-dō, men-taiatari-hiki-men, men-taiatari-hikidō,* and finally *men*—from a proper *ma'ai.*

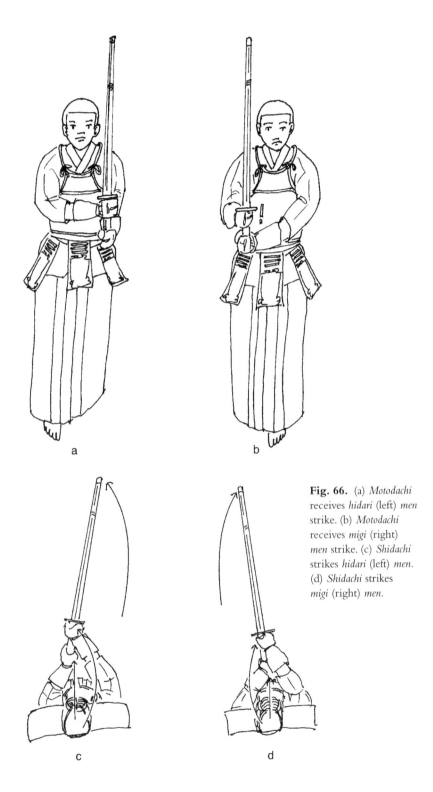

a

b

Fig. 66. (a) *Motodachi*
receives *hidari* (left) *men*
strike. (b) *Motodachi*
receives *migi* (right)
men strike. (c) *Shidachi*
strikes *hidari* (left) *men*.
(d) *Shidachi* strikes
migi (right) *men*.

c

d

Fig. 67. *Kihon keiko* (fundamental practice): (a) Step 1: Stand in *issoku ittō no ma'ai*. (b) Step 2: raise the *shinai*, shift your gravity to your left foot and begin to move your right foot forward.

Fig. 68. *Kihon keiko*
(cont.): (a) Step 3: Swing
the *shinai* until you can
see the *uchidachi*'s face
and step forward on
your right foot. (b) Step
4: Step in with your
right foot and begin to
move your left foot for-
ward. (c) Step 5: Strike
the *shōmen* with your
right arm extended at
shoulder level and your
left arm at chest level as
you bring your left foot
close to your right foot
(okuriashi).

Zigzag *Keiko*

In zigzag *keiko, motodachi* space themselves out in zigzag formation. The *shidachi* (students/strikers) practice different techniques with all the *motodachi*. The first technique is *men,* which each student practices with each *motodachi*. The student then races to the beginning of the line to practice the second technique, *kote-men.* This is followed by *kote-men-dō,* and practice ends with *kirikaeshi.*

Kakari Keiko (Charging Practice)

Kakari keiko is the most intense and aggressive practice against the *sensei.* The student must use all of his skills to break the balance of the *motodachi.* If you are the student, strike aggressively from *tōma* (far distance) and continuously with spirit while maintaining correct form, big movement, and follow-through (passing the *motodachi*). You should be concerned with your technique without worrying about being hit by the *motodachi.*

The *motodachi* should let the student know when the movement is incorrect by fending off the strikes. When the strikes are done correctly, the *motodachi* should allow the student to continue. This will enhance the student's self-confidence.

Keep in mind that *kakari keiko* is meant to build the foundations of kendo, including body, spirit, and skills, and is not intended to correct the finer points. Obviously this type of practice will benefit beginners most, but even higher-ranking kendo practitioners should perform with fresh and new determination.

Variation: In *aiuchi kakari keiko* (dual charging practice), both partners practice *kakari keiko* instead of one acting the role of the *motodachi* and other the *shidachi.*

Hikitate Keiko (Encouraging Practice)

The purpose of *hikitate keiko* is to teach correct *datotsu* (striking technique) to beginners. The instructor should open an area for the student to strike. The teacher should make sure that the *datotsu* was done in a correct form with proper *zanshin* (alertness) at the end of the strike. The *motodachi* should let the student strike freely without fear, so he will learn the correct technique. The student may practice *ippon uchi* (single strike) or *renzoku waza* (sequence of strikes). The *motodachi* should correct the student's bad habits and point out good techniques. No matter how high the *motodachi's dan* (rank) may be, he should lower his level of practice to about one *dan* above the student. It is very important for the instructor to lift up the spirit of the student, to encourage further practice. Instructors should aim to become good teachers through this type of practice.

Gokaku Keiko (Equal Partner Practice)

Gokaku keiko is done between the partners of equal strength. It aims to help them improve *tokui waza* (forte) and practice defense against an opponent's *waza*. This practice is like a *shiai* (match) with careful strikes and defenses done in a correct manner, learned from other exercises. You should choose as many opponents with different styles and skills as possible so that both may improve their skills and spiritual discipline. Through this practice you can learn your weaknesses and gain confidence.

Jigeiko (Match-like Practice)

Jigeiko is a most common practice, involving a wide variety of opponents. With an equal opponent you can practice *gokaku keiko;* with a higher-ranking opponent you can practice *kakari keiko;* and with a junior student you can practice *hikitate keiko. Jigeiko* is intended to improve your techniques. The high-ranking kendo practitioner stands at *kamiza* and the student stands at *shimoza;* each may practice according to their own preferences. Usually practice begins with *kirikaeshi keiko* and goes on to *kakari keiko* or *gokaku keiko* and *ippon shōbu.* It usually ends with *kirikaeshi.* During this practice one can usually find the level of the opponent's skills and change style accordingly.

Shōbu Keiko (Match Practice)

Shōbu keiko is usually taken once, but when an *ippon* is scored you may ask for another *("Mō ippon!").* Put your skills into the match and strive to improve, whether you win or lose. Follow the rules and show respect for your opponent. Usually the players decide whether an *ippon* has been scored, but there may be a *shinpan* (referee). Learn to adapt to different *dōjō* environments. Do your best to win but do not let winning be your only goal. Although you may score first, keep fighting hard and do not stall for time to win. Stay in the best physical and spiritual condition.

Shiai Keiko (Tournament Practice)

Shiai keiko is done prior to a tournament to help the players prepare for the event. Usually it is done according to the format of the tournament. For a *dantai sen* (group match) *shiai keiko* is used to decide the order of players: *senpō* (first player), *jihō* (second player), *chūken* (middle player), *fukushō* (subcaptain), and *shushō* (captain). It is a good idea to have several *shiai keiko* prior to the tournament, to point out players' weaknesses or areas they need to improve. After the *shiai keiko,* the players should gain confidence in their own skills.

Mitori Keiko (Observation Practice)

In essence, everyone in *mitori keiko* is a teacher regardless of rank or length of training. In this exercise, you carefully watch others practice. Study their strong points, techniques, manners, and grace, but also learn from their mistakes.

Hitori Keiko (Lone Practice)

Although it is ideal to practice kendo with an instructor and other students, it is not always possible to do so. You can practice *uchikomi* (striking) using a *uchikomidai* (striking stand) or simply by tying a *shinai* to a desk or tree and practicing various techniques. Probably the most common type of *hitori keiko* is *suburi,* such as *senbon* (thousand) *suburi*. *Kata* practice can be done alone very well. There are various other types of training that aim at strengthening the body, increasing endurance, and correcting form using a mirror, enhancing concentration, and understanding *ki* through Zen training. Many famous kendo masters such as Miyamoto Musashi practiced their kendo alone, deep in the mountains, and yet became the most skilled of all the kendo practitioners.

Tachigiri Keiko (Continuous *Motodachi* Training)

Tachigiri keiko is one of the most vigorous and exhausting training methods and is not done too often. In *tachigiri keiko* you practice against different opponents as a *motodachi* for approximately three hours. Your partner, however, changes every three minutes. The legendary kendo master Yamaoka Tesshu is said to have done 200 matches a day for seven consecutive days. This type of *keiko* challenges one's spiritual and physical limits.

Musha Shugyō (Martial Traveling)

Travel for the purpose of seeking training from different teachers of different schools was once very common and popular among students of kendo. The kendo masters of olden days spent ten to fifteen years on the road for *musha shugyō* and often risked their lives at it. It is not too difficult to imagine an inexperienced kendo practitioner being punished by students of different schools, or a skillful one who has beaten everyone meeting an unfortunate end in an ambush by disgruntled opponents. These travelers often spent many years deep in the mountains for spiritual training as well. They also met many challengers who were in similar training. The more skilled and well known they were, the more challengers they had, and a match was often fought to the death. We may imagine that unknown challengers would eagerly seek a chance to beat a famous kendo master. Miyamoto Musashi defeated over sixty opponents before he was twenty-eight or twenty-nine years old and Tsukahara Bokuden defeated over two hundred challengers during three of his *musha shugyō*. They both emerged victorious from all their matches, without a scratch, which sounds like a miracle. To have survived such training must have taken superhuman abilities, and they should be truly respected.

Musha shugyō is no longer practiced in Japan, but the concept is still useful. You can go to different *dōjō* in different regions or countries to experience different styles of kendo and break the monotony of practicing the same way, year after year.

Tanrenbō (Strengthening Pole)

Keiko with a *tanrenbō* improves *tenouchi* (holding of handle) of the sword or *shinai*. It also helps you learn to come to a complete stop after swinging down. The *tanrenbō* weighs between 2,250 g and 3,750 g, four to seven times the weight of an adult man's *shinai* (~510 g). You should choose a weight commensurate with your strength.

The type of *keiko* with *tanrenbō* includes, straight swing *(shinchoku suburi)*, left-right diagonal swing *(sayū kesa suburi)*, repeat cut with both hands *(morote kirikaeshi)* and repeat cut with one hand *(katate kirikaeshi)*.

The End of *Keiko*

To show respect and to develop endurance, students should not remove the *men* while the *sensei* are still practicing, unless physiologically or medically necessary. When the end of practice is signaled, students should line up promptly in the order described for the beginning of the practice and remain standing until the *sensei* is seated. Then the highest-ranking student orders *"Chakuza!"* to tell students to sit in *seiza*. When the *sensei* has removed his *men*, the highest-ranking student directs *"Men o tore"* (remove your *men*) to tell students to remove their *kote* (right one first) and *men*. The highest-ranking student directs everyone to *"Seiza!"* for about 45 seconds, then directs *"Yame!"* (stop). After the closing remarks or announcements, the highest-ranking student directs *"Sensei ni rei!"* (bow to the *sensei*) and *"Shōmen ni rei!"* (bow to the front). Each student should approach the *sensei* who has given him *keiko* to express appreciation by bowing *(zarei)*, then listen to his advice.

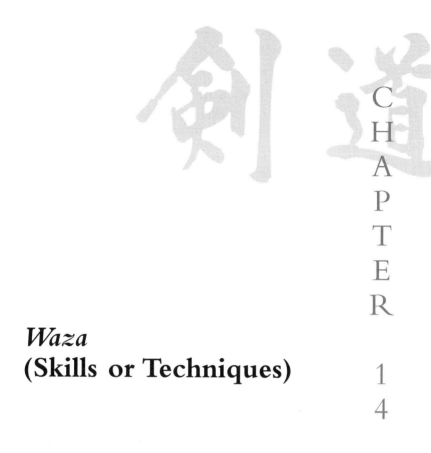

Waza
(Skills or Techniques)

An effective strike is called *yūkō datotsu*. For a strike to be effective you must first strike the *datotsubui* (target) with the cutting zone (*monouchi* or *datotsubu*) of the *shinai* in a correct direction of the blade *(hasuji)*. Also, at the time of the strike you must have full *ki* (spirit), good *kiai* (exclamation), and good posture. After a good strike you must also have alertness *(zanshin)*. Without *zanshin* an *ippon* (point) is subject to cancellation *(torikeshi)*. Accuracy becomes even more important in one-handed technique *(katate waza)*, retreating technique *(hiki waza)*, and *waza* after hand guard fight *(tsubazeriai)*.

One important concept to remember in delivering an effective strike is spirit of offense *(seme)*. You may strike your opponent by chance, but if you have no *seme* it is not considered a good strike. It is very important to pressure opponent with *seme* and *ki*, thus winning even before striking.

Waza (Technique) and *Suki* (Opening)

Waza can be delivered when your opponent shows a *suki*. *Suki* appears and disappears in a fleeting moment. Such moments are as follows:

1. *Degashira* (beginning of the *waza*): When your opponent tries to strike, he is open to your strike.

2. *Hiku tokoro* (retreating): When your opponent retreats in the face of a *seme,* you have a chance to strike.

3. *Waza no tsukita tokoro* (ending of the *waza*): At the end of the *waza* or *renzoku waza* (sequence of techniques), your opponent needs to take a breath or assume a new *kamae*. This creates a *suki* for a strike.

4. *Itsuita tokoro* (settled): A break in your opponent's attention or concentration creates a *suki*.

5. *Uketometa tokoro* (the moment of blocking the strike): At the moment when your opponent has just defended himself from attack, he is vulnerable.

6. Others: When your opponent feels *kyo, ku, gi,* or *waku* (surprise, fear, doubt, or hesitation) or when your opponent has just taken a deep breath, he cannot deliver an effective strike.

The *waza* can be divided into either *shikake waza* (offensive techniques) or *ōji waza* (counter techniques) depending on who makes the first move.

Shikake Waza

It is nearly impossible to deliver a good *waza* if your opponent is in a good *kamae* (stance), with the *kensen* (sword tip) pointing toward your throat or left eye, keeping to the centerline *(seichū sen)*. You must find your opponent's *suki* or force your opponent to make a *suki,* then strike. This is called *shikake waza,* and it is an aggressive offensive technique. Attempt to create *suki* by *renzoku waza* (sequence techniques), *harai waza* (slapping technique), or *katsugi waza* (shouldering technique). It is important to maintain good posture and form, to watch your opponent's movements, and to strike quickly and swiftly. You must also seize the opportunity, for example, when your opponent begins or ends his *waza*.

Renzoku Waza (Sequence of Techniques)

Renzoku waza is a sequence of either *nidan waza* (two-sequence *waza*) or *sandan waza* (three-sequence *waza*) (Fig. 69). When a first strike is not effective, you should immediately follow with *renzoku waza*. In

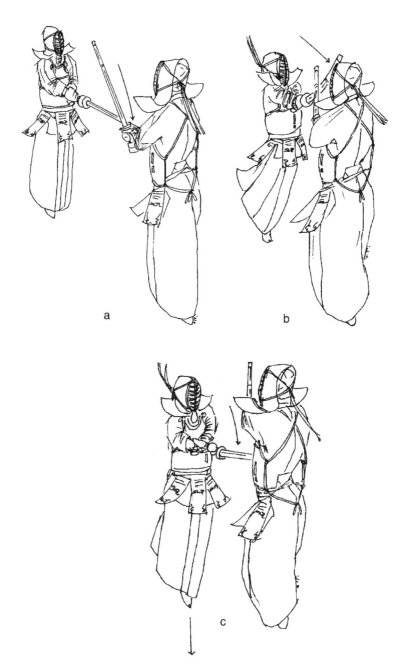

Fig. 69. *Shikake waza* (offensive techniques): (a) Striking the opponent's *kote* was not effective. (b) Attempting to strike the *men* was not effective. (c) Finally, a decisive strike to the *dō*.

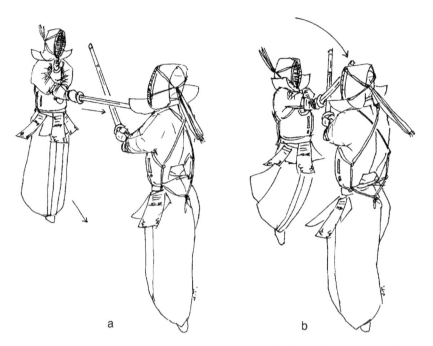

Fig. 70. (a) A stab to the opponent's *tsuki tare* is not effective, so (b) make a decisive strike to the *men*.

another example, you might feint an attack to one area to draw your opponent's attention and immediately strike from the opposite direction toward another area (Fig. 70). For *renzoku waza* to be successful you must use correct footwork (parallel and no *shumoku ashi*) and keep pursuing your opponent until you make a good strike.

Harai Waza (Slapping Technique)

In *harai waza* you slap your opponent's *shinai* from the side to distract his guard from *omote* (your left, your opponent's right) or from *ura* (your right, your opponent's left), or downward or diagonally upward in a slapping motion (Fig. 71). The *harai* and *datotsu* (striking) are in one smooth sequence. Also it is important to strike your opponent's *shinai* below the midsection. The *kensen* (sword tip) should remain at the center of your opponent's body and your left fist at the center of your own body immediately after slapping.

Harai Men (Sweeping *Men* Technique)

From a *chūdan no kamae*, raise your *kensen* slightly as you begin to lift your right foot and strike downward or sideways to the left of your

a   b

c   d

Fig. 71. An example of *harai waza* (slapping technique): (a) From *ura,* (back, one's right, opponent's right); (b) *harai men;* (c) *harai kote;* (d) *harai dō.*

opponent's *shinai* to throw him off guard, then immediately strike your opponent's *shōmen* as you step with your right foot (Fig. 71b).

Katsugi Waza (Shouldering Technique)

Katsugi waza is used as a ploy. Your opponent tends to change *kamae* (stance) and show *suki* when you bring the sword to the shoulder. Step forward and to the right with your right foot, bringing your *shinai* to your left shoulder and swing it down in a direction parallel to your opponent's *shinai*. See Fig. 72.

Debana Waza (Attack-at-the-Start Technique)

The moment an opponent starts a *waza* is called *debana*. The *waza* to strike your opponent at this vulnerable moment is called *debana waza*. When your opponent begins to attack, his mind is set and he is defenseless against the strike. It is most effective when *ki* and *seme* are strong and force opponent to attempt to strike first. At the moment of strike use a snapping motion of wrists and strike lightly. Good posture and *zanshin* are required. See Fig. 73.

Fig. 72. *Katsugi waza* (shouldering technique): (a) Raise the *shinai* to your shoulder. (b) When your opponent shows *suki,* strike the *men* (c) or *kote.*

Katate Waza (One-handed Technique)

Katate waza is effective when your opponent is at a far distance such as when he has retreated, or when you have dodged your opponent's attack *(nuki).* Keep *seme* on opponent's center, take a step with your left foot, and bring your *shinai* to the *jōdan no kamae* (above stance) and strike your opponent's *migimen* while stepping in (Fig. 74b). When you bring down your *shinai,* twist your body slightly to the right, extend your left elbow, and bring your right fist to your right side to keep your balance. When your opponent comes in to strike your right *kote* (forearm) or to *tsuki* (thrust), you can turn your body to the right to deliver a *katate waza.* A variation on this technique is the *katate tsuki* (one-handed thrust). When you find a *suki* in your opponent, extend your left elbow and stab at your opponent's *mendare* area while stepping in with your right foot (Fig 74a). At this time

a

b

Fig. 73. *Debana waza* (attack at the start technique): (a) From *chudan*, as your opponent begins to attack your *men,* (b) strike the *kote.*

your navel, left hand, and *kensen* should be in a straight line. When thrusting your *shinai*, you should twist your wrist internally about 45 degrees. Immediately step back on your right foot and take the center again with *zanshin*. This *waza* is also effective against Nitō ryū or *jōdan waza* but requires practice for accuracy.

Jōdan Waza (*Shinai* **Above Technique**)

In order to deliver *jōdan waza* (Fig. 75), you must constantly have a feeling of superiority and *seme*. The moment your opponent begins to strike or retreat is the opportune time to bring down your *shinai*. Keep *seme* with the *tsukagashira* (butt end of tsuka) and find a *suki* in your opponent (Fig. 75a); push your *shinai* with your right hand toward your opponent's *men* and bring it down with your left hand (Fig. 75b). Keep your left fist in front of your chest and close the distance to your opponent. When your opponent raises a *kote* to block the *men* strike, step in with your left foot, turn your body to the right slightly, and strike your opponent's right *kote* (Fig. 75c). It is important to keep your left hand along the centerline when striking. See Fig. 76a for the direction of the *shinai* with respect to that of fist when delivering *kote waza* from *jōdan*.

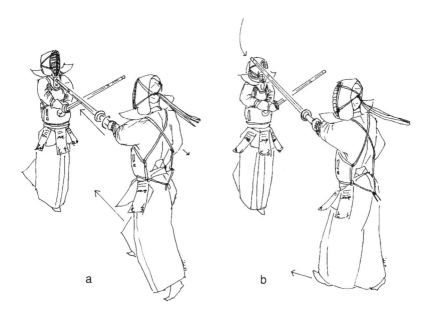

a   b

Fig. 74. *Katate waza* (one-handed thrust): (a) When you see a *suki* (opening), strike the *tsuki dare* with one hand (b) or strike your opponent's *migi* (right) *men*.

Fig. 75. (a) *Jōdan waza* (*shinai* above technique): (b) striking the *men* from *jōdan;* (c) striking the *men* from *kote*.

a

b

c

Fig. 76. *Jōdan waza:* (a) Note the curved path of *kensen* (sword tip) and the straight path of the left fist in striking the *kote* (b) *dō* from *jōdan* and (c) strike.

a

b

c

Taiatari Waza (Body Crush Technique)

Taiatari waza is used to create a proper *ma'ai* when you are too close to your opponent or you want to get your opponent off-balance and create a *suki*. Also, you can meet an opponent's strike with a *taiatari* to put him off balance, thus creating an opportunity to strike back (Fig. 77a). A *taiatari* most commonly follows the *shōmen* but also can be done from the *kote-men, tsuki-men, kote,* or *dō*. After a *taiatari*, make sure you get enough *ma'ai* before striking, either by pursuing or by stepping back from an advancing opponent. This is called *hiki waza*

Fig. 77. *Taiatari waza* (body crush technique): (a) A moment of proper *taiatari*. (b) After breaking opponent's balance, execute *men,* (c) *kote,* (d) or *dō*.

(retreating technique). At the time of the *taiatari*, your feet should be very close to your opponent's and your back should be straight with your chin tucked in. This is done with the entire body and not just the arms, which is why it is called a body crush. Your left hand should drop to the level of your navel and your right to the midchest area. When your opponent raises his fists, his *dō* becomes open. Conversely, if your opponent keeps his fists down, then the *men* becomes a good target. For safety reasons this technique should be avoided against lighter-weight and elderly teachers or practitioners.

Hiki Waza **(Retreating Technique)**
After a *taiatari* or a *tsubazeriai* (hand guard fight), you can create a proper *ma'ai* by taking a step back to strike. During a *tsubazeriai*, both contestants try to take the center and break the other's balance to create a *suki*. To step back with your left foot, you can press your fists above your opponent's, push your opponent's fists upward, or press diagonally to the left or right to create a *suki* and hit your opponent's *men* as you step back with your right foot. When opponent blocks the *men*, you may immediately strike his *dō*. An important point to remember during *tsubazeriai* is not to press your opponent's shoulder with your *shinai,* and not to use *tsuka* to press your opponent's *tsuba* or to use it as a delaying technique. There are many other variations to this *waza*.

Tobikomi Waza **(Jumping-by-Sending-Footwork Technique)**
Tobikomi waza is used from *tōma* (far distance). Bending your right knee and keeping *seme* from below, jump with your right foot and strike your opponent's *shōmen* as your left foot follows. When your opponent raises his arms, keep *seme* and jump to strike the *dō*. See Fig. 78.

Ōji Waza **(Counter Technique)**
Ōji waza includes counter techniques in general. When your opponent attacks, parry his *shinai,* then strike back. Fend off your opponent's *shinai* to neutralize the attack by *suriage waza* (sliding up), *kaeshi waza* (returning technique), *uchiotoshi waza* (striking-down technique), *maki waza* (coiling technique), *osae waza* (pressing technique), or *nuki waza* (evading technique), then immediately strike back. Except in the case of *nuki waza*, the *shinai* makes contact with the opponent's *shinai*. It is essential to synchronize with your opponent's strike. Strike from a proper *ma'ai*. Wrist motion is very important in *ōji waza* because it requires small, quick movements. It is also critical to maintain correct posture during this *waza*. The most important

Fig. 78. *Tobikomi waza* (jumping-by-sending-footwork technique): (a) *tobikomi men;* (b) *tobikomi dō.*

a

b

point is not simply to wait for your opponent's attack but to approach and press your opponent aggressively until he can no longer tolerate the *seme* (spirit of offense) and therefore has to attack.

Nuki Waza (Evading Technique)

In *nuki waza* you evade your opponent's strike and, at this vulnerable moment, immediately strike back. You must be able to anticipate your opponent's strike in order for this *waza* to be successful. You can dodge *(nuki, nuku)* by moving your left foot straight back, diagonally back, or diagonally forward. If you are successful, your opponent's strike will miss its target completely. Step in with your right foot, forward or to the right. This *waza* is the only *ōji waza* in which the *shinai* do not come in contact with each other. See Fig. 79.

Amashi Waza (Evade-by-Withdraw Technique)

Amashi waza is a variation of *nuki waza* in which you take a big step straight back, diagonally left, or to the right rear with your *shinai* lowered. This increases *ma'ai,* thus dodging your opponent's *shinai.* Your opponent will have exhausted his *waza,* so this is the time for you to strike back. When your opponent tries to recover and tries for a new *waza,* strike his *debana,* or strike when your opponent loses momentum and is momentarily unprepared for *waza* or defense.

Kaeshi Waza (Returning Technique)

In *kaeshi waza,* block your opponent's *shinai,* twist your wrist to the opposite side of your opponent's *shinai,* and strike back while stabilizing your stance. In this *waza,* deflect your opponent's *shinai* using the end half of your *shinai* by raising it. You can step to the right or left, depending on whether you deflect with *omote* or *ura.* See Figs. 80 and 81.

Suriage Waza (Sliding Upward Technique)

Suriage waza is similar to *harai waza.* As your opponent's *shinai* is coming down, bring your own *shinai* up and forward to deflect it so you can strike back. You can step back or to the side. You can also slide up with the *omote* or *ura* of your *shinai.* The best *suriage waza* is done by using the natural curvature of the *shinogi* (sword ridge) of the *monouchi* (cutting zone) of the *shinai,* but it is important to keep the *kensen* (sword tip) close to the center. You can *suriage* (slide up) from *omote* and strike your opponent's *men,* or *suriage* from *ura* and strike your opponent's *migi* (right) *men* or *kote,* or flip your wrist and hit your opponent's *hidari* (left) *dō.* The *suriage* and strike should be done in one single motion. This particular *waza* can be used as *shikake waza* or *ōji waza,* depending on who starts the offensive move first. See Fig. 82.

Fig. 79. *Nuki waza* (evading technique): (a) Step back to evade *(nuku)* your opponent's men strike. (b) Immediately strike your opponent's *men*. (c) Opponent readies to strike the *men*. (d) Step to the side to evade *(nuku)* and strike your opponent's *dō*.

Fig. 80. *Kaeshi wasa* (returning technique): (a) Blocking opponent's *men* strike, (b) immediately spin the *shinai* to strike your opponent's *men*.

Fig. 81. *Kaeshi wasa* (cont.): (a) Block your opponent's *men* strike (b) and immediately stroke your opponent's *dō*.
(c) Block your opponent's *men* strike from the *ura* (back) of your *shinai* (d) and immediately strike your opponent's *gyaku* (reverse) *dō* or (e) *hidari* (left) *men*.

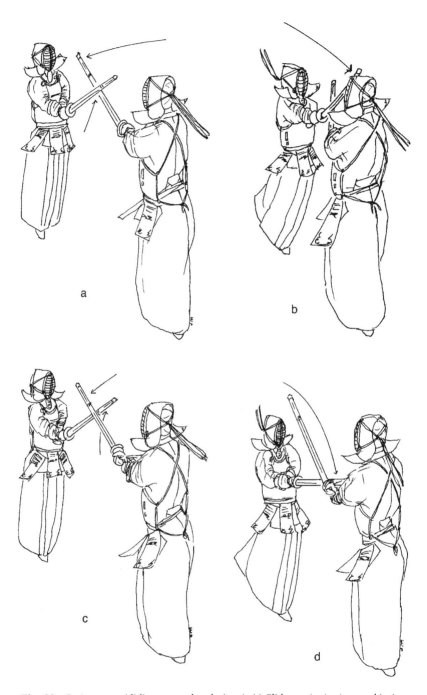

Fig. 82. *Suriage waza* (sliding upward technique): (a) Slide up *(suriage)* your *shinai* from *omote* (your left) as your opponent strikes your *men* and (b) immediately strike your opponent's *men*. (c) Slide up *(suriage)* from *ura* (your right) and (d) immediately strike your opponent's *kote*.

Uchiotoshi Waza (Striking Down Technique)

As your opponent's *shinai* is coming down, sidestep and strike his *shi-nai* from the *omote* or *ura* of your own *shinai*. It is important to strike your opponent's *shinai* down but keep your own *shinai* in the center. You may step to the right, left, and diagonally back to the right or to the left to strike your opponent's *shinai* down. Using the *monouchi* of your *shinai*, strike between the *nakayui* (middle strap) and the middle portion of our opponent's *shinai* at the right moment. The *uchiotoshi* (striking down) and strike should be done in a single smooth movement. See Fig. 83.

Maki Waza (Coiling Technique)

As your opponent's *shinai* comes down or comes in by *tsuki*, open your body and block your opponent's *shinai* by drawing a circle with your own *shinai* around your opponent's center. You can do this from the *omote* or *ura* side of own *shinai*, and you can open your body to the right or left by stepping to either from side or back or forward. See Fig. 84.

Osae Waza (Pressing Technique)

As your opponent comes to strike your *men*, open your body to your own right by stepping to the right side (or diagonally forward or

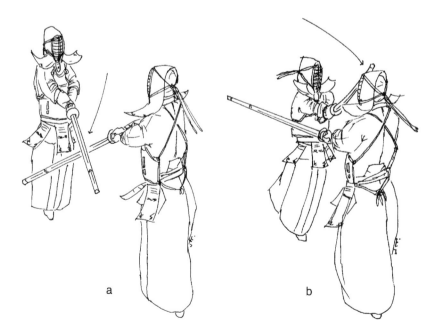

a   b

Fig. 83. *Uchiotoshi waza* (striking down technique): (a) Strike down your opponent's *shinai* as he tries to attack your *kote*. (b) Immediately strike your opponent's *men*.

Fig. 84. *Maki waza* (coiling technique): (a) Step to the side and block your opponent's *shinai* with a circular movement of your *shinai*. (b) Ready to strike. (c) Execute *men*.

back). Deflect your opponent's *shinai* by *kaeshi waza* (returning technique) and press your opponent's *shinai* with the *omote* (front) of your own *shinai*. Immediately strike your opponent's *men* or, if your opponent tries to raise his *shinai* against your *shinai*, strike your opponent's *migi* (right) *kote* or *migi dō*. If you want to *osae* (press) with the *ura* of the *shinai*, step to your left side (or diagonally forward or back) to open your body to the left.

Harai Waza (Slapping Technique)

Harai waza was mentioned earlier in the section on *shikake waza*. It also can be used as *ōji waza*. As your opponent strikes your *men*, *dō*, or *kote*, you can *harai* or *harau* (slapping or slap) from the *omote* (front) or *ura* (back) of the *shinai* by stepping forward, backward, right, left, or diagonally in any direction. Immediately strike your opponent's *men*, *migi* (right) *dō*, *hidari dō* (left *dō*), or *gyakudō* (reverse *dō*). When doing a *harai* (slapping) movement, draw a semicircle to deflect your opponent's *shinai*. At this time the *kensen* should not move out of the *chushin sen* (centerline).

Seme and *Uchikomi* (The Spirit of Offense and the Strike)

Aside from the techniques already discussed, there is a fundamental technique to the *seme* and strike. The *uchikomi* is similar to the *kihon uchi* technique in basic practice but it is done with much more *seme*. It is essential to assume a correct *chūdan no kamae* with the correct foot position, arm position, *metsuke* (focal point), and so on. However, you must be ready to take action as if you were on a spring. Keep a strong *seme* and assume a superior posture both in *kamae* and spirit, and find a *suki* in your opponent. There is a *chushin sen* (center line) or *seimei sen* (lifeline), an invisible thread between you and your opponent; the kendo practitioner who places his *shinai* on this line will have the live *shinai* and the opponent will have a dead *shinai*. This line is not big enough for two *shinai*, so you must compete for this limited space. The following basic *waza* are technically considered *shikake waza* (offensive techniques).

1. *Shōmen* (front *men*): Get into an *issoku ittō no ma'ai* (one-foot one-sword distance) in *chūdan no kamae* from *tōma*. Keep your *kensen* at the center with a strong *seme* until your opponent raises his *shinai*. Immediately step in and strike your opponent's *shōmen* as soon as you raise your *shinai* in a snapping motion. Return to a *chūdan no kamae* and maintain *zanshin*.

2. *Sayū men* (left and right *men*): Feint toward your opponent's right *men*, and as your opponent tries to defend himself, quickly strike the left *men*.

3. *Migi* (right) *kote:* From a *chūdan no kamae* and an *issoku ittō no ma'ai*, raise your *shinai*. As your opponent begins to raise his *shinai* in response, step in as if to step on your opponent's right foot and strike the *migi kote* immediately. Keep your *kensen* in the center.

4. *Migi* (right) *dō:* This is similar to *migi kote*. Pressure your opponent with strong *seme*. When your opponent raises his *shinai*, step in immediately and strike the *migi dō*.

5. *Tsuki:* With strong *seme*, keep your *kensen* in the center. When your opponent begins to retreat, immediately strike *tsuki* to the *mendare*. Then, just as rapidly, withdraw your *shinai* and resume the *chūdan no kamae*. Maintain *zanshin*. A *tsuki* (thrust) to the *dōmune* area is not considered a point even if one's opponent is in *jōdan* or Nitō ryū.

Fundamental Techniques in Nitō Ryū
The following are the basic Nitō ryū techniques.

1. *Men* (head), *dō* (torso), and *kote* (forearm): Close in the *ma'ai* and *osaeru* or *harau* with your short *shinai*, simultaneously hitting your opponent's *kote, men,* or *dō*. See Fig. 85a.

2. When your opponent closes the *ma'ai*, slap with your short *shinai* and immediately strike your opponent's *kote* with your long *shinai*. See Fig. 85b.

3. When your opponent attacks your *men*, block with the short *shinai* and step to the side to strike your opponent's *dō*. See Fig. 86. *Variation:* From *zangetsu* (crescent moon) stance, deflect your opponent's *shinai* in *ukenagashi* (deflecting technique), step to the side and hit the *men*.

4. When your opponent attacks your *dō*, the side with the short *shinai*, block with your short *shinai* and hit your opponent's *men* or *dō* with your long *shinai* as you twist your body to the side of your short *shinai*.

Fig. 85. Nitō ryū techniques: (a) Use the small *shinai* to control your opponent's *shinai* and strike the *men* or (b) *kote*.

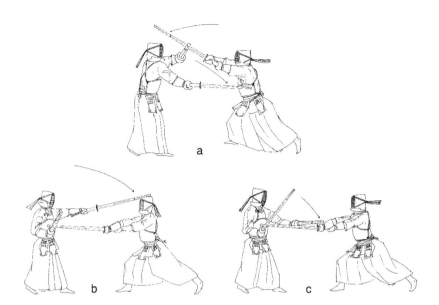

Fig. 86. Nitō ryū techniques (cont.): (a) Block your opponent's *men* strike with your short *shinai* and simultaneously strike the *dō*. (b) Block your opponent's *dō* strike with your short *shinai* and strike the *men* or (c) block with your long *shinai* and strike the *kote*.

5. When your opponent strikes your *dō* on the side with the long *shinai*, lower your long *shinai* to protect your *dō* and strike the *kote* or step back and *tsuki* (thrust) with your short *shinai*, or block with your short *shinai* across your *dō* and hit your opponent's *men* with your long *shinai*.

6. When your opponent strikes your *men* as you are in *jūji* (cross) stance, block with your short *shinai* and *tsuki* with your long *shinai*. See Fig. 87. *Variation:* Hit your opponent's *men* or *dō* with your long *shinai* after blocking or slapping with your short *shinai*.

7. You must pay extra attention to your opponent's *tsuki*. When you sense a *tsuki* from your opponent, increase the *ma'ai*. If your opponent makes a *tsuki* after your *seme*, slap it to the side and hit the *shōmen*.

8. When your opponent strikes your *kote* on the short *shinai* side, pull back your short *shinai* or put it in *yoko ichimonji* to avoid being hit. To counter, use your short *shinai* in *maki otoshi* (coiling and dropping technique) and strike your opponent's *men*, or block with the mid portion of your short *shinai* and strike your opponent's *men* or *dō* with your long *shinai*. See Fig. 88a and b.

Fig. 87. Nitō ryū techniques (cont.): (a) Block your opponent's *men* strike with *jūji* (cross) stance and (b) immediately strike the *dō*.

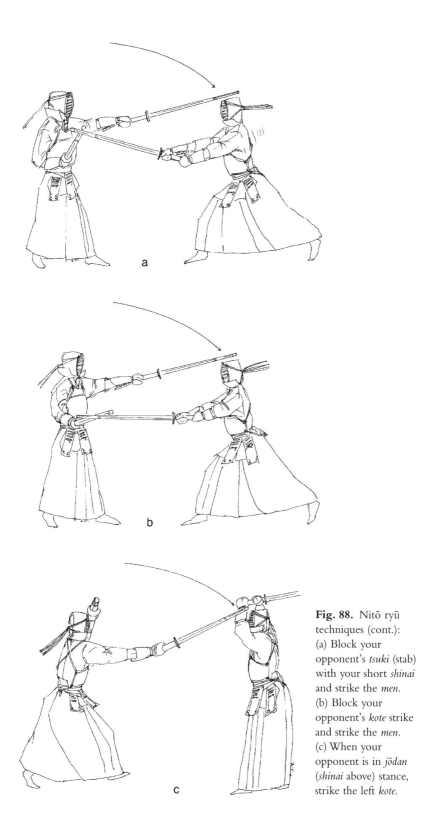

Fig. 88. Nitō ryū
techniques (cont.):
(a) Block your
opponent's *tsuki* (stab)
with your short *shinai*
and strike the *men*.
(b) Block your
opponent's *kote* strike
and strike the *men*.
(c) When your
opponent is in *jōdan*
(*shinai* above) stance,
strike the left *kote*.

9. Offense with the short *shinai:* Avoid striking lightly and consecutively with your short *shinai* from a close distance. If the *ma'ai* is too close, immediately step back to keep a proper *ma'ai.* When your opponent is in *chūdan no kamae, fureru* (touch) your opponent's *shinai* with your short *shinai* and if there is a *suki* (opening), immediately close in the *ma'ai,* and strike the *kote* with your short *shinai.*

10. When your opponent is in *jōdan no kamae,* lure him with your short *shinai,* and strike the *men* or *kote* with your long *shinai.* It is difficult to strike while your opponent is still in *jōdan no kamae.*

   a. When your opponent is in a *jōdan no kamae,* thrust with your long *shinai* from *chūdan no kamae.* You opponent will have difficulty maintaining the *jōdan* stance to block the *tsuki* and thus cannot attack.

   b. If your opponent strikes anyway, proceed to *tsuki* or assume the *zangetsu* stance and immediately strike the *dō, kote,* or *men* in *kaeshi waza.* Against an opponent in the *jōdan no kamae,* assume the *jūji* stance, close in the *ma'ai,* and hit the *dō* as you withdraw one step back. When your opponent is forced to change to *chūdan no kamae* to counter the *jūji* stance, continue to press. Take one step back and strike the *men* with your long *shinai* or the *dō* with your short *shinai.*

   c. It is generally easier to strike your opponent's *kote* in the *jōdan* stance (Fig. 88c). If your opponent strikes your *men,* block with your short *shinai* and strike the *dō* with your long *shinai.*

11. *Tsubazeriai* (hand guard fight): If you are at *tsubazeriai* with your long *shinai,* strike your opponent's *kote, dō,* or *men,* or *tsuki* with the short *shinai.* Or step backward slightly to the side and hit your opponent's *men* with your long *shinai.* From the *tsubazeriai* with your short *shinai,* strike the *han men* (left or right *men*) or *dō* with your long *shinai* as you step back.

Forms and Rules

Nihon Kendo Kata

The Kendo kata evolved from ancient combative techniques. With the development of Japanese swords, *kata* (form) practice, also called *kumitachi* (sword form of sparring), became a way to master the proper handling of the *katana* (Japanese sword). Experts shaped many methods of attacking and defending into various *kata*. During the Tokugawa era, a relatively peaceful time when real duels were rare, there were around two hundred kinds of *kata*. *Shinai keiko* (practice with the bamboo sword), which is similar to present-day kendo practice, was used to test the *kumitachi* techniques by actually striking the opponent. Obviously, striking with the *katana* (Japanese sword) or wooden sword was dangerous.

In the late nineteenth century, the Metropolitan Police Department in Tokyo first organized the *kata* from the various schools into a ten-form Keishi-ryū. In 1906, Dai Nippon Butoku Kai (see Chapter 1) selected three basic *kata* to be taught in schools. When kendo was incorporated into the Japanese school curriculum during the educational reform in 1911, Butoku Kai established a ten-form *kata* with input from many experts from all over Japan under the leadership of five officials: Negishi Shingorō, Tsuji Shinpei, Naitō Takaharu, Monna Tadashi, and Takano Sasaburō. This is the Dai Nippon Teikoku Kendo Kata, the archetype of the Nihon Kendo Kata. Although the Kendo Kata was initially intended for young students, committee members were extremely serious about the process. There were many heated discussions about every detail, and some wanted to have nuances of their own schools preserved in the new *kata*.

In 1917, an attempt was made to standardize the Dai Nippon Teikoku Kendo Kata. It underwent additional refinements, and the text was published in 1933. After World War II, it was renamed simply Nihon Kendo Kata.

It is interesting to note how the original *kata* was revised. For example, thrusting of the solar plexus *(suigetsu)* in *Tachi no Kata Yonhonme* (long sword form, fourth technique) was changed to thrusting of the right chest to prevent accidental injury. The term *seigan* (middle stance with variations) in *Tachi no Kata Gohonme, Ropponme,* and *Nanahonme* was changed to *chūdan no kamae* to avoid confusion about the direction of the *kensen* because there are many kinds of *seigan*. When we see film clips of performances by earlier teachers, differences between the original and current *kata* are apparent.

Studying the Kendo Kata

The Nihon Kendo Kata (or simply Kata) was developed by compiling the best techniques of various kendo schools. It teaches the fundamental sword technique. As you become more skilled, you will realize the depth and significance of the Kata. It is highly recommended that you study the Kata in conjunction with *shinai* practice.

In studying the Kata, you should

1. Refine your composure and mannerisms.
2. Develop proper posture.
3. Become aware of the thoughts and actions of others.
4. Become agile.
5. Lose undesirable technical habits.
6. Understand the proper *ma'ai*.
7. Develop spirit and energy.

8. Comprehend the principles of *katana*.

9. Cultivate grace, refined character, and dignity.

Furthermore, as a basis of *shinai keiko*, Kata practice is valuable for learning the various *waza*, such as the *nuki, suriage, kaeshi,* and *ukenagashi*. Although Kata movements are prearranged, you should always practice as if you were in actual combat. In general, the *uchidachi* leads by assuming the role of a teacher who encourages and shows the *shidachi* how to win. However, the *shidachi* must not be on the defensive. The *shidachi* should perform with full spirit to draw out the *uchidachi's waza*.

The following are the general rules of Kata:

1. The *uchidachi* and the *shidachi* look at each other's eyes and are alert from beginning to end.

2. Advance from the front foot; retreat from the back foot.

3. In *Tachi no Kata,* the *uchidachi* initiates the movement at the right moment. In *Kodachi no Kata,* the *uchidachi* strikes as the *shidachi* encroaches *(irimi)* into the *ma'ai*.

4. Regardless of the outward form, the *shidachi* must show sufficient *zanshin* (alertness) before the *uchidachi* begins the next movement.

5. Walk in *suriashi* (sliding footwork); do not stomp.

6. Always bring the back foot up to the proper distance after a *datotsu* so that the feet are not wide apart.

7. On *datotsu,* strike the *datotsubui* with the *monouchi* (cutting zone) accurately to a distance of about 10 cm (closer with practice).

8. In *jōdan no kamae* or when the *katana* is swung up, you should be able to see your opponent between your arms and your *kensen* should not drop back.

9. Employ a *en-kyū-kyō-jaku* (slow–fast–strong–weak) cadence appropriately.

10. Hold your breath when advancing into *ma'ai* or retreating; use shallow abdominal breathing.

11. Each *kiai* or *kakegoe* (exclamation), such as *"Yah!"* and *"Tōh!"* should be loud and sharp, and full of energy.

Tachi no Kata (Long Sword Form)

Tachiai (Preparation)

1. The *uchidachi* and *shidachi* face each other three steps apart in the *dōjō's shimoza* (lower seat). They sit in *seiza* (left knee first, then the right). They each place their *bokken* on the floor gently, the *kojiri* (butt end) first. The *bokken* should be one fist away from the right thigh, the blade toward the thigh, and the *tsuba* at knee level. They place their *kodachi* (short sword) on the inside, blade facing the thigh. They bow to each other from a sitting position *(zarei)*. The *shidachi* starts the bow before the *uchidachi,* to show respect. Rising up from *zarei,* the *shidachi* keeps his hands on the floor until the *uchidachi* raises his hands.

2. Each grasps the *bokken* with the right hand, a few inches away from the *tsuba* to leave space for the left hand when transferring the *bokken* to the left side. The *shidachi* holds the *kodachi* between the thumb and index finger and the *tachi* between the index and middle fingers. Both bring the *bokken* to the right hip, stand up, assume *sagetō* (at rest), and move to the starting position at a nine-step distance from each other. If the *katana* are used, the *shidachi* should place his left hand over the *tsuba* from below when standing up to prevent the swords from accidentally falling forward.

3. At about five steps diagonally to the right and back (or away from the *kamiza*) of the starting position, the *shidachi* kneels on the right knee (or on the one away from the *kamiza*), places the *kodachi* on the right side (or away from *kamiza*) with blade turned inward and parallel to the performer, and comes to the starting position with a *bokken* or *tachi* in *sagetō*. Although not a requirement, the right side facing the *kamiza* is ordinarily the *uchidachi*'s position. See Fig. 89.

4. Both face the *kamiza* of the *dōjō* and bow from a standing position (*ritsurei* at 30 degrees). Then they face each other and bow (*ritsurei* at 15 degrees). Their eyes should be directed naturally to the floor when they are bowing to the *kamiza* and toward each other when they are bowing to each other.

5. The players now each transfer the *bokken* to the left side, hold it at the left hip with the blade up, place the left thumb on the *tsuba* (hand guard), and unlock the sword. Each brings the right hand up to chest level to transfer the *bokken* to the left hand. *Taitō* is equivalent to placing the *katana* in the *obi* (sash). Placing the left thumb on the *tsuba* is equivalent to preparing to draw the *katana* by pushing the *tsuba* forward to unlock the sword.

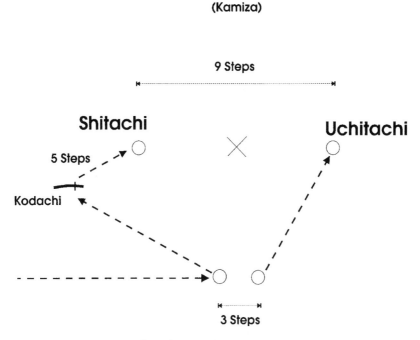

Fig. 89. Starting position for Nihon Kendo Kata.

6. Starting on the right foot, the players advance three large steps in *ayumiashi* (walking footwork) using *suriashi* (sliding footwork), and draw the *bokken* while assuming the *sonkyo* (squatting position). They must be careful not to pause at *chūdan* before *sonkyo*. The *kensen* should cross each other about 5 cm (2 in.). The distance at which the tips of the blades barely touch is called *shokujin no ma* (swords touching interval). When the players are standing up, the tips of their blades cross a little more to a distance called *kōjin no ma* (swords crossing interval), which is closer to *issoku ittō no ma* (one foot one sword interval) in *chūdan* (middle stance).

7. *Kamae o toku* (disarm): The player lowers the *kensen* while gradually turning the blade to the left and down until the *kensen* is 3 to 6 cm below the level of the opponent's left knee, take five small steps back in *ayumiashi,* then resumes *chūdan*. This final move is repeated at the end of *tachi*.

Ipponme (First Technique)

Ipponme teaches *gi* (honesty, virtue, conviction, faith, justice, truth, and power) and *sen* (fore). Therefore, *ipponme* is performed with large, all-out *waza* without apprehension. See Fig. 90.

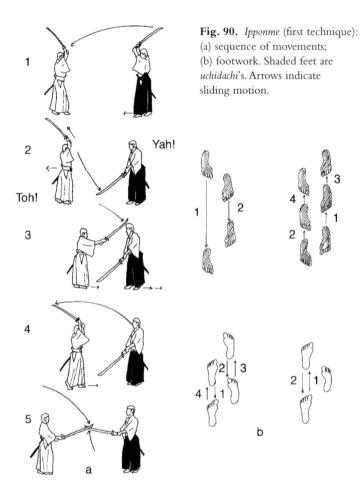

Fig. 90. *Ipponme* (first technique): (a) sequence of movements; (b) footwork. Shaded feet are *uchidachi*'s. Arrows indicate sliding motion.

1. The *uchidachi* is in *morote hidari jōdan* (upper stance with the left foot forward). Direction of the *kensen* is slightly to the right and back at about 45 degrees from horizontal. The *shidachi* is in *morote migi jōdan* (upper stance with the right foot forward). The direction of the *kensen* is straight back at about 45 degrees from horizontal. The right foot may be advanced slightly. The *uchidachi,* starting on the left foot, and the *shidachi,* starting on the right foot, advance three large steps into *issoku ittō no ma* in *ayumiashi.*

2. The *uchidachi* checks the *shidachi*'s readiness, then initiates the *waza* when the opportunity is present. The *uchidachi* chooses the right moment, steps in with the right foot, and strikes the *shōmen* as if cutting through the *tsuka* to lower than the *gedan*

(lower stance) level while yelling *"Yah!"* The *uchidachi's* strike should be fast and strong. The *shidachi* withdraws slightly in *okuriashi* (sending footwork) starting on the left foot, pulls the hands back to evade the *uchidachi's bokken (nuki waza),* then steps forward without pause, starting on the right foot, to strike the *shōmen* while yelling *"Toh!"*

3. The *uchidachi,* with the *kensen* still lowered and leaning slightly forward, retreats a half step in *okuriashi.* The *shidachi* alertly lowers the *kensen* to the center of the *uchidachi's* face (between the eyes). The *uchidachi* takes another half step back in *okuriashi.* The *shidachi* moves the left foot forward and takes *hidari morote jōdan* to show *zanshin* (alertness).

4. The *uchidachi* confirms the *shidachi's zanshin,* straightens up, and then begins to raise the *kensen* to *chūdan.* The *shidachi* retreats, starting with the left foot. After the *shidachi* shows sufficient *zanshin,* the *uchidachi* begins to return to *chūdan,* and the *shidachi* follows.

5. The players each lower their *kensen* (tip of the sword), take five small steps back in *ayumiashi* to their starting positions, and resume *chūdan no kamae* to prepare for the next *kata.*

Nihonme (Second Technique)

Nihonme teaches *jin* (benevolence, endurance, and patience). Thus, although the *shidachi* is capable of fatally striking the *uchidachi,* he strikes the *kote* instead and spares the *uchidachi's* life. See Fig. 91.

1. While both are at *chūdan,* the *uchidachi* and *shidachi* advance three large steps, starting on the right foot in *ayumiashi,* to the proper *ma'ai.*

2. The *uchidachi* chooses the right moment, then strikes the right *kote* with a large *waza* in *okuriashi,* yelling *"Yah!"* The *uchidachi's kensen* after the strike should be just below the *kote* level. The *shidachi* withdraws to the back and left, starting on the left foot in *okuriashi;* the right foot follows, and the *shidachi* simultaneously lowers the *kensen* to evade the strike *(nuki waza)* as if drawing a semicircle under the *uchidachi's bokken.* The *shidachi* swings the *bokken* up until the *uchidachi's kote* is visible under the arms, then takes a large *okuriashi* step forward with the right foot to vertically strike the *uchidachi's* right *kote,* yelling *"Toh!"* The *shidachi's* motion should be continuous and the *bokken* should not swing diagonally.

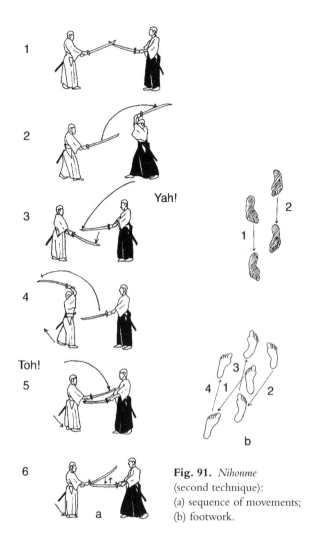

1

2

Yah!

3

4

Toh!

5

6

a

b

Fig. 91. *Nihonme* (second technique): (a) sequence of movements; (b) footwork.

3. With *zanshin,* the *uchidachi* starts on the left foot and the *shi-dachi* starts on the right, returning to the center as both assume the *chūdan* position. There is no overt *zanshin* (alertness) but it must be present. The *uchidachi*'s *kensen* moves under the *shidachi*'s as a show of submission.

4. The players lower their *kensen,* take five small steps back in *ayumiashi* to their starting positions, and resume *chūdan no kamae* to prepare for the next *kata.*

Sanbonme (Third Technique)

Sanbonme teaches *yū* (courage) and how to win without injuring the opponent *(kuraizume).* See Fig. 92.

1. While both are at *gedan,* the *uchidachi* and *shidachi* advance three large steps, starting on the right foot, to the proper *ma'ai.* Both unyielding, they naturally assume *chūdan.*

2. Choosing the right moment, the *uchidachi* thrusts at the *shi-*

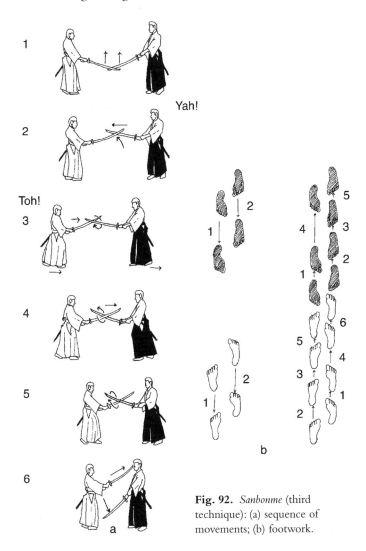

Fig. 92. *Sanbonme* (third technique): (a) sequence of movements; (b) footwork.

dachi's suigetsu (solar plexus) with both arms extended and the blade slightly to the right in *okuriashi* with the right foot, yelling *"Yah!"* The *uchidachi* should use *suriashi* (sliding footwork), not stomp. The *shidachi* takes a large step back, starting on the left foot in *okuriashi,* and wards off the *uchidachi's bokken* with the *omote shinogi* (left sword ridge) of the *monouchi* (cutting zone) to *nayashi* (weaken) the thrust, then immediately thrusts back at the *uchidachi's* chest with both arms extended and the blade down, yelling *"Toh!"* The *uchidachi's* sword must be sufficiently deflected in *nayashi* (weakening) technique. When thrusting back, the *shidachi* should not stomp. The *uchidachi,* withdraws the right foot, moves the *kensen* around to the left side from under the *shidachi's bokken,* and with somewhat extended arms takes a *hidari shizentai* (a variation of *chūdan*) and wards off the *shidachi's* thrust with the *ura shinogi* (right sword ridge) of the *monouchi.* The *kensen* should be at the throat, but the *uchidachi* should not slap the *shidachi's* sword as in *harai waza* (slapping technique).

3. The *shidachi,* keeping the arms extended with unyielding spirit, presses with a step forward using the left foot, in *kuraizume,* or *kiate,* without actually thrusting. *Kuraizume* (seize with superior poise) is a feeling of dominating without actually thrusting. The *shidachi* should be careful not to stomp. The *uchidachi* retreats, starting with the left foot, then moves the *kensen* around to the right side from under the *shidachi's bokken* taking a *migi shizentai* to ward off the *shidachi's bokken* by pressing it to the left with the left *(omote) shinogi* of the *monouchi.* The *kensen* is to the throat.

4. The *uchidachi* moves the sword to the right and down (the *kensen* points away from the *shidachi* in resignation), and retreats three steps, starting on the left foot, in *ayumiashi.* The *shidachi* quickly chases with three steps in small *ayumiashi,* starting on the right foot, and then gradually raises the *kensen* to the center of the *uchidachi's* face (between the eyes).

5. The *uchidachi* confirms the *shidachi's zanshin,* then begins to raise the *kensen* to *chūdan no kamae.* The *shidachi* retreats five steps in *ayumiashi,* starting on the left foot. On the *shidachi's* third step, the *uchidachi* advances three steps in *ayumiashi,* and both return to the center as both assume *chūdan.* They should take sufficiently large steps in order to come back to the center.

6. They should both lower their *kensen,* take five small steps

back in *ayumiashi* to their starting positions, and resume *chū-dan no kamae* to prepare for the next *kata.*

Yonhonme (Fourth Technique)

The *hassō no kamae* (eight-faceted stance) represents wood or trees. The *wakigamae* (hip stance) represents gold or metal, which can smash wood. *Yonhonme* teaches large *aiuchi waza* (simultaneous striking technique). *Kirimusubi* (chaffing) relates to a sense of proper *tsubazeriai* (hand guard fight) in *shinai* kendo. See Fig. 93.

1. The *uchidachi* beings in *hassō no kamae.* (*Hassō* is a variation of *jōdan:* Step forward with your left foot, bring your hands up to face level, and then hold the *bokken* with your left fist in front of your chest, with the *tsuba* one fist distance to the right of your mouth. The blade should face forward and the right foot should be slightly angled to the right.) The *shidachi* begins in *wakigamae.* To assume *wakigamae,* move the *bokken* in an arc with your right fist passing near the level of your mouth. Your right hand should be at your right hip with the palm open (the fingers and thumb support the *tsuka*). The *kensen* should face toward the back and down, and the blade faces the right and down. Your body should be in a *hanmi* (half-body stance), with the right shoulder pulled back. (The *bokken* should not be visible from the front. You should feel as though you were hiding a precious treasure in your bosom.) Both advance three small steps in *ayumiashi,* starting on the left foot, toward the proper *ma'ai.*

2. The *uchidachi,* choosing the right moment, changes to *morote hidari jōdan.* The *shidachi,* without delay, also changes to *morote hidari jōdan.* Without pause, both step forward with the right foot and swing the *bokken* to strike each other's *shōmen* in *aiuchi* or *kirimusubi* with arms extended. To come to a proper *ma'ai,* each should aim at the other's face (or nose) rather than at the top of the head. The *bokken* cross at head level.

3. From *aiuchi,* both are unyielding, and as if chafing the *shinogi,* naturally assume *chūdan.* If they are too close, the *uchidachi* should adjust. The *uchidachi* chooses the right moment, steps forward with the right foot as the left follows, and thrusts at the *shidachi's* right chest with the blade facing the right, yelling *"Yah!"* The *shidachi* moves the left foot to the left and front, with the right foot behind it, evades the *uchidachi's* sword in a large *maki kaeshi* by lifting the left hand above the

head with the blade to the back, and immediately strikes the *uchidachi's shōmen*, yelling *"Toh!" Maki kaeshi* means to "coil over." With a rotating motion, the *uchidachi's* sword, which is initially on the left side of *shidachi's* sword, is deflected to the right side by and away from the *shidachi*.

4. After the *uchidachi* confirms the *shidachi's zanshin* (alertness), the *uchidachi,* starting on the left foot, and the *shidachi,* starting on the right, return to the center as both assume *chūdan no kamae.* There is no overt *zanshin* but it must be present.

5. Both lower their *kensen (kamae wo toku),* take five small steps

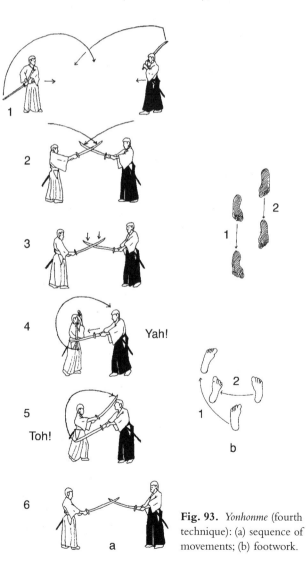

Fig. 93. *Yonhonme* (fourth technique): (a) sequence of movements; (b) footwork.

back in *ayumiashi* to their starting positions, and resume *chū-dan no kamae* to prepare for the next *kata*.

Gohonme (Fifth Technique)

Jōdan no kamae represents fire. *Chūdan no kamae* represents water, which can put out the fire. See Fig. 94.

1. The *uchidachi* begins in *morote hidari jōdan*. The *shidachi* begins in *chūdan no kamae* with the *kensen* pointing at the *uchidachi's* left fist and the blade facing down. The *uchidachi,* starting on the left foot, and the *shidachi,* starting on the right, both advance three large steps to the proper *ma'ai*.

2. Choosing the right moment, the *uchidachi* steps in from the

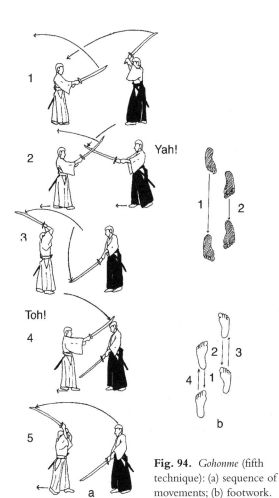

Fig. 94. *Gohonme* (fifth technique): (a) sequence of movements; (b) footwork.

right foot to strike the *shōmen,* yelling *"Yah!"* Unlike the first *tachi* technique, this strong and fast cutting is only to the chin. The *bokken* is then naturally deflected to the lower right. The *shidachi* steps back, starting on the left foot in *okuri-ashi,* and simultaneously sweeps up the *bokken* using the left *shinogi* (sword ridge) in *suriage* (semicircular motion). The *shidachi* should be careful not to let the *kensen* drop down below horizontal in the back at *suriage.* Then, without delay, the *shidachi* steps forward on the right foot and strikes the *shōmen,* yelling *"Toh!"*

3. The *shidachi,* after a pause, retreats, starting with the right foot, lowering the *kensen* to the middle of the opponent's face, then raises the *bokken* to *hidari jōdan* to show *zanshin.*

4. The *uchidachi* after confirming the *shidachi's zanshin,* begins to raise the *kensen* to *chūdan.* The *shidachi* steps back with the left foot and lowers the *kensen.* The *uchidachi* begins to return to *chūdan* after seeing sufficient *zanshin* from the *shidachi,* and the *shidachi* follows. The *uchidachi,* starting on the left foot, and the *shidachi,* starting on the right, return to the center in three small steps in *ayumiashi.*

5. Both lower their *kensen,* take five small steps back in *ayumiashi* to their starting positions, then resume *chūdan* to prepare for the next *kata.*

Ropponme (Sixth Technique)

Chūdan represents water and *gedan* represents earth, which can cover up the water. When the *uchidachi* takes the *jōdan* (fire) stance, the *shidachi* responds with the *chūdan* stance. See Fig. 95.

1. With the *uchidachi* in *chūdan* and the *shidachi* in *gedan,* both advance three large steps, starting on the right foot, to the proper *ma'ai.*

2. The *shidachi* chooses the right moment and raises the *kensen* to *chūdan,* pressuring the *uchidachi's* fists. The *uchidachi* responds by slightly lowering the *kensen,* then just as the *bokken* are about to touch (unable to contain *shidachi's* pressure) retreats, starting with the right foot, to take *morote hidari jōdan.* The *uchidachi's kensen* is slightly lowered to contain the *shidachi's* pressure, but the blades do not touch. The *shidachi,* without delay, advances one large step with the right foot (left follows) and points the *kensen* at the *uchidachi's* left fist.

Fig. 95. *Ropponme* (sixth technique): (a) sequence of movements; (b) footwork.

3. The *shidachi* shows *debana* (readiness to strike) if the *uchidachi* advances. Thus, the *uchidachi* retreats, starting with the left foot, to *chūdan* instead. The *shidachi* also retreats back to *chūdan*. The *uchidachi* chooses the right moment and strikes the *shidachi*'s right *kote* in a small *waza*, yelling *"Yah!"* The *uchidachi* attempts to capture the *shidachi*'s *debana kote*, to which the *shidachi* responds with a *suriage kote* (deflecting and *kote* strike technique). The *shidachi* then moves the left foot to the left, simultaneously deflecting the *bokken* with a small *suriage* (smoothly without pause, yet sharply) using the right *shinogi* (sword ridge) as if drawing a semicircle. The *shidachi* steps forward with the right foot to strike the *uchidachi*'s right *kote*, yelling *"Toh!"*

4. The *uchidachi* opens the *kensen* to the left and down, with the blade facing right and down, then takes a large step to the left and back. The *uchidachi* does not face the *shidachi* directly. The *shidachi* steps toward the *uchidachi* with the left foot, pointing the *kensen* gradually from the throat to the face, assumes *morote hidari jōdan,* and shows *zanshin.*

5. *Zanshin* confirmed, both return to the center. The *uchidachi* takes a large step to the front and right with the left foot. The *shidachi* takes two large *ayumiashi* steps, with first the left then the right foot, to the back and left. The steps should be sufficiently large to return him to the center. Both assume *chūdan.*

6. Both lower their *kensen,* take five small steps back in *ayumi-ashi* to the starting positions, then resume *chūdan no kamae* to prepare for the next *kata.*

Nanahonme (Seventh Technique)
See Figs. 96 and 97.

1. Both begin at *chūdan* and advance three large steps, starting with the right foot, to the proper *ma'ai.*

2. The *uchidachi* chooses the right moment, lightly steps forward with the right foot in *okuriashi,* and thrusts at the *shidachi*'s chest using the left *shinogi* (sword ridge), with the blade turned slightly to the right and down. The *shidachi* parries the *uchidachi*'s thrust by retreating, starting with the left foot, simultaneously stretching the arms and supporting the *uchidachi*'s *bokken* as if thrusting back, with the blade turned to the left and down.

Fig. 96. *Nanahonme* (seventh technique).

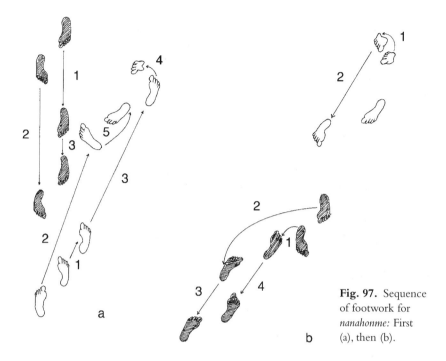

Fig. 97. Sequence of footwork for *nanahonme:* First (a), then (b).

3. Both assume *chūdan* with equal spirit. The *uchidachi* steps straight forward with the left foot, then as the right foot steps forward in *ayumiashi,* strikes the *shidachi's shōmen* boldly with the whole body, yelling *"Yah!"* Eye contact with the *shidachi* is momentarily lost but regained immediately after missing the *shōmen*. The *shidachi* moves the right foot to the right and front. The *shidachi* then places the left foot in front of the right foot and strikes the *uchidachi's* right *dō* as they pass each other, yelling *"Toh!"* The *shidachi* keeps an eye on the *uchidachi* at all times, striking the *dō* on the second step. At the end, the *bokken* and the arms are nearly horizontal (the *kensen* is slightly lower) in the right and front with the blade to the right. After striking, the *shidachi* drops the right knee lightly to the floor in front of the left foot, keeping the right foot on its toes and the left knee raised, and with both arms extended.

4. After a slight pause, the *shidachi* turns over the *bokken* to assume *wakigamae* (hip stance) and to show *zanshin*.

5. The *uchidachi* turns to face the *shidachi* as the *shidachi* assumes *wakigamae* and straightens up to swing the *bokken* overhead. The *uchidachi* retreats with the left foot, using the right foot

as a pivot, and faces the *shidachi* in *chūdan*. The *uchidachi* must be careful not to assume a *wakigamae* when turning to face the *shidachi*. The *shidachi* simultaneously swings the *bokken* overhead, turns to the left using the right knee as a pivot (move left foot to the left) to face the *uchidachi,* and points the *kensen* as in *chūdan*.

6. The *uchidachi,* feeling the *shidachi*'s force, retreats, starting with the left foot. Both assume *chūdan*. Without breaking the link, both return to the center, starting with the left foot. The *shidachi* is closer to the center, so he must take smaller steps. The *uchidachi* circles around, using the *shidachi* as the axis.

7. Both assume *sonkyo,* return the *bokken* to *taitō,* stand up, and take five small steps back to their starting positions. Each transfers the *bokken* to the right hand, then bows to the other (15-degree *ritsurei*).

Kodachi no Kata (Short Sword Forms)
Changing *Bokken* and *Tachiai*

1. The *uchidachi* waits in *sonkyo*. The *shidachi* retreats to the *kodachi* (short sword), kneels down on the right knee (or the one away from the *kamiza*), places the *tachi* (long sword) on the floor on the outside of the *kodachi,* picks up the *kodachi,* and returns to the starting position.

2. At the starting position in *sagetō,* they bow to each other (15-degree *ritsurei*), then transfer the *bokken* to the left side, with the left thumb on the *tsuba*.

3. They advance three large steps, starting with the right foot, to the proper *ma'ai*. Assuming *sonkyo,* the *shidachi* draws the *bokken*. The *shidachi* holds the *kodachi* in the right hand and places the left hand on the left hip with the thumb pointing backward, fingers together.

4. The *uchidachi* lowers the *kensen* 3 to 6 cm below the *shidachi*'s left knee with the blade facing left and downward. The *shidachi* lowers the *kodachi* to the right with the *kensen* pointing away from the *uchidachi,* maintaining the angle of the wrist. Simultaneously, the *shidachi* lowers the left hand to the left side. They take five small steps in *ayumiashi* back to the starting position. This final move is repeated at the end of the first two *kodachi* techniques.

Ipponme (First Technique)
See Fig. 98.

1. The *uchidachi* begins in *morote hidari jōdan*. The *shidachi* begins in *chūdan hanmi* with the *kensen* slightly raised and pointing to the *uchidachi*'s face, the left shoulder pulled back, and the left hand on the left hip. In *chūdan hanmi*, the tip of the *kodachi* should reach to where a *tachi* tip would be. The *shidachi* should not shift weight to the back foot or lean too far forward. The *uchidachi* starts with the left foot while the *shidachi* starts with the right; both advance three large steps to the proper *ma'ai*.

2. The *shidachi* threatens to further encroach. The *uchidachi*, not allowing the *shidachi* to encroach, steps forward with the right foot to strike the *shidachi*'s *shōmen*, shouting *"Yah!"* Unlike the first *tachi* technique, the strike should be strong and deliberate.

Fig. 98. *Ipponme* (first technique): (a) sequence of movements; (b) footwork.

The *shidachi* moves the right foot to the right and front, with the left foot behind it to open the body to the left, simultaneously moving the right hand overhead with the blade back to deflect the strike in *ukenagashi* with the left *shinogi* (sword ridge). The *shidachi* then strikes the *uchidachi's shōmen*, shouting *"Toh!"* The *shidachi* should be careful not to block. Rather, the *uchidachi's* blade should graze the *shidachi's shinogi*.

3. After a slight pause, the *shidachi* retreats one step in *okuriashi* to take *jōdan* (without lowering the *kensen*) and shows *zanshin*. Both assume *chūdan*, then, both starting with the left foot, return to the center.

4. Both lower their *kensen*, take five small steps in *ayumiashi* back to their starting positions, and resume *chūdan* to prepare for the next *kata*.

Nihonme (Second Technique)
See Fig. 99.

1. The *uchidachi* begins in *gedan*. The *shidachi* begins in *chūdan hanmi* with the *kensen* slightly lowered and pointing to the *uchidachi's* chest. The left shoulder is pulled back, and the left hand is on the left hip. Both advance three large steps, starting with the right foot, to the proper *ma'ai*.

2. The *uchidachi* raises the *kensen* to *chūdan* in defense. The *shidachi* prevents this by covering the *tachi* with the left *shinogi* (sword ridge) of the *kodachi* and threatens to encroach. The *uchidachi* retreats with the right foot to take *wakigamae* by moving the blade directly to the back and right, not by arcing upward as in the fourth *tachi* technique. The *shidachi* immediately assumes *chūdan* with the blade down and forward pressure.

3. The *uchidachi*, without pausing at *wakigamae*, changes to *hidari jōdan* and strikes the *shidachi's shōmen* by stepping forward with the right foot, yelling *"Yah!"* The *shidachi* moves the left foot to the left and front, with the right foot behind it to open the body to the right. Simultaneously the *shidachi* brings the right hand overhead (close to the face) with the blade back to deflect the strike, in *ukenagashi*, using the right *shinogi*. The *shidachi* then strikes the *uchidachi's shōmen*, yelling *"Toh!"*

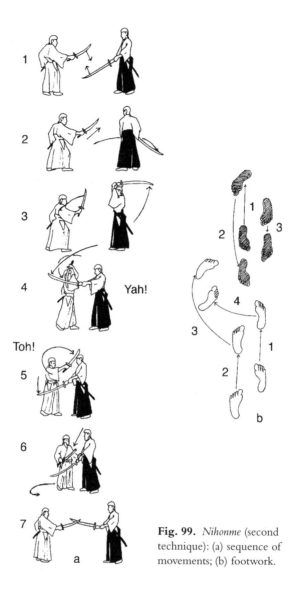

Fig. 99. *Nihonme* (second technique): (a) sequence of movements; (b) footwork.

4. The *shidachi*, after a slight pause, grasps the *uchidachi* by the upper arm and presses downward just above the elbow with the left hand to immobilize it, brings the right hand to the right hip with the blade facing right and down, and points the *kensen* to the throat of *uchidachi* to show *zanshin*. At that, the *uchidachi*, starting on the left foot, and the *shidachi*, starting on the right, return to the center and assume *chūdan*.

5. Both lower their *kensen,* take five small steps back in *ayumi-ashi* to their starting positions, and resume *chūdan* to prepare for the next *kata.*

Sanbonme (Third Technique)

This *kata* teaches the value of life. The ultimate goal of kendo is harmonious existence, not annihilation. No one is injured in this *kata.* See Fig. 100.

1. The *uchidachi* begins in *chūdan.* The *shidachi* begins in *gedan hanmi* with the *kensen* down, the left shoulder pulled back, and the left hand on the left hip. This *kamae* is said to express *mugamae* (stance of void), a sense of superiority where overt *kamae* is irrelevant.

2. The *uchidachi* advances toward the proper *ma'ai* starting with the right foot, and on the third step assumes *morote migi jōdan* and strikes the *shidachi's shōmen,* yelling *"Yah!"* The *uchidachi* strikes because the *shidachi* threatens to continue encroaching. The *shidachi* advances to the proper *ma'ai* with the *uchidachi,* starting with the right foot. At the *uchidachi's* strike on the third step, the *shidachi* sweeps up *(suriage),* then coils down *(suriotoshi)* the *uchidachi's bokken* toward the *uchidachi's* right. The height of the right hand at *suriage* is above and in front of the forehead. At *suriotoshi* it is at the abdomen.

3. The *uchidachi* immediately steps forward with the left foot to strike the *shidachi's* right *dō.* The *shidachi* steps forward on the left foot, turns the body to right, and sweeps across *(surinagashi)* the *uchidachi's bokken* with the left *shinogi.* The *shidachi* then slides up *(surikomi)* to the *uchidachi's tsuba* with the left *shinogi.* The *shidachi* presses the *uchidachi's tsuba* area with the *kodachi's* metal sleeve. Then the *shidachi* closes in on the *uchidachi,* simultaneously pressing and immobilizing the *uchidachi's* arm just above the elbow from the side, with the left hand, yelling *"Toh!"* The *shidachi* must be careful not to block the *uchidachi's dō* strike at *surinagashi,* but swing the *kodachi* sideways to the right as if sweeping across the *uchidachi's* chest. When the *uchidachi's* arm is immobilized, the *kodachi's kensen* points up slightly so that the *uchidachi* is unable to free his *bokken.*

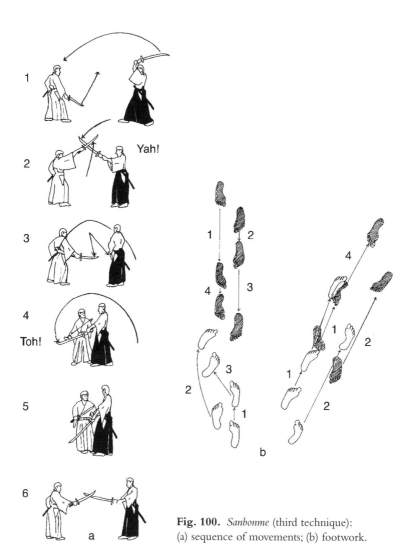

Fig. 100. *Sanbonme* (third technique):
(a) sequence of movements; (b) footwork.

4. The *uchidachi* retreats three steps to the back and left, starting on the left foot. The *shidachi* chases the *uchidachi* with three steps, starting with the right foot. The *shidachi* holds the right hand on the right hip with the blade to the right and down and the *kensen* to the *uchidachi*'s throat to show *zanshin* (alertness). The stance should be firm but not aggressive at *zanshin*. The *uchidachi*, starting with the right foot, and the *shidachi*, starting with the left, return to the center as both assume *chūdan*.

5. Both assume *sonkyo*. They return their *bokken* to *taitō*, stand up, and take five small steps back to their starting positions. They then transfer their *bokken* to the right. They bow to each other (15-degree *ritsurei*), then bow to the upper section of the *dōjō* (30-degree *ritsurei*).

6. The *shidachi* retreats to where the *tachi* is, kneels down on the right knee (the one away from the *kamiza*), and picks up the *tachi*. Both come to the *shimoza* of the *dōjō*, kneel in *seiza* at a three-step distance, then bow to each other. Both stand up and exit the performance area.

Shiai (Match)

Skills learned through diligent *keiko* are tested in the *shiai,* which is an extension of *keiko,* not simply a contest to see who can strike the opponent first. An appropriate point must be captured accurately according to the principles of the *katana.* To win in a *shiai* is not the goal of kendo *keiko,* rather a *shiai* is a means of improving, a part of the training process.

In an unfamiliar arena with spectators and against an unfamiliar opponent, you may feel awe or fear. You may become confused, timid, or frozen. To overcome these feelings, you should relax, remember the basics (e.g., *kamae,* footwork, and posture), and give a good sharp *kiai.* Try to control your breathing by using deep abdominal breathing. You should try to win, but remember fairness and sportsmanship, and be courteous and respectful.

It is expected that all competitors understand and follow the rules of the *shiai,* so that the matches proceed fairly and smoothly. Referees *(shinpan)* are expected to be thoroughly familiar with the rules and regularly practice refereeing. The following is based on the 1997 International Kendo Federation Rules and its 1999 revision. Note that the rules may be modified to accommodate the requirements of the sponsoring organizations (e.g., size of the court, time limit, etc.).

General Rules

Shiai-Jō (Match Court)

The *shiai-jō* (Fig. 101) is a square with each side measuring 9 to 11 m (27 to 33 ft.). White boundary lines are 5 to 10 cm (4 to 8 in.) wide. An X made of tape strips 30 cm long marks the center. Starting lines *(kaishi sen)* on the left and right sides of the X measure 50 cm (20 in.) to mark the contestants' positions at the start and end of a match. Each starting line is 1.4 m from the X. There should be a 1.5 m (5 ft.) clearance all around the court for safety.

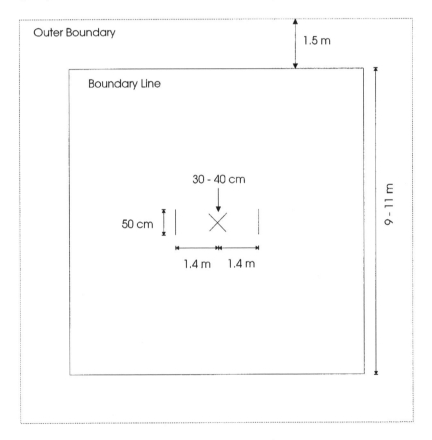

Fig. 101 *Shiai-Jō* (match court).

Shinai

The *shinai* must be made of bamboo or a synthetic material approved by the All Japan Kendo Federation. The length, weight, and tip diameter are checked prior to the match. The *tsuba* must not be more than 9 cm (3.5 in.) in diameter.

Bōgu (Gear) and Fukusō (Attire)

Kendo *bōgu,* or *gu,* are *men, kote, dō,* and *tare.* The *fukusō* consists of the kendo *gi (dōgi)* and *hakama.* Contestants will have a red or white cloth strip marker (5 cm by 70 cm, folded in half) called the *mejirushi* tied where the *dō* strings cross in the back. A *zekken* (name tag) is worn to identify the contestant. Athletic supporters and taping are allowed for medical reasons, if they are tidy and not hazardous to the opponent.

Shiai/Shinpan Kisoku (Match and Refereeing Regulations)

The official English edition of the *Regulations of the Kendo Match and Its Refereeing* (*Shiai* and *Shinpan Kisoku*) is available from Zen Nihon Kendo Renmei.

The standard duration of a match is five minutes, and an extension *(enchō)* is three minutes. The clock is stopped if the chief referee announces a point (e.g., *"Men ari"*) or stops the match *("Yame")*. The clock does not stop if the chief referee separates the contestants *("Wakare")*.

A referee director *(shinpanchō)*, and presiding referees *(shinpan shunin)* for a multicourt *shiai*, will oversee the procedures. A match is judged by a chief referee *(shushin)* and two subordinate referees *(fukushin)*. The *shushin* makes the announcements, but all three referees have an equal vote in calling the points or fouls. Each court will also have a timekeeper, recorders, and a contestant announcer.

Red and white square flags *(shinpanki)* are used to signal decisions. A flag is 25 cm square with a 10-cm stem. Triangular flags may be used by the timekeeper (yellow) and a contestant's manager (red).

Scoring

Decision

In *sanbon shōbu,* the contestant who scores two points first, or one point within the time limit if the opponent has not scored, is the winner. In *ippon shōbu,* the one who scores a point first will be the winner. There are times when the winner may be determined by a majority decision *(hantei).* Criteria for *hantei* are demonstrating superior skill (nearly a *yūkō datotsu*), and superior posture and movement.

Yūkō Datotsu

A point is awarded when the majority of referees agree on its validity *(yūkō).* A point is valid if an appropriate place *(datotsubui)* was struck with full spirit and proper posture, using the *monouchi* portion of the *shinai (datotsu bu)* with the blade directed correctly, and followed by *zanshin* after the strike. Correct blade direction means that the path of the strike and the direction of the blade are the same, which means that the side opposite the *tsuru* must be used to strike.

A point made as the opponent steps out of the court, or immediately after the opponent falls, is valid. If both contestants strike each other simultaneously, neither will count. This is called *aiuchi.*

The announcement of *yūkō datotsu* may be revoked after a referees' conference, usually for a lack of alertness after the *datotsu,* for a superfluous gesture, or for verbalizing boisterously. In this case, the *shushin* will announce *"Torikeshi"* and wave flags in the lower front.

Individual *(Kojin Sen)* and Team *(Dantai Sen)* Matches

Individual matches are usually fought in a tournament format. Each winner advances to the next higher tier until a champion is determined. Semifinals are called *jun-kesshō sen.* The championship match is called *kesshō sen.*

Team matches are fought according to a predetermined order within the teams. Usually, each member fights *sanbon shōbu* without an extension. The team with the most winners wins. In case of a tie, the team with the most points wins. If points are also equal, a representative from each team will compete to determine the winning team. The positions in a five-person team are named (from the first contestant): *senpō, jihō, chūken, fukushō,* and *taishō.*

In tournament format, the winning team advances to the next higher tier until a champion team is determined. In a *kachinuki* team match, a contestant who wins a match continues to fight the subsequent opponents until he loses. The team with the contestant who defeats the last opponent *(taishō)* wins.

Beginning, Stopping, and Ending

A match begins when the *shushin* announces *"Hajime"* and stops when the *shushin* announces *"Yame."* In case of an emergency, a *fukushin* may announce *"Yame."* A competitor who needs a time out may request one but must immediately explain the reason to the *shushin;* unreasonable stoppage can result in a foul *(hansoku).* If the *tsubazeriai* (hand guard fight) comes to a stalemate, the *shushin* will separate the contestants by announcing *"Wakare"* but the clock does not stop. The match is over when the *shushin* announces *"Shōbu ari"* or *"Hikiwake."*

Prohibited Acts

When a foul is detected, a referee signals by holding the offender's flag down at 45 degrees. If two or more referees acknowledge the foul, the flags are held out until the *shushin* stops the match and announces *"Hansoku ikkai"* (first foul) or *"Hansoku nikai"* (second foul). The referees will confer if the foul is not obvious.

The following acts will result in an automatic loss with two points awarded to the opponent. The offender is not allowed to continue the match and points earned by him during the match will be nullified.

- Use of illicit drugs: Previously earned points will be canceled.

- Disrespectful words or acts toward the referee or the opponent: Previously earned points will be canceled.

- Use of illegal equipment: Does not apply to the points earned prior to discovery of the illegal equipment.

The following acts will result in *hansoku* (foul). One point is awarded to the opponent for every two *hansoku* determined by the *shushin,* who announces *"Ippon ari"* with the proper flag raised.

- Deliberate tripping: Leg sweeps or tripping constitute *hansoku.*

- Unfairly pushing the opponent out of the court with unreasonable force.

- Carelessly stepping out of the court *(jōgai):* A foot or other part of body must be completely outside of the court (not just stepping on the line). Supporting a fall with the *shinai* with the *kensen* outside of the court, being pushed outside after a reasonable contact involving a *waza* are also fouls. If you step out of the court during *renzoku waza* a strike becomes *ippon.*
- Dropping the *shinai:* Completely dropping the *shinai* to the floor or losing control of it so that it is in the air even if it is caught before it hits the floor. It does not constitute *hansoku* if the *shinai* momentarily leaves the player's hands or bounces off the floor if the player has good control of the *shinai.* The opponent has a moment to strike before a referee declares *"Yame"* when the *shinai* is dropped.
- Stopping the match unreasonably.
- Grasping or holding the opponent.
- Grasping the opponent's *shinai* or the *jinbu* (blade portion) of one's own *shinai.*
- Holding the opponent's *shinai* in one's arms.
- Deliberately placing the *shinai* on the opponent's shoulder.
- Prostrating (lying prone to avoid being hit) after a fall without attempting to counter the opponent's attack or without getting up immediately.
- Deliberately wasting time.
- Doing an unfair *tsubazeriai.*
- Deliberately striking an improper place.

If simultaneous fouls result in a loss of points for both contestants, the *shushin* announces *"Sōsai"* and does not count the *hansoku.*

Injury or Accidents

In case of an injury or accident, a contestant may request medical assistance. If unable to continue within five minutes, the disabled contestant loses the match. If it is clear that the opponent deliberately caused the injury, the opponent loses and all his points are invalidated. The injured player in this case gains two points or one point in extension and wins the match. A player pronounced incapacitated may be reinstated in remaining matches if a medical doctor or referee allows it. However, a player who has caused deliberate injury is not permitted to play in the remaining matches.

Protest

No one can protest the referees' decisions. However, the contestant's manager may call a questionable point, such as raising the wrong flag, to the attention of the referee director *(shinpanchō)* or presiding referee *(shinpan shunin)*, before the end of the match. After a referee's conference *(gōgi)*, a final decision will be rendered.

Match and Referee Procedures

Entrance

At the start of the individual matches, referees *(shinpan-in)* enter the court, move to their respective spots with both their flags in their right hands, face the center of the court, and unfurl their flags. (Fig. 102 shows the *shinpan-in* lineup.) The chief referee *(shushin)* holds the red flag in the right hand and the other referees hold their red flags in their left hands. Contestants enter the court to the *ritsurei* position (nine steps apart) and wait for direction.

At the start of team matches, the referees enter the court, line up facing the *shōmen* (front section of the arena), and direct both teams to line up facing each other at the *ritsurei* position with the first two contestants wearing all of their kendo *gu* and holding their *shinai* in *sagetō* (Fig. 103).

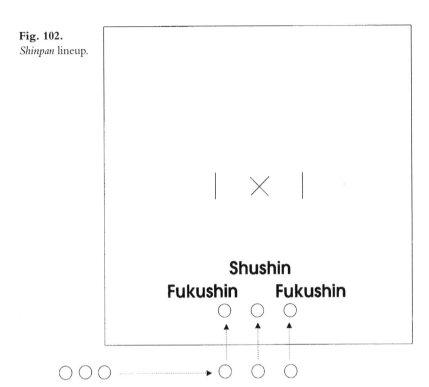

Fig. 102.
Shinpan lineup.

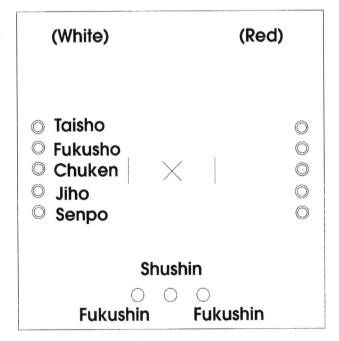

Fig. 103.
Team lineup at
the beginning
and end.

Bow to *Shōmen*

Before the start of the first match of the day, and at the start and end of the final match, under the direction of the *shushin,* all bow *(rei)* to *shōmen.*

At the start of individual matches, referees will be at their respective spots and contestants at the *ritsurei* positions (Fig. 104). When the *shushin* announces *"Shōmen ni,"* everyone faces the front. When the *shushin* announces *"Rei,"* everyone bows (30 degrees). Then the referees turn to face the center of the court while the contestants turn to face each other.

At the start of team matches, the referees line up facing the *shōmen* and the first teams line up at the *ritsurei* positions. When the *shushin* announces *"Shōmen ni,"* everyone faces the front, and when the *shushin* announces *"Rei,"* everyone bows (30 degrees). Then the teams retreat to the waiting areas, and the referees move to their posts and ready their flags.

At the start of the final individual match, when the contestants arrive at the *ritsurei* positions and referees are at their posts, the *shushin* conducts the *shōmen ni rei* (30 degrees). At the end of the final match, the contestants bow to each other first (15 degrees), then the *shushin* conducts the *shōmen ni rei* (30 degrees). The contestants exit the

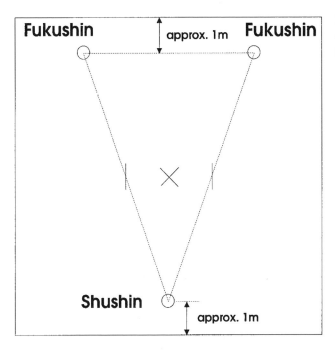

Fig. 104. *Shinpan* starting positions.

court. The referees wind their flags with the red one on the outside, line up with the *shushin* facing the *shōmen,* turn to the exit, and leave.

Start of the First Match

After the *shōmen ni rei,* the referee director *(shinpanchō)* will signal the start of the first match by standing up (or will whistle if multiple courts are used) when all the contestants (or the first contestants in team matches) are ready at the *ritsurei* position. The contestants bow to each other (15 degrees), take three steps to the starting line, and then take *sonkyo* (squatting) positions as they are drawing their *shinai.* The match begins when the *shunin* announces *"Hajime."*

Start of Other Matches

The contestants step into the court, bow to each other at *teitō* stance (hold *shinai* with the left hand), take three steps, and draw their *shinai* while assuming the *sonkyo* position. The *shushin* announces *"Hajime"* and the match begins.

Yūkō Datotsu

If a referee raises a flag to acknowledge a score, other referees must either raise a flag to agree, wave a flag across in the lower front to disagree, or cross their flags in the lower front (red one in front) to indicate their inability to see the point. If a majority of referees agree on the score, the flags are kept up and the *shushin* announces the point, *"Men ari."* If a point was not agreed on, the referee will lower his flag immediately and the match will continue.

When a point is announced, the contestants immediately return to the starting lines and wait in *chūdan.* To resume the match, the *shunin* announces *"Nihon me"* for the second point, *"Shōbu"* for the final deciding point, or *"Hajime"* if the point was revoked (after an announcement of *"Torikeshi"*). Then the flags are lowered. If a winner has been determined, the *shushin* announces *"Shōbu ari."*

Ending a Match

When a match ends, the *shushin* announces *"Shōbu ari"* with the appropriate flag raised if a winner has been decided, or *"Hikiwake"* with the flags crossed overhead (red in front) if the match ended in a draw. The contestants assume the *sonkyo* position, withdraw their *shinai,* retreat to the *ritsurei* position, bow to each other (15 degrees), and then exit the court.

Stoppage/Halt *(Chūshi)*

In the case of an emergency, or to avoid accidents, or if a foul is detected, a referee may stop the match. If a contestant needs a time out, he may get the attention of the *shushin*. The *shushin* will announce *"Yame"* and the contestants will return to the starting lines and the referees to their respective spots. If untied strings or loose clothing needs adjusting, the contestant will withdraw his *shinai* and retreat to the nearest boundary lines to adjust the equipment in *sonkyo* or *seiza* while the opponent waits in *sonkyo* near the boundary lines. When ready, the contestant will return to the starting lines and assume *chūdan*. The match is resumed when the *shushin* announces *"Hajime."*

Referees' Conference *(Gōgi)*

Gōgi, the referees' conference, is used to verify *hansoku* (illegal act or foul), to correct a mistake (e.g., wrong flag color), to consider revoking a point, or to clarify other procedural problems. To begin a *gōgi,* a referee raises both flags straight up in the right hand. The contestants withdraw their *shinai,* retreat to the nearest boundary lines, and wait in *sonkyo* or *seiza.* The referees gather in the center of the court to confer. When the conference is over, they direct the contestants to return to the starting lines. The *shushin* announces the decision (e.g., *hansoku,* indicating with the correct flag, *torikeshi,* or none if no action is to be taken) and resumes the match by announcing *"Hajime."*

Wakare

When the *tsubazeriai* (hand guard fight) comes to a stalemate, the *shushin* announces *"Wakare"* with both flags horizontally in front. The contestants immediately separate and assume *chūdan* and do not resume until the *shushin* announces *"Hajime."* The clock does not stop, so the contestants must separate promptly.

Referee's Duties

The referees judge the outcome of the match. The contestants have put all their energy and skills into a short period of time. Therefore, the referees must be fair in deciding victory or defeat and not be influenced by anything other than the match itself. It is especially important not to judge the contestants on their past achievements, on the name of their *dōjō,* or on personal feelings or preferences. Because all judging has a subjective component, the referees must have training in kendo and have a thorough understanding of the *waza* and rules. The referee must have keen vision because the speed of a strike is measured in milliseconds. The referee must also have good ears to differentiate the sounds of strikes to the different *datotsubui* as well as the *kiai* of the contestants. A referee must be accurate, precise, and prompt in the decision.

Besides deciding the outcome the referees must pay attention to the safety of the contestants and the orderly conduct of the matches. The referees must check the appropriateness of the contestants' *chakusō* as well as the *shinai* and *bōgu* prior to the match. The chief referee must correct inappropriate manners, speech, or behavior during and after the match.

Use of Flags

See Figs. 105 through 108 for flag positions.

1. Effective *datotsu:* Raise the flag of the contestant with the *datotsu* at a 45-degree angle. In a draw, raise both flags overhead, crossing them with the red one in front.

2. Ineffective *datotsu:* Wave both flags (red in front) to the lower front and sideways.

3. Abstaining: Cross both flags (red in front) in the lower front.

4. Reversing an effective *datotsu:* The main judge waves both flags (red in front) at the lower front.

5. Terminate the match: Raise both flags straight up.

6. Request conference: Raise both flags straight up in the right hand and declare *"Gōgi."*

7. When the *tsubazeriai* stalemates, the shushin extends both flags forward and declares *"Wakare."*

8. The flag is taken diagonally down and to the side of a contestant who has committed *hansoku.*

9. Declaration of *hansoku:* Hold the flag in one hand and indicate by the number of fingers the number of *hansoku* (i.e., *hansoku ikkai, hansoku nikai*) to the offending contestant.

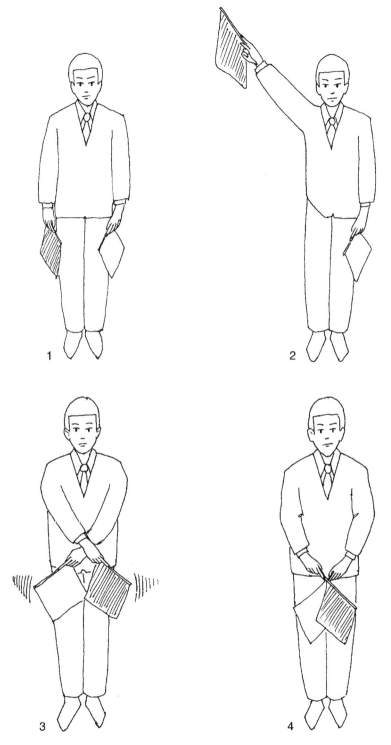

Fig. 105. Refer to the table for the meaning and declaration of all flag positions shown in the following illustrations. Flag positions: (a) two flags to sides; (b) flag diagonally above; (c) flags crossed below and waving; (d) flags crossed.

Table 3

Declaration and Use of Flags

Item	Declaration	Flags	Picture#
Commence the match	*Hajime*	Two flags to sides	1
Resume the match	*Hajime*	Two flags to sides	1
Terminate the match	*Yame*	Two flags overhead	6
Recognize *datotsu*	*(Men, kote, dō, tsuki) ari*	Flag diagonally above	2
Not recognize *datotsu*		Wave both flags below crossing	3
Abstain		Both flags crossed below	4
Canceling *datotsu*	*Torikeshi*	Wave both flags below crossing	3
Commence *nihonme*	*Nihonme*	Lower the flag	13
Both earned *ippon*, final point	*Shōbu*	Lower the flag	13
Winner is determined	*Shōbu ari*	Lower the flag	13
Enchō/ extension	*Enchō hajime*	Both flags to the side	1
Ippon gachi/ winner by one point	*Shōbu ari*	Raise the flag diagonally above	2
Declare *hantei*	*Hantei*	Raise the flag diagonally above	2
Winner by *hantei*	*Shōbu ari*	Lower the flag	13
Fusengachi/ winner by default	*Shōbu ari*	Raise the flag diagonally above	2
Tie, draw	*Hikiwake*	Both flags crossed overhead	5
Unable to continue the match	*Shōbu ari*	Raise the flag diagonally above	2
Judges to confer	*Gōgi*	Raise both flags with right hand	8

Item	Declaration	Flags	Picture#
Results of *gōgi*		*Shushin* indicates by flag	2
Use of drugs	*Shōbu ari*	Raise the flag diagonally above	2
Disrespectful (words/ behavior)	*Shōbu ari*	Raise the flag diagonally above	2
Use of illegal *shinai/bōgu*	*Shōbu ari*	Raise the flag diagonally above	2
Leg sweep	*Hansoku "x-kai"*	Lower the flag diagonally below and show number by fingers	9, 11, 12
Push opponent to *jōgai*	*Hansoku "x-kai"*	Lower the flag diagonally below and show number by fingers	9, 11, 12
Stepped out to *jōgai*	*Hansoku "x-kai"*	Lower the flag diagonally below and show number by fingers	9, 11, 12
Dropped *shinai*	*Hansoku "x-kai"*	Lower the flag diagonally below and show number by fingers	9, 11, 12
Inappropriate time out	*Hansoku "x-kai"*	Lower the flag diagonally below and show number by fingers	9, 11, 12
Simultaneous first *hansoku*	*Hansoku ik'kai*	Same as above	10, 11, 12
Simultaneous second *hansoku*	*Sōsai*	Wave both flags below, crossing	3
Subsequent *sōsai*	*Onajiku sōsai*	Wave both flags below, crossing	3
Second illegal move	*Hansoku nikai*	Lower the flag diagonally and show number by fingers	9, 11, 12
Win by *hansoku*	*Shōbu ari*	Raise the flag diagonally above	2
Kōchaku jōtai (frozen)	*Wakare*	Thrust both flags forward	7a
To resume from above	*Hajime*	Lower both flags to sides	7b
Injury prevents match	*Shōbu ari*	Raise the flag diagonally above	2

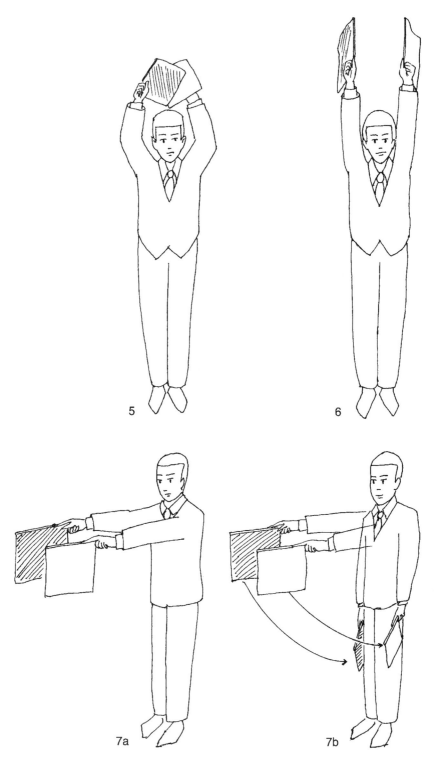

Fig. 106. Flag positions (cont.): (a) both flags crossed overhead; (b) two flags straight up overhead; (c) both flags thrust forward; (d) both flags lowered to sides after (c).

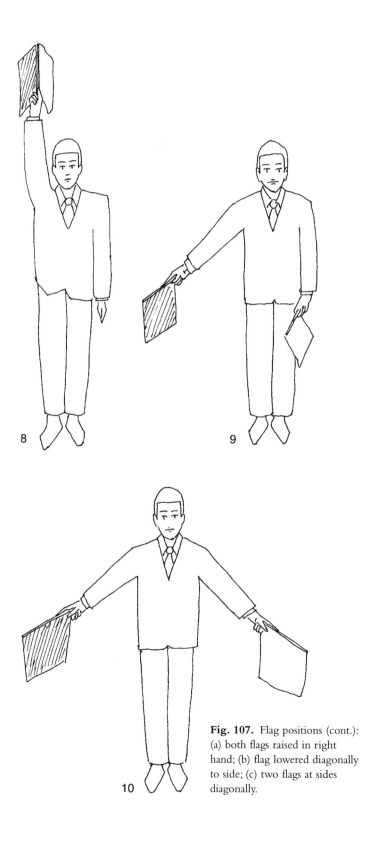

Fig. 107. Flag positions (cont.): (a) both flags raised in right hand; (b) flag lowered diagonally to side; (c) two flags at sides diagonally.

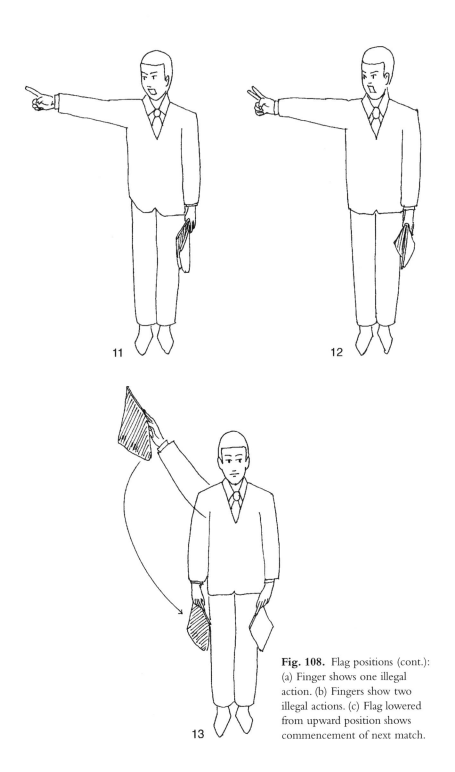

Fig. 108. Flag positions (cont.): (a) Finger shows one illegal action. (b) Fingers show two illegal actions. (c) Flag lowered from upward position shows commencement of next match.

Methods of Declaration

1. Commencing the match: *"Hajime."*
2. An effective *datotsu*: *"Men," "Kote,"* or *"Dō ari,"* with the contestants at the position of play.
3. Reversing an effective *datotsu*, as in a case of showing disrespect: *"Torikeshi,"* with the contestants at the center.
4. Commencement of *nihonme*: *"Nihonme,"* with the contestants at the center.
5. After each contestant has earned *ippon* and at the beginning of the final point: *"Shōbu,"* with the contestants at the center.
6. Declaration of a winner: *"Shōbu ari,"* with the contestants at the center.
7. Commencement of extension *(enchō)*: *"Enchō hajime,"* with the contestants at the center.
8. Declaration of winner by *ippon*: *"Shōbu ari,"* with the contestants at the center.
9. Winning by default *(fusengachi)*: *"Shōbu ari,"* with the winner at the center.
10. Winning by judgment *(hantei)*: *"Shōbu ari,"* with the contestants at the center.
11. Termination of the match: *"Yame,"* with the contestants at the center.
12. Declaration of foul play *(hansoku)*: *"Hansoku ...* (times)," with the contestants at the center. For simultaneous foul play, the red side is addressed first, then the white side. This is followed by declaration of offset *(sōsai)*. For second and subsequent offsets, the declaration of offset and flag signals are made simultaneously.
13. *Ippon* by *hansoku*: *"Ippon ari"* first declares *hansoku*. The referee then turns to the winner, raises the flag, and declares *"Ippon ari,"* with the contestants at the center.
14. Winner by *hansoku*: *"Shōbu ari,"* first declares *hansoku* to the offending contestant, then declares *"Ippon ari . . . shōbu ari,"* with the contestants at the center.
15. When contestants request time out by raising their hands the main referee raises his flags straight up and declares *"Yame,"* then asks for the reason for the time out.
16. Excessive *tsubazeriai*: *"Hansoku,"* with the contestants at the center. The second time will be counted as an *ippon*.

17. Draw or tie: *"Hikiwake."* The main referee crosses both flags overhead with the contestants at the center.

18. Any other incident may be decided by a conference of the judges; the main referee will declare the decision.

Igi (Clarification or Protest)

When a contestant's manager signals to question an application of the rules, a referee immediately suspends the match. The manager explains the problem to the *shinpanchō* or the *shinpan shunin,* who then directs the referees to conference. The *shushin* conveys the outcome of the conference to the *shinpanchō* or *shinpan shunin,* who then conveys the final decision to the manager. The *shushin* then allows the match to resume.

Hantei (Majority Decision)

If a match is to be determined by the referees' decisions after a conference, the contestants stand at the starting lines in *chūdan* and await the *shushin's* declaration. The *shushin* announces *"Hantei"* (majority decision), and all three referees raise their flags simultaneously for the contestant determined to be superior (a referee cannot abstain from a vote). The *shushin* raises the winner's flag (majority vote) and announces *"Shōbu ari."*

Fusengachi (Win without Match)

In the case of an individual match, if the opponent is unable to compete (e.g., no-show, disabled), the contestant bows, advances to the starting line, assumes *sonkyo,* and then stands up in *chūdan.* The *shushin* raises this contestant's flag, announces *"Shōbu ari,"* and lowers the flag. The contestant assumes the *sonkyo* position, withdraws the *shinai,* stands up, retreats, bows, and exits the court. In the case of a team match, if the opposing team is unable to compete, the team lines up with the referees as usual. The *shushin* raises this team's flag, announces *"Shōbu ari,"* and lowers the flag. The team bows when the *shushin* so directs, then exits. The contestant who loses by default is prohibited from being reinstated in the remaining matches.

Kōtai (Rotate)

Referees periodically rotate *(kōtai)* in a counterclockwise direction, holding their flags in their right hands (Fig. 109). The referees may be replaced individually or all at once (Fig. 110 and Fig. 111).

Ending

At the end of an individual match, the contestants return to the starting lines, await the *shushin's* announcement (*"Shōbu ari"* or *"Hikiwake"*), assume *sonkyo,* withdraw their *shinai,* stand up in *taitō,* retreat to the *ritsurei* position, lower their *shinai* to *sagetō,* bow to each other (15 degrees), and exit the court. At the end of a team match, both teams line up at the *ritsurei* position with only the last contestants in full kendo *gu* and holding their *shinai.* They bow to each other (15 degrees) when the *shushin* so directs, then exit the court.

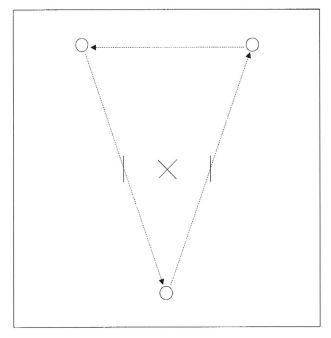

Fig. 109.
Shinpan
rotation.

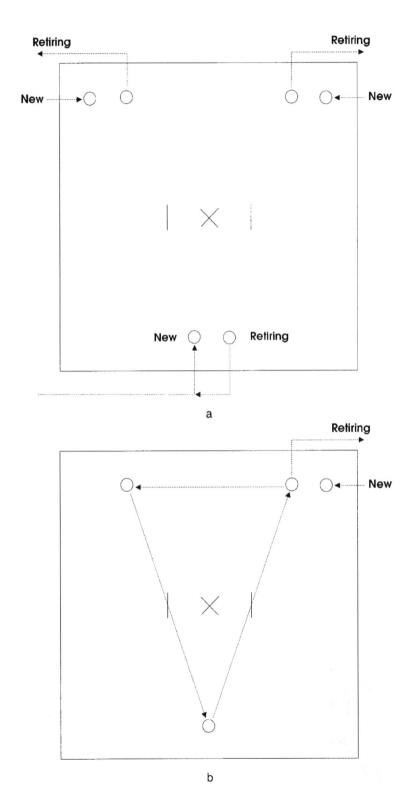

Fig. 110. *Shinpan* (a) alternation A; (b) alternation B.

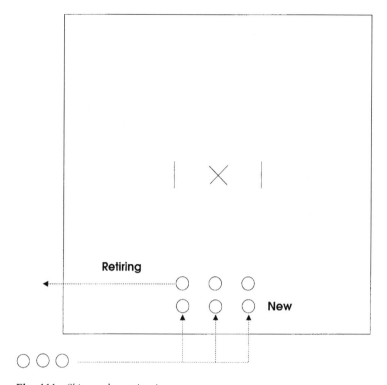

Fig. 111. *Shinpan* alternation in group.

Miscellaneous

- To draw *nitō* (two swords) from both *shinai* in *sagetō,* first draw the *shinai* for the left hand with the right hand and place it in your left hand, then draw the *shinai* for your right hand.

- To withdraw, first withdraw the *shinai* in your right hand, then the *shinai* in your left hand.

- Affix equipment securely so that it will not become undone during a match. Clothing should be neat, without rips or tears. The straps tying the *men* should measure 40 cm from the knot. The referees should note that the contestants' equipment, their *shinai* (including *tsuba*), and their clothing are appropriate.

- The contestants should bow only to each other in the court, and refrain from bowing to the referees or doing *zarei* privately in the court. As the contestants pass each other between matches, they should refrain from overzealous behavior such as *dō* bumping or shaking hands. The contestants should remain off court until the previous contestants have exited and the referees have finished rotating to their new spots.

- The managers and contestants are not allowed to bring a timer to the contestants' waiting area. They must not signal instructions or vocalize encouragement to the contestants. During the first and the last match of a team match, it is preferable that the other members sit in *seiza*.

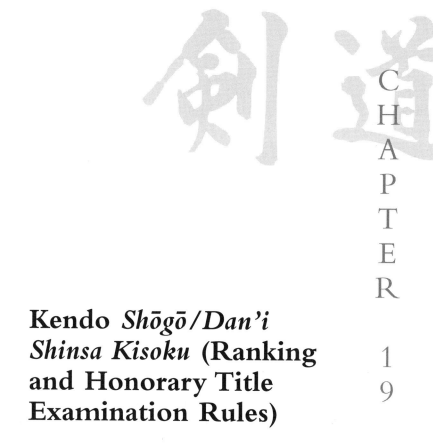

Kendo *Shōgō/Dan'i Shinsa Kisoku* (Ranking and Honorary Title Examination Rules)

CHAPTER 19

The kendo ranks are divided into *kyū* and *dan*. Beginners start at the tenth *kyū* and rise to the first *kyū*. Originally, *dan* ended at the fifth *dan* and was followed by the ranks *renshi, kyōshi,* and *hanshi,* but in 1957 this was extended to tenth *dan,* although the honorary titles were retained. This was done to make the kendo ranking system correspond to the judo ranking system. However, the dual honorary titles and the revised ranking system created problems. The *hanshi* is the highest rank in personal character, leadership, and kendo skills. Some feel that it is inconsistent to have *hanshi hachidan* and still have the higher ranks of *kyūdan* and *jūdan.* In fact, no *jūdan* has been awarded in the past thirty years or so, and it is not likely that a candidate will appear. The 1988 revision in the ranking system requires a year of extra training added between *nidan* and *nanadan* and two extra years for *hachidan.* This extra training is to improve the overall level of kendo.

The Kendo Shōdan Shiken (ranking examination) and the *shōgō* (honorary title) have changed numerous times since their inception in 1889 at the first Butoku Kai Enbu Tournament in Kyoto. The last major change occurred in November 1999, following the bylaws of the All Japan Kendo Federation (AJKF) aimed at improving and promoting kendo. The changes went into effect on April 1, 2000. The rules that pertained to the ranking examination, the honorary title examination, and the selection standard of the examiners were three separate entities, but in the new regulations they are brought together under the Kendo Shōgō/Dan'i Shinsa Kisoku (the Kendo Honorary Title and Ranking Examination Rules). Under the old regulations, the kendo ranking system allowed *shodan* (first *dan*) to *jūdan* (tenth *dan*). Under the new rules *hachidan* (eighth *dan*) became the highest *dan,* and ninth *dan* and *jūdan* were eliminated. The honorary title *hanshi* became the highest title in the kendo ranking system. The regulations of 1969 were abolished, but the honorary titles and *dan* bestowed under the old rules continue to be honored.

The examiners for the honorary title are selected by the Examiner Selection Committee of AJKF and appointed by its president. The panel of examiners for the *renshi* title consists of seven members who are *hanshi* or *kyōshi* and 71 years old or younger. For the *kyōshi* title, the panel consists of seven members, five of whom must be *hanshi* and 71 or younger. Two other members must be chosen from scholars. The *hanshi* title requires ten examiners. Seven of the ten members must be *hanshi* aged 80 or younger. Three additional members must also be scholars.

The examiners are appointed by the president of the local kendo organization and report to the AJKF. They examine the *shodan* (first) to *godan* (fifth) applicants. The examiners for the *rokudan* (sixth) to *hachidan* (eighth) are selected by the examiner selection committee and are appointed by the president of the AJKF.

The *shodan* (first) to *sandan* (third) are examined by the five-member committee who are all *rokudan* or above. For *yondan* (fourth) and *godan* (fifth), the seven examiners are *nanadan* (seventh) or above. For *rokudan* (sixth) and *nanadan* (seventh) the panel consists of ten members, seven of whom examine performance and *kata,* and three who consider the written examination. In the *hachidan* (eighth) examination the panel of examiners has twenty members. Seven examine the first performance and ten examine the second performance. Three members consider the *kata* and written examination.

The examinees for the honorary titles must be members of the participating organization and have special qualifications, including mastery of kendo, superior knowledge, and outstanding character. All the candidates must be recommended by presidents of the participating organizations and the *renshi* candidates must be *rokudan* (sixth), the *kyōshi* candidates must be *nanadan* (seventh), and the *hanshi* candidates must have *hachidan* (eighth). The president of the AJKF can also recommend a candidate for *hanshi* if he considers it appropriate. Exceptions include the *renshi* title given to a *godan* (fifth) holder when recommended by presidents of the participating local organizations, subject to meeting other requirements. Examinees are given the *renshi* or *kyōshi* title when five out of the seven examiners approve. For the *hanshi* title, the agreement of eight out of the ten examiners is needed. As an exception, the *hanshi* title may be bestowed on a *nanadan* (seventh) holder who is over 70 years old and meets all other requirements. It is within the power of the president of the AJKF to withdraw or bestow the *hanshi* title under very special circumstances. It should be noted that posthumous awards of honorary titles have been abolished.

The candidates for all the *dan* examinations must be members of participating local organizations and must fulfill the requirements shown in Table 4 in addition to skill, knowledge, and maturity commensurate with each degree.

Alternatively, if the candidates are recommended by the president of the local organization and meet the requirements shown in Table 5, they may take the examination for *nidan* (second) to *godan* (fifth).

When recommended by the president of the local organization and considered appropriate, the candidates listed in Table 6 may take the examination for *shodan* (first) to *godan* (fifth).

If the candidates for *rokudan* (sixth) to *hachidan* (eighth) are over 60 years old, the exception shown in Table 7 may apply for the examination.

Table 4
Requirements for Candidates for *Dan* Examinations

First *dan*	*shodan*	Must have *ikkyu* and be over eighth grade
Second *dan*	*nidan*	1 year after passing *shodan* examination
Third *dan*	*sandan*	2 years after passing *nidan* examination
Fourth *dan*	*yondan*	3 years after passing *sandan* examination
Fifth *dan*	*godan*	4 years after passing *yondan* examination
Sixth *dan*	*rokudan*	5 years after passing *godan* examination
Seventh *dan*	*nanadan*	6 years after passing *rokudan* examination
Eighth *dan*	*hachidan*	10 years after passing *nanadan* examination

Table 5
Requirements for Candidates for *Nidan* to *Godan* Examinations

Second *dan*	*nidan*	Above 35 years old
Third *dan*	*sandan*	Above 40 years old
Fourth *dan*	*yondan*	Above 45 years old
Fifth *dan*	*godan*	Above 50 years old

Table 6
Requirements for Candidates for *Shodan* to *Godan* Examinations

First *dan*	*shodan*	Holder of *ikkyu*
Second *dan*	*nidan*	35 years old or 3 months of training after *shodan*
Third *dan*	*sandan*	40 years old or 1 year of training after *nidan*
Fourth *dan*	*yondan*	45 years old or 2 years of training after *sandan*
Fifth *dan*	*godan*	50 years old or 3 years of training after *yondan*

Table 7
Requirements for Candidates for *Rokudan* to *Hachidan* Examinations

Sixth *dan*	*rokudan*	2 years after passing *godan* examination
Seventh *dan*	*nanadan*	3 years after passing *rokudan* examination
Eighth *dan*	*hachidan*	5 years after passing *nanadan* examination

The examination covers technical skill, Nihon Kendo Kata, and written examinations. When a candidate for *shodan* (first) to *nanadan* (seventh) fails the written part, he may retake it. For the *hachidan* (eighth), only the candidate who has passed the first performance examination may proceed to subsequent examinations and only after attending a special seminar.

For *shodan* (first) to *sandan* (third), the candidates pass when three of five examiners agree. The *yondan* (fourth) and *godan* (fifth) candidates need five out of seven examiners. *Rokudan* (sixth) and *nanadan* (seventh) candidates need five out of seven examiners to pass the performance test and two out of the three examiners for the written examination. The *hachidan* (eighth) examinee must have the consent of five out of seven examiners for the first performance test, and seven out of ten for the second performance test. The *kata* and written examination for *hachidan* (eighth) require the agreement of two out of the three examiners. The president has the power to withdraw the ranks between *rokudan* (sixth) to *hachidan* (eighth) if the results of the examination or conduct of the candidate before and during the examination are considered inappropriate. It is also within the power of the president to bestow the rank of *rokudan* (sixth), *nanadan* (seventh), or *hachidan* (eighth) under special circumstances.

PART IV

Kendo Philosophy and Concepts

Kendo as a Spiritual Art

One major difference between kendo and Western martial arts is kendo's philosophical and spiritual emphasis. I believe that unless one understands and includes the spiritual dimension in one's training, kendo is merely a game of hitting an opponent with a stick. When we understand its spiritual and philosophical roots, kendo becomes an art and contributes to our growth, helping us acquire grace and harmony. Without insight into the philosophy of kendo one may practice it for many years and fail to reach the quality called *kihin* (character, refinement, grace, elegance, and poise).

Kendo and *Gorin no Sho*

Because kendo has been practiced for hundreds of years, a wealth of adages and axioms left by famous swordsman-teachers has accumulated. Miyamoto Musashi, who was born in the latter part of the sixteenth century, when Japan was about to emerge from centuries of internal warfare, collected many of these in his writings entitled *Gorin no Sho (Book of Five Rings)*. Although *Gorin no Sho* is in some ways a technical manual, Musashi discusses the concepts and philosophy of kendo.

In this book, Musashi shows a deep general knowledge of Zen and the art of strategy.

Kendo and Zen

Many of the books written by great kendo samurai show strong Zen influences. It was a common practice for a kendo master to write the secrets of his kendo style with the help of a scholar, usually a Buddhist monk. Yagyū Tajima no Kami Munenori, for example, wrote a book called *Yagyū Hyōhōka Densho*. Munenori was a student of Zen master Takuan Sōhō, who was invited to teach at Edo castle by the third Tokugawa *shōgun*, Iemitsu. Munenori explains his philosophy of kendo by using Zen concepts. Many of these wise sayings still pertain in our daily activities and add a new dimension to our practice of kendo.

Kendo Adages

Kendo adages include not only concepts but also the technical aspects of kendo, such as *suki, ma'ai, sen,* and *seme.* Some of the adages and concepts mentioned here are not necessarily mentioned elsewhere in this book, but you may encounter them in a *dōjō* or in books related to Japan.

Concepts

A-un no kokyū (exhaling inhaling timing): Synchronization of timing with the opponent. *A* and *un* come from Sanskrit. *A* represents exhaling and *un* represents inhaling.

Budō (the way of martial arts): Way or study of martial arts such as kendo, *iaido,* aikido, judo, karate, sumo, *jūjutsu, jōjutsu, naginata, bōjutsu, kusarigama, kyūjutsu,* and *yabusame.*

Bunbu ryōdō (academics and martial skill dual way): A duality of academic and martial skills that is considered essential to the good samurai.

Bushidō (the way of the samurai): The way of life for a samurai based on Zen Buddhism and Confucianism. It emphasizes righteousness, courage, honor, mercy, courtesy, faith, and loyalty.

Byōjōshin (calm mind): A mind in perfect balance. Tranquility, serenity, and calmness are to be maintained all the time. According to Yagyū Munenori's *Hyōhōka Densho, byōjōshin* is a state of mind devoid of deviated thoughts such as wishing to win or defending oneself.

Chakin shibori (**wringing the tea-ceremony towel**): This is a technique of grasping the sword handle *(tsuka)* with both hands, as if one were wringing the soft tea-ceremony towel.

Chi (**knowledge or wisdom**): Knowledge and wisdom are important virtues of a samurai.

Dasō kyoda (**strike the bush and threaten the snake**): This Yagyū Shinkage ryū technique tries to show the opponent your intention of moving, causing him to move, thus giving you an opportunity to strike back.

Dō chū sei, sei chū dō (**calmness in movement, movement in calmness**): To maintain a calm mind and alertness while moving.

Dokumyō ken (**sword to cut oneself**): To consider yourself an enemy and win over yourself. Only by overcoming self-doubt and uncertainty can you defeat the enemy.

Fudōshin (**unmovable mind**): A state of mind that is not moved by an external force.

Gi (**doubt**): *Gi* is not allowed in kendo. If you have uncertainty in facing your opponent, you cannot make a proper decision.

Gi (**duty**): One of the five virtues of the samurai. A strong sense of duty was considered the philosophical backbone of the good samurai.

Hōshin (**empty mind**): The opposite of *shishin,* or a halted mind. A flexible mind, which is able to meet any change of the opponent, is an ideal state of mind for kendo.

Hyakuren jitoku (**hundred practices acquired spontaneously**): Practice a hundred times, and you will acquire the skills. Continuous and arduous practice is needed to improve oneself.

Hyakuri no michimo ippo kara (**the journey of a thousand miles starts with one step**): The practice of kendo is like a long journey, and one must take the first step.

Ichigo ichie (**one life, one meeting**): This is an expression from the tea ceremony. It means do your best with your opponent as if this were the only encounter in your lifetime.

Iwao no mi (**a body like rock**): The body and mind are a massive rock, not easily moved. According to Miyamoto Musashi, this state of mind can be accomplished by arduous training in the martial arts.

Jin (compassion): Compassion or thoughtfulness toward fellow human beings is considered one of the virtues of a good samurai and leader.

Kanken no metsuke (look with mind and eyes): Miyamoto Musashi recommends seeing more with one's mind and less with one's eyes. *Ken* means to see with the eyes, but *kan* means to understand the true state of things with the mind.

Katte ute; utte katsuna (win then strike, don't strike to win): This refers to the importance of overcoming the opponent's *ki, ken,* and *waza* before striking. Avoid using excessive and unreasonable *waza* simply to capture a point.

Kenchū tai; taichū ken (offense in defense; defense in offense): In the middle of an offence one must not forget to defend himself, and in defense one may not forget to take offensive action.

Ken Zen ittchi (sword and Zen in harmony): The ultimate goals of kendo and Zen are the same.

Kigurai (loftiness): A loftiness of the mind, a superiority of spirit and *seme,* a state of mind that pressures the opponent without drawing the sword or using *waza.*

Kihin (grace): Character, refinement, grace, elegance, and poise—*kihin* is an important virtue of a samurai or kendo practitioner. After years of practice, one can reach a physical and spiritual grace and dignity.

Ku (fear): *Ku* is not allowed in kendo. *Ku* describes panic, trepidation, and alarm. When one has *ku,* one grows timid and is not able to move freely.

Kyō (surprise): *Kyō* is not allowed in kendo. When an opponent's unexpected movement surprises a person, the mind becomes confused and the body may become unbalanced.

Makura o osaeru (press down the pillow): This is the concept of *debana waza.* When an opponent's head is on a pillow it is easy to press down his head against an effort to raise it.

Meikyōshisui (mirror-like water surface): Ability to respond to changing situations rapidly just like they reflect in a mirror. It describes the state of mind of a person who has achieved a high level of training in kendo.

Mōshin (confused state of mind): A state of mind inflexibly fixed on a certain point.

Munen musō (**absence of thoughts**): An empty, clear, and enlightened state of mind that is free from any harmful and detrimental thought, fear, or evil wishes.

Mushin no Kokoro (**nonexistent state of mind**): Similar to *hōshin,* this state of mind is detached and does not stop at any particular point. In this state of mind one can respond to any changes.

Rei (**etiquette**): One virtue of a good samurai is to know the etiquette appropriate to all the activities of daily life, even of dying.

Rei ni hajimari rei ni owaru (**begins with *rei* and ends with *rei***): A practice that emphasizes the importance of *rei* in the Japanese martial arts, especially kendo.

Ri no shugyō waza no shugyō (**training of mind and training of skills**): Takuan Sōhō's phrase, which means that one must train to clear the mind so that the body can move freely.

Sekka no ki (**moment of flint stone sparks**): This teaching of Takuan Sōhō refers to rapid speed, like the sparks flying as flint stones are struck together. It does not describe the speed of the *waza* so much as a state of mind that reflects one's surroundings instantaneously. It does not mean that one's mind should be set as fast as sparks.

Setsunintō (**killing sword**): Killing is against the way, but there are instances in which killing an evil person is justified to save a hundred good people. Yagyū Munenori explains this in the first chapter of *Hyōhōka Densho.*

Shishin (**halted mind**): The opposite of *hōshin,* this means a blocked or halted mind, a state of mind not allowed in kendo. A mind focused on a single detail cannot see the entire picture.

Waku (**doubt/indecision**): *Waku* is not allowed in kendo. Doubt and lack of confidence make prompt decisions and movements impossible.

Yū (**courage**): Courage is one of the important virtues of a samurai and kendo practitioner. When it was commonplace to die in a combat, a man needed courage.

Zanshin (**leaving the mind upon the fallen opponent**): *Zanshin* is the rebirth of *ki.* After the completion of a *waza,* one rebuilds *ki* in preparation for the next offensive or defensive move against one's opponent. There must be an alertness of mind, even after the completion of the task. At the end of an action, save some *ki* for the next movement.

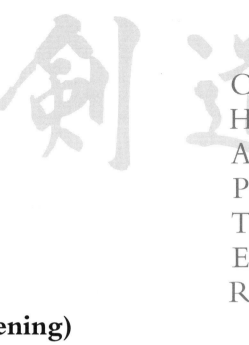

Suki (Opening)

Suki is a common concept in Japanese life, used by people who do not practice the martial arts as well as by those who do. It means a fleeting moment in which one is vulnerable to attack. It also means the time one needs to recover, a moment during which no defensive movement is possible. Being able to open a *suki* in an opponent can lead to victory.

Suki literally means a slit or an opening between objects. When you are performing a task, you may relax or rest between activities. When you are preoccupied with your opponent's move, you may lose your concentration. This moment of relaxation is *suki,* a period of time when you are unprepared for the next action. The time is usually very short, measured in milliseconds in kendo.

Another dimension to *suki* is space. You may encroach on your opponent without your opponent noticing. You can bring your *kensen* so close to your opponent it becomes impossible for your opponent to counter. This is a *suki*.

As mentioned before, *suki* is the sliver of time when you cannot protect yourself from attack. Ordinarily, it takes only half the time to defend as to attack, if both parties are equal in training. For example, it takes 0.3 second to initiate and complete a good *datotsu*, but only 0.15 second to defend against one. Clearly you need to force your opponent into *suki* if you are to deliver a clean *datotsu*. For example, when you try to strike your opponent's *kote*, you may see him dodging your *shinai* in *nuki waza* and his *shinai* coming straight at your *men*, but it is impossible to defend yourself against this attack because your opponent has forced you into *suki*. Although your eyes can clearly see what is happening, your body is in a brief period of immobility.

You can force your opponent to create a *suki* by using *harai waza* or *makikaeshi waza*. This move either will make your opponent drop his *shinai*, or make your opponent's *kensen* deviate from *chushin sen*. This will create a *suki*.

Debana (beginning), *waza no tsukita tokoro* (moment a technique ended), and *itsuita tokoro* (settled) are good examples of *suki*. At the beginning of an action, you commit yourself both mind and body, and are unable to alter this commitment even when your opponent makes a sudden defensive movement. This is obviously a *suki*. When you have committed to a *waza* or have just completed one, you cannot, for a moment, physically or mentally move on to the next action. This is a *suki*.

Every action has a beginning. At the moment your opponent is on the verge of executing a technique, you have an opportune moment to strike. Your opponent is likely to focus entirely on the technique he is about to execute. Once your opponent is committed to taking an action, he has reached a point of no return. If you attack at that instant, your opponent will not be able to avoid your strike. *Debana-men, debana-tsuki,* or *debana-kote* are all effective strikes of this nature, occurring at the start of the opponent's movement. *Debana* techniques are considered to be the most sophisticated. Kendo practitioners who can foresee the opponent's intentions and quickly strike are considered to have clear insight and extraordinary talent.

The second opportune moment to strike occurs at the conclusion of your opponent's action. At this moment, there is a very short period of immobility before your opponent recovers and begins another action, whether offensive or defensive, when he is vulnerable. *Kaeshi, nuki,* and *suriage* techniques are examples of this.

The third type of *suki* occurs when your opponent is settled, called *itsuita tokoro*, which means lost concentration or *zanshin*. *Itsuita tokoro* often occurs after a number of successive actions when your opponent pauses for breath. It can also occur when your opponent blocks a strike and opens a part of the body to a counter strike. Other instances are when your opponent delivers an unsuccessful strike or tries to retreat from an unsuccessful strike.

Kensen, Ma'ai, and Sen

The *kensen,* or *kissaki,* is the tip of the sword. Used skillfully, it will
"kill" or suppress three things. First, it kills the opponent's sword so
that it cannot be used to strike. Second, it kills the spirit of the opponent so that he cannot take steps to strike. Third, it kills the opponent's *waza* so that he cannot effectively deliver it.

If you wave the *kensen* too widely, your opponent can take advantage of its rhythm and strike. It is likely that your opponent will
attack on the upswing, and you will be hit as the sword goes down.
Chiba Shūsaku is known to have shaken his sword tip in a small
rhythmic manner, as in *sekirei-no-o* (tail of wagtail). His intent was to
keep his *kensen* active and intimidate as well as confuse his opponent.
If you do this correctly, in a small rhythmic motion at midline, your
opponent will not be able to detect the start.

The tip of the sword is always the beginning and ending of the
waza. Use the center of your *kote* or *tenouchi* as a fulcrum, and make a
semicircular motion with the center of *monouchi* of your *shinai.* You
will gain speed and the *waza* will be crisp and effective.

The length of the sword is relative. Some say that rather than lengthening the sword, you should step forward so that your sword will give you an unlimited reach.

The proper *ma'ai* depends on the size of your body, the level of your skill, and the length of your *shinai*. Envision the *ma'ai* so that you appear far enough from your opponent, but close enough from your point of view. Obviously, the *ma'ai* is equal in distance from either side, but with *ki* and mind, you can shorten the distance.

Sen means "fore" or "ahead of time." In kendo, it means "ahead of an opponent's *waza*." When practicing kendo, make it a habit to think of striking before your opponent thinks of it. Keep your opponent from starting first. There are several refinements of *sen* that you should become familiar with.

- *Sen no sen:* Strike a split second before your opponent commences a *waza*. *Debana waza* is a typical example of this technique.

- *Tai no sen:* Sense your opponent's strike, and strike back at the same time so that the match ends with *aiuchi*. If your *ki* is stronger, your sword will prevail by warding off your opponent's strike.

- *Go no sen:* When your opponent strikes, use *ōji waza* to ward off the attack, then strike immediately to take the advantage of the moment when your opponent has settled after completing the *waza*.

About *Seme*

In kendo, *semeru (seme)* means to attack spiritually as well as physically. When you assume an attack stance, you must be full of *ki* directed toward your opponent. In general, *datotsu* (striking) can be targeted at three parts: the *men,* the *kote,* and the *dō.* The choice of which part to target depends on the movements of your opponent's *shinai* or arms. When your opponent's *kensen* is lowered, the most effective *datotsu* can be at the *men.* When the *kensen* starts to rise, the most effective *datotsu* can be at your opponent's *kote.* When your opponent's arm rises, the most effective *datotsu* can be at the *dō.*

When striking from *tōma,* first take one step to close the *ma'ai* to *issoku ittō no ma'ai,* then strike your target. If you raise your *shinai* from *tōma* to strike, your opponent will detect your intent and have ample time to defend himself, or even to counterattack.

Timing a strike is extremely important to delivering an effective *datotsu.* When your opponent is in motion or beginning an action, he will be preoccupied by thoughts of the movement and will be less prepared to defend himself. This is your chance to strike.

When your opponent is beginning to withdraw, you can strike the *men, ni,* or *san* (two or three), *dan men uchi (men-men, men-men-men), kote-men, kote-dō, tsuki-men,* or *kote-men-dō.* When your opponent is about to initiate a *waza* by stepping in, use the following *waza: debana-men, debana-kote, debana-tsuki, harai-men, hari-men, harai-kote, hari-kote, harai-dō,* and *uchiotoshi-men. Debana* means "at the moment of commencement." *Harai* is a sweeping or brushing movement, and is most effective if applied to the half of the *shinai* closest to the opponent. *Hari* is slapping in a quick and forceful manner.

Uchiotoshi literally means "to strike it down." For example, when your opponent comes at your *kote* or *dō,* strike his *shinai* down to parry as well as make a *suki* with which to strike back, as in *dō-uchiotoshi-men.*

Similar *waza* can be also applied when your opponent is stepping in with a strike. In order to deliver an effective *datotsu,* you must have a sound *kamae* and watch your opponent carefully to find an opening. Certain moves can be made from the *kamae* position to fracture the stability of your opponent or to distract the *shinai.*

- *Fureru* **(to touch):** Hold the *shinai* lightly and gently touch your opponent's *shinai* to learn his emotional or mental state. When you find confusion or imbalance in your opponent's mind, go in for a good *datotsu.*

- *Osaeru* **(to press down):** Let the *kensen* of your *shinai* lightly ride your opponent's *shinai* and press forward. When your opponent begins to withdraw, strike a *datotsu.*

- *Hataku* **(to slap):** Slap your opponent's *shinai* using a snapping motion of the wrist, forcefully but in a small motion. This is effective in terminating your opponent's intention to strike especially when you slap hard at the moment of your opponent's *debana.*

- *Uchiotoshi* **(to strike down):** When your opponent's *kamae* is shallow, tentative, or cursory, strike diagonally downward in a light snapping movement of the *kensen* of your *shinai.* When your opponent's *kamae* is unbalanced with *uchiotoshi,* go in for a *datotsu. Note:* Maintain the balance of your *kamae* when using this technique. Make sure your *kensen* is always within the centerline. While making a *datotsu,* swing your arms in a large motion and propel your body forward. When the *datotsu* is over, return your *kensen* to the centerline.

- *Harai* (**to slap in large motion**): *Harai* is an exaggerated *hari* or *hataku*. Approach from *omote* or *ura* and strike with a snapping motion, knocking your opponent's *shinai* off the centerline, as if you were drawing a semicircle with the tip of your *shinai*.

- *Maku* (**to wrap around**): A *maku* is effective when used on an opponent who has a solid and firm grip on his *tsuka*. Hold your *shinai* lightly and make a coiling movement around your opponent's *shinai,* like a snake. As your opponent's *shinai* rises, use a swift, snapping motion of your wrist to lift upward.

- *Shinai ashisabaki* (*shinai* **footwork**): When you attack with your *kensen* do not grasp your *tsuka* tightly or fix the *kensen* in one place. Hold your *shinai* lightly. Your feet should be placed to allow easy and swift movement to the front and back, and to the left and right. When stepping forward, you should feel your left foot propelling your body forward.

- *Sansappo* (**three killing techniques**): Three techniques to attack to win are killing *ki* (spirit), killing *ken* (sword), and killing *waza* (technique).

Tokui Waza (Forte)

A kendo practitioner may develop over the years certain *waza* that he prefers to use more frequently than others because they have been successful. These are called *tokui waza* (forte). Some kendo practitioners favor certain maneuvers because of a physical characteristic. This is also called *tokui waza*. When used too frequently *tokui waza* can be appropriately called *kuse* (habit) and can be disadvantageous because an opponent can prepare for them. When a habit is acquired early and persists throughout a career it is called *waruguse* (bad habit). A *waruguse* is difficult to erase, so it is essential that instructors correct their students' bad habits before they become fixed.

A tall person is accustomed to being attacked on the *kote* and *dō*. For that reason, tall players are usually most proficient at defending those areas. By the same token, a tall player is rarely attacked on the *men* and so may be vulnerable to a *men* attack.

A short opponent, on the other hand, is accustomed to being attacked on the *men* and is usually well prepared for a *men* attack. You may therefore be successful in striking the *kote* or *dō,* where a short person is least guarded.

An opponent with a wide stance who holds the *tsuka* with widely separated hands tends to be skilled in using *waza* from *chu-ma* (middle distance) or *issoku ittō no ma'ai* (one-foot one-sword distance). An opponent with a *shumoku ashi* (T-shaped stance) tends to be more skilled in *ōji waza* than in *shikake waza*. You should break his *kamae* for a successful offense; otherwise, this opponent will be ready with a counterattack. An opponent with a narrow stance who holds the *tsuka* with hands close together is usually skilled in offense by jumping in from *tōma*. Such opponents are often not as skilled in *ōji waza*. Instead of retreating when this opponent attacks, go forward with your own offense. You may well score a *datotsu*, or at least end with an *aiuchi*.

An opponent with a center of gravity in a forward position is often skilled in *debana waza*. On the other hand, an opponent with a center of gravity in a back position is often skilled in *go-no-sen* and is ready to deliver a counteroffensive.

An opponent who has lowered the *shinai* in *gedan* is tempting you to attack the *men*. Do not strike the *men* carelessly. If you strike the *men*, be aware that this opponent is ready with an *ōji waza* such as *kaeshi waza*. It may be more effective to use a technique such as *hata-ki waza* or *harai waza* before striking the *men*.

An opponent who has a wide stance, holds the *tsuka* lightly with the left hand, and slightly opens the *kensen* tends to be skilled in *omote ōji waza* and *kaeshi waza*, and good at *debana waza*.

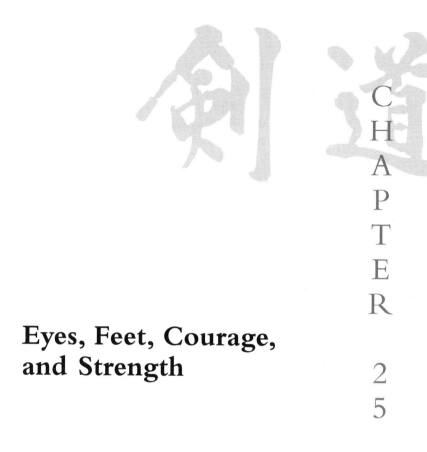

Eyes, Feet, Courage, and Strength

In kendo, there is an axiom, *"Ichi gan, ni soku, san tan, shi riki,"* or "first eyes, second feet, third courage, and fourth skill or strength."

- *Gan* **(eyes):** An ability to observe and forecast is obviously very important not only in kendo but also in other martial arts and life in general. With a strong power of observation, and the ability to perceive the truth through pretence, you can conquer an opponent. Miyamoto Musashi instructs us to use our physical eyes less and our mind's eyes more *(kanken no metsuke)*.

- *Soku* **(feet):** *Ashisabaki* (footwork) is considered the second most important item in kendo, as in all martial arts. The significance of footwork dates back to ancient times. The character *bu* as in *budō* consists of two separate characters; the top part means "halberd" and the bottom means "foot." (The bottom character means "stop" in modern language.) Miyamoto Musashi explains the importance of footwork in *Gorin no Sho.* He says that footwork decides the winner and loser of a match.

- *Tan* (**courage**): Courage can be an inborn characteristic or it can be acquired through practice and training. Because kendo, traditionally, was the discipline of a samurai who used his kendo skills as a soldier, it is easy to imagine that courage was important.

- *Ryoku* (**strength**): Strength is not simply physical strength, because you cannot become the best from muscular strength alone. Nor will a lack of muscular strength keep you from becoming the best. The most appropriate interpretation of this term is skill or *giryoku*.

When you have all these and have finally acquired a good technique, your performance will become perfect.

PART V

Personages

Japanese literature is filled with stories of swordsmen, both fictional
and factual. The Japanese fascination with swordsmen is old and deep.
Many stories are based on real swordsmen, albeit the ability of the
swordsman or the number of his opponents is inflated. Some were
active during the Kamakura (1185–1333), Muromachi (1336–1573),
and Azuchi-Momoyama (1568–1600) periods, and into the Edo period. These include Itō Ittōsai Kagehisa, Tsukahara Bokuden, Miyamoto
Musashi, Yagyū Munenori, and Kamiizumi (Kōzumi) Nobutsuna. The
modern period has also produced fine kendo masters, although the
actual use of swords in combat has diminished since Meiji and there
has been none since the end of World War II.

Itō Ittōsai Kagehisa, who according to legend floated across the
Sea of Sagami from the island of Ōshima, established Ittō ryū (one-
sword-technique school). Mikogami Tenzen and Ono Zenki, his two
best disciples, had to duel to the death to see who would succeed
Ittōsai. Tenzen, favored by his master, won the duel by killing Zenki.
Tenzen changed his name to Ono Tadaaki and served as fencing
instructor to the Tokugawa Bakufu with Yagyū Munenori, another
famous swordsman. Ono Tadaaki was later known for Onoha Ittō ryū
(Ono-style one-sword technique). Tadaaki lacked political skill and
was not favored by the shōgun, Ieyasu, in spite of his obviously outstanding swordsmanship. Chapter 26 tells the story of Itō Ittōsai
Kagehisa in greater detail.

Good at espionage, the fifth son of Yagyū Sekishūsai Muneyoshi,
and a master of Yagyū Shinkage ryū, Yagyū Tajima no Kami
Munenori was retained by Shōgun Tokugawa Ieyasu as a kendo
instructor for his son, Tokugawa Hidetada, as a reward for his achievements in the battle of Sekigahara, a battle that secured Ieyasu's power.
Yagyū became chief kendo instructor of the Tokugawa Shōgunate
when Hidetada succeeded his father, to become the second Tokugawa
shōgun. Chapter 28 describes the life and teachings of Yagyū.

The tragic vendetta story of the 47 rōnin has fascinated the
Japanese for many generations, but one rōnin, Nakayama Yasubei,
stands out. He gained his fame at Takada no Baba when he helped his
adopted uncle, Sugano Rokurōzaemon, in an unfair duel. After this
incident Yasubei was adopted by Horibe Yabei of Akō and became
Horibe Yasubei. The leader of the 47 rōnin, Ōishi Kuranosuke, was
pushed into the center stage of history by the tragic death of his lord
Asano Takumi no Kami. Ōishi, a seemingly ordinary minister of Akō
in peacetime, had vowed in secrecy to avenge his lord's untimely
death. He, along the rest of the rōnin, committed seppuku after carrying out what was considered a morally correct if illegal vendetta.

A trio of commoners turned samurai were recruited in Edo and sent to Kyoto with other *rōnin* to form a band of fierce, semi-official armed police. Through manipulations and assassinations, Kondō Isami, the head of a small *dōjō* in Edo called Shieikan, became the leader of the group and ran the organization under a very strict code of conduct. Hijikata Toshizo, a boyhood friend of Kondō, became his lieutenant, and Okita Sōshi, the youngest of the Shinsengumi and Kondō's student, became one of the squadron leaders. Kondō succeeded in having the government sanction the group, and the Shinsen Gumi was placed under the lord of the Aizu Matsudaira, who was in charge of the security of the capital city. The armed police force patrolled the city of Kyoto during the last years of the declining Tokugawa government. Members of Shinsen Gumi excelled in kendo. They patrolled Kyoto and hunted down the *rōnin* who favored the reform of the emperor's government. Kondō Isami, Hijikata Toshizo, and Okita Sōshi have been the subjects of many novels and movies in spite of, or perhaps because of, their extremely bloody story.

Late in the Edo period, Chiba Shūsaku founded Hokushin Ittō ryū (northern-star one-sword technique) and taught thousands of students his style of swordsmanship. Yamaoka Tesshū, the son of a Tokugawa retainer, and a student of Chiba Shūsaku, is well known for his mission during the Meiji Restoration War to meet Saigō Takamori, a general of the imperial army who was determined to crush the Tokugawa forces. The fifteenth and last shōgun, Tokugawa Yoshinobu, personally asked Tesshū to undertake this mission, and Tesshū was instrumental in sparing Edo from ruin by the war. Tesshū eventually became a chamberlain to the Emperor Meiji.

Another famous student of Chiba Shūsaku is Katsura Kogorō, who excelled in kendo but never drew his sword to harm anyone because he felt that his mission in life was much greater than individual fights. He escaped from trouble whenever he could, even when he was a target of the Shinsen Gumi during the days of unrest at the end of Tokugawa era. He played a major role in the establishment of the Meiji government in 1868.

The legendary Nakayama Hakudō was a well-known, accomplished, and revered kendo master who also excelled in *jōdo* and *iaido*. Mochida Moriji was a modern swordsman known for his gentleness and kendo skills. Mochida Moriji and Saimura Goro demonstrated Dai Nippon Teikoku Kendo Kata before the emperor. In a film clip their performance is very impressive.

Sasamori Junzō was a scholar and Christian who studied in the Unites States for many years. He received a doctorate from the

University of Denver. After he returned to Japan he discharged his duties as the president of Aoyama Gakuin University, served in the Lower House of Diet, was a home minister, and continued to teach and work for the public until his death at 89. He wrote a book entitled *Ittō Ryū Gokui (The Secrets of One-sword School)* and co-authored *This Is Kendo* with Gordon Warner. Mori Torao, known as Tiger Mori in the United States, came to the United States and became fencing champion. The other prominent kendo masters from this time include Takano Sasaburo, Ogawa Kinnosuke, Ōasa Yuji, Negishi Gorō, and Noma Seiji.

Itō Ittōsai Kagehisa

On the island of Izu Ōshima located some thirty kilometers east of the Izu Peninsula, Itō Ittōsai was born on August 5, 1550, a descendent of the Kamakura samurai family. Ōshima is known for its active volcano, Mt. Mihara, and as an island of exile from ancient times. Kagehisa was named Maehara Yogorō when he was born. As Yogorō was growing up he proved to be quite an athletic and tough youngster. He could not wait to escape from the tiny island, and finally he swam to the Izu Peninsula.

When he was 14 years old, Yogorō defeated a notorious kendo master named Tomita Ippō. Oribe, a priest of the area, appreciated Yogoro's action and gave him a sword forged by the renowned swordsmith Ichimonji of Bizen province (Okayama prefecture). While Yogorō stayed with Oribe as his houseguest, Tomita's students attacked him at night. Yogorō hunted down and defeated all but one, who hid behind a big water pot. In one stroke Yogorō's sword cut down his enemy and sliced through the pot; henceforth, his sword was known as Kamewari Ichimonji (Ichimonji's pot-splitting sword).

Yogorō traveled around the country for *musha shugyō* (martial traveling) and trained under several outstanding kendo masters.

Kanemaki Jisai, a renowned kendo master in Edo (Tokyo) gave him his first formal kendo instruction. Yogorō learned quickly and made remarkable improvement. Five years into his training he told Kanemaki that he understood the fundamentals of swordsmanship. Kanemaki replied scornfully that it was impossible to master swordsmanship in five years. However, in a match between the teacher and the student, Yogorō emerged victorious over Kanemaki. The latter recognized Yogorō's ability and gave him the five secret precepts of swordsmanship of his school. Yogorō felt forever indebted to his teacher for this gift. When Yogorō established his own school, he put the five precepts at the top of his own precepts. After facing many opponents and after years of training, Yogorō decided to establish his own school, which he called Ittō ryū (one-sword school) and named himself Itō Ittōsai Kagehisa.

Ittōsai never settled in one place but continued to travel under a banner that read "The best in Japan, Supreme expert of kenjutsu Itō Ittōsai." Although this may seem rather odd, Ittōsai did it in hopes of finding a good teacher. He beat all his challengers, and they ended up becoming his students. One night at Kuwana in Ise province (Miye prefecture), as Ittōsai caught a ferry to cross a river, the mean-looking ferryman named Choshichi challenged him to a match. Ittōsai easily defeated the ferryman, who attacked him with a long oar from *jōdan,* which appeared very primitive and immature to Ittōsai. Ittōsai struck the *migi kote* (right forearm) of the ferryman quite easily with his *shinai.* The ferryman screamed with pain and begged Ittōsai to take him as his student. Ittōsai agreed, hoping that Choshichi would reform. Choshichi took the name Ono Zenki and traveled the land with Ittōsai. Zenki eventually became one of the two disciples qualified to fight to succeed Ittōsai.

As Ittōsai traveled he met renowned swordsmen but was never defeated. In the town of Okamoto in Awa province (Tokushima prefecture), Ittōsai met a young samurai named Mikogami Tenzen for a match. Ittōsai quickly closed in the *ma'ai* and wrenched the sword from Tenzen's hands. Tenzen grabbed a *bokken* to fight. Kagehisa picked up a piece of firewood to fight back. This piece of firewood measured 1 *shaku* 5 *sun* and 5 *bu,* which became standard length of *kodachi* for Ittō ryū thereafter. No matter how many times Tenzen tried to hit Ittōsai his *bokken* was knocked to the ground by Ittōsai's piece of firewood. Tenzen knew the teacher he was seeking was Ittōsai and he became a disciple.

Tenzen had to duel to the death with his senior disciple Ono Zenki on a spring day in 1588 in a field called Koganegahara in Shimōsa (Chiba prefecture). Ittōsai told Tenzen that he would like to give the scroll of secret precepts to him, in spite of Zenki being the next in line. Because of Tenzen's outstanding character, Ittōsai favored him over Zenki. Ittōsai gave Tenzen the Kamewari Ichimonji and the secret of winning against a superior disciple. As they were passing by the field Ittōsai announced to his unsuspecting disciples that one of them was to succeed him. He would bestow the scroll of secret precepts on the victor of the duel. As he spoke, he placed the scroll on the ground. Zenki, who felt the title rightfully belonged to him, reached for the scroll and ran. As Tenzen and Ittōsai were chasing him, he hid behind a large water pot under a big pine tree. Zenki was prepared to strike Tenzen if he removed the pot. Seeing this, Ittōsai commanded Tenzen to cut Zenki and the large pot at the same time. Tenzen, as ordered, cut Zenki and the large pot with *kiai*. Zenki fell with the scroll still in his mouth. Ittōsai felt pity for Zenki, who wished to have this scroll even at his death. Ittōsai told Zenki that he would give the scroll to him first, then to Tenzen. Zenki dropped the scroll from his mouth with a smile and closed his eyes. Tenzen became the one and only successor of Ittōsai.

Unlike Miyamoto Musashi or Yagyū Munenori, Itō Ittōsai Kagehisa never wished to obtain religious enlightenment, prestige, or employment. He only wanted to improve his swordsmanship. Ittōsai parted with Tenzen and withdrew from the world. Tenzen left for Edo to further his training. He met Yagyū Tajima no Kami Munenori in Edo. After a match, Munenori recommended Tenzen for the position of kendo instructor to the Tokugawa *bakufu* government.

Miyamoto Musashi

In spite of the numerous books written about Miyamoto Musashi, only a few facts are known about him. Those who want to read exciting fiction should turn to *Musashi* by Yoshikawa Eiji. Musashi, in this account, was born in 1584 as the third child of Hirata Muni. We are certain that he died in 1645, presumably at the age of 62. He was named Hirata Bennosuke when he was born. The place of his birth is controversial partly because Musashi's mother died after his birth and his stepmother raised him. Musashi's stepmother left him at a nearby temple, where he learned to read and write. Although his father Muni was cold toward Musashi, he saw young Musashi's god-given talent and trained him relentlessly until Musashi reached 13. Because of this complicated childhood, Musashi probably did not have an accurate recollection of his birthplace. Though he stated in *Gorin no Sho* that he was from Harima (Hyogo prefecture), there is a theory that he was actually born in the Miyamoto village of Mimasaka (Okayama prefecture).

Musashi's father, Hirata Muni, and grandfather Hirata Shogen, were both well known for their martial skills besides being good swordsmen. They were both renowned masters of *jitte* (a metal club with an L-shaped projection for catching swords). Muni served under the lord Shinmen Iga no Kami and participated in several campaigns. He married a daughter of Shinmen family and was allowed to use the name Shinmen Munisai. Muni also used the name Miyamoto Munisai after he moved to Miyamoto village. Probably the reason Musashi called himself Shinmen Miyamoto Musashi no Kami Fujiwara no Genshin in *Gorin no Sho* was because of his father's affiliation with both Shinmen and Miyamoto. Musashi did not use the name Hirata in his writing.

At 13 Musashi fought Arima Kihei, an expert of Shintō ryū, and killed him, to the surprise to everyone in the village. At 15 he was renamed Miyamoto Musashi Masana from Hirata Bennosuke, as a rite of passage. He gave up his father's lord's name, Shinmen, and his father's name, Hirata. He left home the following year for *musha shugyō* (martial traveling) and won over sixty consecutive matches without losing once before he was 28 or 29 years old. His opponents included Akiyama from Tajima, the Yoshioka family of Kyoto, In'ei of Hōzoin, and Shishido Baiken of Iga.

When Musashi was 21 he challenged the renowned Yoshioka family, kendo instructors for generations to the Ashikaga shōgun in Kyoto. He disabled the eldest son, Seijūro, with a *bokken* and killed the second son Denshichiro. He was challenged at the pine trees of the Ichijōji temple but successfully defended himself against the rest of the Yoshioka family.

Musashi's most famous duel took place on an island of Ganryū with Sasaki Kojirō of Kokura, Kyushu. Musashi sought to have a duel with Kojirō, a kendo instructor to the Hosokawa clan of Kyushu. Kojirō was an expert at the ultra-long sword and *tsubame gaeshi* (swallow-cutting technique). They finally met at the small island of Funashima (now called Ganryū Island), though Musashi showed up much more than fashionably late. Musashi's decisive and lethal stroke with an oar on Kojirō's head determined the match.

We have an image of Musashi as an eccentric man with a phobia against cleanliness. It is said that he never or hardly ever took a bath in his life and did not change his filthy clothing. He did not shave or wash his hair. This may have had to do with a skin condition related to the congenital syphilis he suffered all his life. In any event, this habit added to his famous bizarre appearance. However, we cannot deny that he had colossal talent in swordsmanship as well as writing, sculpture, painting, metallurgy, *nō* dancing, tea ceremony, and carpentry. Although he wrote, "I had no teacher in the way of various arts," he must have been exposed to the experts of the arts and religion of the day. Through his writing, we can see his personality and philosophy.

The *Gorin no Sho (Book of Five Rings)*

Musashi's famous *Gorin no Sho* shows not only the technical aspect of swordsmanship and strategy but also the philosophy behind the man. The *Gorin no Sho* was written two years before his death and was based on the *Hyōhō Sanjūgo Kajō (Thirty-Five Articles of the Martial Arts),* written in February of the eighteenth year of *Kan'ei* (1641) at the request of Lord Hosokawa Tadatoshi, who invited Musashi to stay in a house he had prepared for Musashi as houseguest/instructor near Kumamoto Castle. The *Gorin no Sho* has five sections: "Earth," "Water," "Fire," "Wind," and "Sky."

The "Book of the Earth" begins ". . . I call my way of the martial arts Niten Ichi ryū (Two-Heavens, One School). After many years of training, I, Shinmen Musashi no Kami Fujiwara no Genshin, a warrior born in Harima province (Hyogo prefecture), at the age of 60, decided to express the way of the warrior in writing for the first time early in the tenth month, in the twentieth year of *Kan'ei* (1643), atop Iwato Mountain of Higo (present-day Kumamoto prefecture), Kyushu, after praying to the heaven, bowing to Kuan-Yin the goddess of mercy, and facing the Buddha's altar."

The "Book of the Earth" is a general statement of the philosophy of Niten Ichi ryū and explains why it is superior to other techniques. The "Book of the Water" further pursues Musashi's reasons for calling it Niten Ichi ryū and offers more details on the actual technique of swordsmanship. In the "Book of the Fire," Musashi gives details of actual combat by citing 27 examples. He points out the differences between his school and other schools in his "Book of the Wind." Finally, in the "Book of the Sky," Musashi summarizes his enlightened state of mind in a relatively few words. The term "sky" goes well with the previous books, but it also means void or emptiness. There is an excellent translation of *Gorin no Sho* by Victor Harris.

Here, I would like to mention examples from the "Book of the Earth" and "Book of the Sky" as Musashi wrote the fundamental attitudes for training and the final result of training. In the "Book of the Earth" Musashi advises those who want to learn his school of swordsmanship:

1. Do not have evil thoughts.
2. Train intensely according to the way.
3. Acquaint yourself with all kinds of arts.
4. Have knowledge in the ways of different professions.
5. Appreciate the gain and loss in each and every one.
6. Develop the ability to appraise the value in all matters.

7. Learn to see the unseen.
8. Pay attention to details.
9. Do not waste effort on futile matters.

Musashi aptly sums up the results of lifelong training in the last sentence of *Gorin no Sho:* "There is good and no evil exists in a void. Mind becomes void with knowledge, principle, and the way."

Dokgyōdō (The Way of Walking Alone/Twenty-one Articles of Self-discipline)

Among Musashi's best writings is *Dokgyōdō (The Way of Walking Alone),* written on May 12, in the second year of *Seiho* (1645), shortly before his death. He knew he was fatally ill, probably from a terminal cancer. His illness was aggravated by the harsh living conditions of the cold cave on Iwato Mountain where he wrote *Gorin no Sho.* On his deathbed, he invited his close friends and students and left them the *Dokgyōdō.* This is collection of his belief in the pursuit of the way. I interpret the title to mean *Twenty-one Articles of Self-discipline.* Musashi died one week later, on May 19, 1645. *Dokgyōdō* amounts to a "motto" of his life and gives us a glimpse into the man. We do not know why he wrote this on his deathbed, but I believe he wrote what he had told himself numerous times during his life. He probably wanted his students and friends to know how he had trained himself and wanted to warn those whose conduct did not measure up to his standard.

In *Dokgyōdō,* Musashi emerges as an honest, lonely, and sensitive man with the feelings, needs, and desires of an ordinary person who through perseverance and self-discipline, overcame strong urges and desires to become a truly enlightened man. His teachings are still very pertinent in today's world:

1. Do not behave contrary to the way of the world.
2. Do not indulge in physical gratification.
3. Do not rely on anything.
4. Think yourself small and the world large.
5. Do not have avarice throughout your entire life.
6. Do not have regrets in personal affairs.
7. Do not resent or complain about the good and evil of others.
8. Do not grieve over separation during the pursuit of the way.
9. Do not hate or think ill of yourself or of others.
10. Do not have love affairs.

11. Do not have likes and dislikes in all aspects of life.
12. Do not desire a permanent private residence.
13. Do not indulge in gourmet meals.
14. Do not possess tools that will last for many generations and become antiques.
15. Do not fast if it harms your body.
16. Except for weapons, do not have preference in any personal items.
17. Do not be afraid to die in defense of the way.
18. Do not wish to possess treasures or land in your old age.
19. Respect the gods and Buddha but do not depend on them.
20. Keep your mind always on the way of the martial arts.
21. Sacrifice your life in defense of honor.

Second Day of Fifth Month, Second Year of Shōho (May 2, 1645)

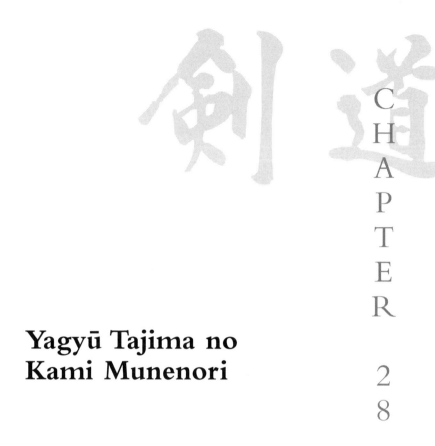

Yagyū Tajima no Kami Munenori

C
H
A
P
T
E
R

2
8

Yagyū Tajima no Kami Munenori was born in 1571, the fifth son of
Yagyū Sekishūsai Muneyoshi, and died in 1646. Munenori was a chief
kendo instructor to the Tokugawa government and author of *Hyōhōka
Densho*. Munenori's father, Muneyoshi, was lord of a small Yagyū castle
in Yamato province. Munenori was licensed in the Yagyū Shinkage ryū
by Kamiizumi (Kōzumi) Ise no Kami Hidetsuna. The Yagyū clan played
an important spying role in the battle of Sekigahara. Tokugawa Ieyasu,
the first Tokugawa shōgun, gave the Yagyū fief, which had been confiscated by Toyotomi Hideyoshi, back to the Yagyū clan after the battle.

Tokugawa Ieyasu wished to retain Muneyoshi to teach his son
Hidetada, but instead kept young Munenori at his father's request.
Munenori taught kendo to Hidetada and became a chief kendo
instructor and *sōmetsuke* (police chief) when Hidetada became
shōgun on Ieyasu's retirement. Munenori excelled in Yagyū Shinkage
ryū, but his skills were polished yet more when he became a student
of the Zen priest Sōhō Takuan (1573–1645), who was invited to
teach by the third shōgun, Tokugawa Iemitsu. Munenori was

apparently Takuan's favorite student. Takuan wrote two books on Zen philosophy at Munenori's request. *Fudōchi Shinmyō Roku (Record of Steadfast Wisdom and Divine Mystery)* and *Taiaki* are guides to Zen for kendo practitioners.

Yagyū Hyōhōka Densho (Book of Swordsmanship for Posterity) is not so much a technical manual of kendo as it is a spiritual or philosophical guide based on Zen Buddhism as taught by Takuan. Munenori concludes that the ultimate in kendo training is to remove "sickness" of mind. This "sickness" includes the desire to win, thinking of techniques to win, wishing to show the result of hard training, and wanting to attack or defend. Even the thought of wanting to eliminate "sickness" from your own mind is considered a "sickness." A state of mind devoid of "sickness" is called *byojōshin* (neutral state of mind). This state of mind is achieved only after many years of kendo training. When one achieves *byojōshin,* the body moves automatically without conscious thought.

In his *Hyōhōka Densho,* Munenori also describes the concept *kentai hyōri* (offensive and defensive front and back). That is, when your body is on the offensive your mind should stay calm and in a defensive mode. If your body is about to go on the offensive and your mind is similarly excited, there is a good chance you will not see your opponent calmly and thus receiving a counterattack. This is a lesson that should be kept in mind not only in kendo but in life in general.

Takuan Sōhō died in 1645, leaving a single character to summarize his life. In response to the question by one of his disciples on the meaning of life he wrote the character *yume* (dream). Three months later Munenori also died, as if following his teacher to the other world.

Tsukahara Bokuden

Tsukahara Bokuden, the second son of Urabe Akikaku, was born in 1488, about a century before Miyamoto Musashi, in Kashima, Hitachi province (Ibaraki prefecture). It was a world of wars, and he was surrounded by people of the martial arts. He was named Shizaemon Takamoto. His father, who mastered Kashima no Hitachi (Secret Sword of Kashima), was a priest of the Kashima shrine and a vassal to Lord Kashima Kagemoto. Tsukahara Tosanokami, also a vassal to Lord of Kashima, adopted Bokuden at 14.

The Kashima shrine and the neighboring Katori shrine were dedicated to the gods of the martial arts and the priests were trained in these arts. The Kashima shrine was a place of training for *sakimori* (frontier soldiers) from ancient times. So, Kashima/Katori was a Mecca for martial practitioners. Iizasa Chōisai, Aisu Hyuga no Kami Ikōsai, and Kamiizumi (Kōzumi) Ise no Kami Hidetsuna were all schooled in Kashima ryū. Iizasa Chōisai, a founder of the Tenshin Shōden Katori Shintō ryū, was married to Bokuden's aunt.

Young Bokuden was robust and trained in kendo at a young age while his peers were free to play. At 17 he set out on *musha shugyō,* visiting many provinces and fighting many renowned swordsmen.

Bokuden enrolled in a school of Kamiizumi Ise no Kami and became the highest-ranking student, above such well-known swordsmen as Marume Kurando, Isobata Banzō, Yagyū Matazaemon, and Jingūji Izu. Bokuden debuted when he was 18 and a student of Kamiizumi Hidetsuna.

When Bokuden was visiting his ailing father, Shinamaru Nyūdō Enkai came to Kamiizumi's *dōjō*. Enkai was an infamous user of *kongōzue* (large club reinforced with steel) and had left a trail of destroyed *dōjō* all over the land. His obvious intention was to destroy the prestige of Kamiizumi and increase his own fame. Kamiizumi was sick but Enkai and his followers insisted on having a match with him. Four high-ranking students were no match for Enkai and were defeated miserably. Enkai left the *dōjō* after making insulting remarks to Kamiizumi. Bokuden, on hearing of this, went to Mt. Haguro to meet Enkai and take revenge. Bokuden defeated eighteen of eighty or so of Enkai's students before he slew Enkai. For this achievement Bokuden received the *Shinkage Ryū Gokui* (the Secrets of New Shadow School) from Kamiizumi Ise no Kami Hidetsuna.

When Bokuden was 27 he stayed at the Kashima shrine for one thousand days to gain enlightenment. During this training he never spoke to anyone and placed himself on a diet consisting only of grains. In the end he reached a state of mind that could not be moved. Bokuden named a new technique Hitotsu no Tachi (one and only sword), indicating the only variety of sword in the world. Armed with this new style he set out to travel the land and teach Shintō ryū.

Another famous episode occurred while he was traveling in a ferry. He encountered a rude and boastful samurai. Bokuden's utter indifference enraged the samurai, who challenged Bokuden to a duel. Bokuden told the samurai that he was from Mutekatsu ryū (School of Winning Without a Sword) and needed no sword. Because the ferry was crowded, he suggested fighting on a tiny island in the middle of the river and let the samurai go off the ferry first. Bokuden, moving slowly, handed the ferryman his two swords. Poling against the bottom of the river, he pushed the ferry away from the island, leaving the samurai stranded. He could have killed the samurai if he had wanted to, but he saved the man's life and taught him a lesson. We see the maturity and wisdom of avoiding a fight.

Beginning in his eighteenth year, Bokuden dueled eighteen times, participated in combat thirty-six times, and killed over two hundred enemies without sustaining any significant wounds himself. Many lords and generals became his disciples.

In the fourth year of Eiroku (1561), at 73, Bokuden visited Takeda Shingen at his castle in Kai province (Kōfu, Yamanashi prefecture). Unlike on a previous trip when he had over one-hundred followers, two falcons, and three horses, on this visit Bokuden was accompanied only by three of his students, Morooka Ippa, Matsuoka Norikata, and Saito Shumenosuke. His first visit, seventeen years earlier, had lasted over a year, during which time he taught kendo to Shingen and his vassals. After that, negotiations between Takeda Shingen and Uesugi Kenshin of Echigo (Niigata prefecture) broke down and there were several border skirmishes. Bokuden in his old age felt that this was his last visit to Shingen and he followed his friend to the famous battle of Kawanakashima. Shingen's plan to divide his army in two and attack from both ends was detected by Kenshin, who led all his troops to attack Shingen's headquarters on the misty early morning of September 10, 1561. Shingen realized his strategic failure, however, and remained calmly seated in his chair. Bokuden is said to have been watching the whole event. As the battle grew hotter, Kenshin with his lieutenants on horseback appeared before the seated Shingen. Kenshin attacked Shingen several times from his horse, but suddenly the horse started to gallop in retreat. It is interesting to think Bokuden may have played a role in this episode.

Bokuden died on the second day of the third month, in the second year of Genki (March 2, 1571) at 83.

Chiba Shūsaku

"Sore ken wa shunsoku. Shin ki ryoku no ittchi." This famous epitaph is inscribed on a stone monument by the grave of the founder of the Hokushin Ittō ryū, Chiba Shūsaku.

When Chiba was in his early twenties and still training under his *sensei,* one of the higher-ranking students asked him, "In one word what is the essence of *ken* (sword)?" Chiba answered, *"Ken* is . . . *shunsoku." Shunsoku* means "speed." Lightning-like speed is the essence of *ken,* according to Chiba. To explain what he meant by *shunsoku,* he said, *"Shin-ki-ryoku no ittchi." Shin* means "heart," *ki* means "spirit, " and *ryoku* means "strength." Chiba said all three had to be *ittchi* or "in harmony." The literal translation, "heart-spirit-power in harmony" is an enigma, but what he appears to have meant by *shin* and *ki* is a union of "perception" and "reaction." Stated differently: One perceives in the heart (eyes to brain) and reacts to that perception with the spirit (brain to muscles). This must be simultaneous and accompanied by power (from the stomach).

Seeing a *suki* or an enemy's sword attacking and reacting to it at the same time, gives the sword speed and the advantage of reaching the enemy sooner. Speed is victory in kendo, in Chiba's words. What is so revolutionary about this explanation is that the old school had the idea of separate entities of *kamae*, eyeing, and movement. This new idea was so distasteful to his teacher that it eventually cost Chiba his license in the Ittō ryū. He later established his own school, Hokushin Ittō ryū (Northern Star One-Sword School), named after his family's tradition of worshiping the northern star.

Chiba was also revolutionary in practicing kendo. He wore what we now call the *bōgu*, including the *men*, *kote*, and *dō*. Though he is not credited with inventing the *bōgu*, Chiba is known to have popularized it. He was very particular about the way his *bōgu* were made. For instance, he requested a specific type of bamboo for the *shinai* and another type for the *dō*. He also required a certain number of stitches per square inch for the *kote* and *men*. The material for the leather and *tsuru* were also strictly specified. He specified the construction of the *mengane* and strongly prohibited tempering the *mengane* for fear it would shatter when struck.

Chiba Shūsaku left a work called *Kenpo Hiketsu (Secret Methods of the Sword)*. In it he analyzed the techniques of kendo, and concluded that there were sixty-eight *te* (techniques). After closely scrutinizing the methods used in kendo, he determined that there were twenty *men waza*, eighteen *tsuki*, twelve *kote*, seven *dō*, ten *tsuzuki waza*, and one *kumite*. Thus he brought down the veil of mystery surrounding kendo.

He also started his students with *uchikomi keiko*, unlike old schools where students learned *kata* for many years before they started *uchikomi keiko*. The result was astounding because his students learned at such a rapid pace. It was said that what would take three years in other schools would only take one year, and what would take five years would only take three years in Chiba's school.

Evidence that he was a good teacher is revealed in *kenjutsu uchikomi jūtoku* (ten merits in striking), in which Chiba outlines the techniques of *uchikomi keiko* in a way a beginner can understand.

1. *Waza* (technique) should be fierce and rapid.
2. Striking should be strong.
3. Breathing should be long (able to hold breath) while performing a *waza*.
4. Swing the arms freely.
5. Move the whole body lightly and freely.
6. Maneuver the long sword freely.
7. Concentrate on *seika tanden* (lower abdomen).
8. See clearly.

9. Strike clearly.

10. Hold the sword lightly.

He adds eight more points, making *juhachi toku* (eighteen merits).

11. Keep a calm mind.

12. See clearly (same as 8).

13. See the opponent's sword clearly.

14. Move freely.

15. Strengthen the body.

16. Squeeze the *tenouchi* (at the time of striking).

17. Receive the opponent's sword cleanly.

18. Strengthen the arms.

With Chiba's exceptional talent in kendo and his modified teaching methods, his popularity soared. It is said that his students numbered five thousand. His *dōjō* became one of the three biggest in Edo (Tokyo), and produced numerous excellent kendo practitioners. Many of his students contributed to the Meiji Restoration.

He had three sons who also became great kendo practitioners, and one was even said to be his superior. Unfortunately, they all died young. Chiba himself died at 62. He was forever remembered as a pioneer and one of the greatest kendo practitioners that Japan has produced.

A story that Chiba liked when he was young was that of a woodcutter who encountered a strange creature in the forest while he was cutting wood. When the woodcutter thought of capturing this strange creature and selling it in town, the creature laughed and said, "Hey, woodcutter! You are thinking of capturing me, aren't you?" The woodcutter wondered how this creature knew what he was thinking. The creature chuckled. "Now you are wondering how I knew what you were thinking." The woodcutter was indignant that the creature knew his thoughts, and started to think about killing it. The creature then laughed and said: "Oh, now you are thinking of killing me because I know your thoughts." The woodcutter felt he could not win if this creature could read his mind. He decided to ignore it. The creature said contemptuously to the woodcutter, "Now you are thinking you cannot win because I can read your mind." The woodcutter continued to ignore the creature and resumed cutting wood. As he was swinging the axe, the head of the axe loosened and sped to the creature's head, killing it. The name of the creature was *satori* (enlightenment).

Chiba told his students that it was not good enough to know what the enemy was thinking. One had to be the head of the axe to achieve the ultimate in kendo.

Mochida Moriji,
Kendo *Hanshi* Tenth *Dan*

Mochida Moriji was a student of Hokushin Ittō ryū. He was awarded the *hanshi* in 1927 and tenth *dan* in 1957, the first person to achieve this rank. He was one of the members of the committee that formed the Dai Nihon Teikoku Kendo Kata. He served as a chief kendo instructor for police headquarters, the Imperial Police Force, Keio University, Gakushūin, and the Kōdansha Noma Dōjō. He left the following passage, which summarizes his kendo training:

> You must practice the fundamentals of kendo until fifty. The basics then become a part of you. When you think of the basics, they are often assumed to be something that was mastered in the early stages of a kendo career. This is a misconception. Many people bury the fundamentals deep in their minds without giving them a second thought. It took me fifty years to learn the fundamentals, and to make them a part of my body and soul. I did not enter the true discipline of kendo until I was fifty. This was because I was determined to practice kendo with my mind.

The back and lower extremities begin to deteriorate at 60. The mind will complement the weakness of the body. I practiced kendo by utilizing my mind to compensate for my physical weakness.

At 70, the whole body begins to weaken. I practiced to make my mind immovable and not to be disturbed. When the mind is immovable and focused, the opponent's mind will reflect like a mirror. I have tried to retain this focus.

When I reached 80, my mind became focused and immovable. I admit that I have occasional distractions. I seek to eliminate interfering thoughts.

PART VI

Appendixes

Dr. Noboru Akagi

Dr. Noboru Akagi was born on January 25, 1928, in Tokyo. Dr. Akagi's illustrious kendo career began at age five. He must have demonstrated great potential: At eleven he was chosen to represent Sumida Ku, Tokyo, in a kendo tournament in the youth division at the prestigious *dōjō* of Sainei Kan in the palace. He was awarded *shodan* in 1941, *nidan* in 1942, *sandan* in 1945, *godan* in 1964, *rokudan* in 1970, and finally *shichidan* in 1977. He was awarded the honorary title of *renshi* in 1968 and *kyōshi* in 1976.

Dr. Akagi started the Aiea Taiheiji Kendo Club, originally called the Taiheiji Godo Kai, on August 29, 1965, with only a handful of students. Two of the original students, Arnold Fukutomi *(shichidan)* and Gerald Matsubayashi, are the principal instructors at the *dōjō* today. Dr. Akagi conducted kendo practice as a chief instructor from the inception of the *dōjō* to 1990, when he retired from this position but remained as a consultant. He continues to teach and practice kendo. He has trained many students who are now proud members of our society. It is particularly rewarding for him to watch the many young students in the *dōjō* today.

Dr. Akagi joined the Hawai'i Kendo Federation (HKF) in 1963. He eventually became chairman of the board of directors and was elected president of the HKF in 1985. He has been an officer of the International Kendo Federation since 1982, and became a board member in 1991. He has been a member of the Japan Physician's Kendo Federation since 1983. He wishes to bring world recognition to the HKF by becoming a member of national and international organizations.

Dr. Akagi established the HFK as an independent organization under the International Kendo Federation in 1988, over the objections of some of the board members. Dr. Akagi made a plea on behalf of the kendo practitioners of Hawai'i, and did not compromise in his determination. He was also instrumental in procuring funds from Kenshiro Otsuka for the establishment of an educational endowment for the Hawai'i Kendo Federation.

Dr. Akagi believes that practicing kendo teaches us self-discipline, respect, and perseverance, and thus prepares us to become productive and respected members of society.

History of Kendo in Hawai‘i

Kendo in Hawai‘i dates back to June 19, 1868, when the first Japanese immigrants arrived on the British sailing ship, HMS *Scioto*. They were called *gannen mono* (first-year men) because it was the first year of Meiji. In 1881, King David Kalakaua stopped over at Tokyo during his world tour and met the Meiji emperor. Subsequently, thanks to King Kalakaua's effort, the first government-contracted immigrants *(kanyaku imin),* consisting of 943 men, women, and children, arrived in Honolulu on the *City of Tokio* on February 8, 1885.

A few days after the first *kanyaku imin* arrived, a very big festival was held at the immigration depot by Japanese immigrants. King Kalakaua and all the dignitaries were invited to participate in the celebration. The main attraction appears to have been sumo wrestling, but kendo was also performed. *The Pacific Commercial Advertiser* reported,

> The wrestling match was preceded by a fencing match called Gekkin [ed. Gekken]. The two combatants were armed with two-handled, straight wooden swords about 5 feet long. Their heads were defended by heavy helmets, the faces being covered by a wire mask. The hands were protected by padded gloves, breastplates and

greaves were worn, and thus protected they went at each other quite scientifically. The attack and defense was very good, one or the other now and then acknowledging a cut or thrust.

From this article we can see that there were immigrants who did sumo as well as kendo. The article also mentions three-stringed-instrument players and drum players, obviously indicating *shamisen* and *taiko* performers. It must have been quite festive. The kendo performers, contemporary with Sakakibara Kenkichi and Yamaoka Tesshū, called their art *gekken,* a common name for kendo in that era. They were wearing the same *bōgu* that we use today and must have used *shinai,* in spite of the reporter writing "two-handled straight wooden swords." I can also imagine that they did *uchikomi keiko,* which appeared to the writer "scientific." This must have been followed by *jigeiko* or *shiai keiko.* Each player recognized a good hit from time to time. What an exciting scene it must have been to the audience and how proud those early kendo practitioners must have felt performing in a foreign country and in front of royal guests.

Kendo enthusiasts of old Hawai'i practiced individually in small groups and clubs in Japanese language schools and temples under Japanese school-teachers and priests. The earlier kendo instructors in Hawai'i were samurai or their descendents. Furuyama Hanzaemon, father of the late Furuyama Chūichi, was one such kendo instructor. He was officially invited to Hawai'i in 1916 to teach kendo after he retired as a Miyagi Prefectural Police kendo instructor. Furuyama used to say that his family had been instructors of Ryūgō ryū kendo for generations. Furuyama Chūichi continued to teach until shortly before he passed away in February 1999 at the age of 90.

Outstanding kendo teachers such as Sugiura Yonematsu (*hanshi,* 1964) and Mikami Shūji (*hanshi,* 1940) helped unite the kendo community in Hawai'i. Older kendo practitioners of Hawai'i like Yasuda Masao practiced vigorously in a modest-sized second-floor *dōjō* located near the house and shop of Mikami in Kapahulu, adjacent to Diamond Head and Waikiki. However, according to Muramoto Tsukasa, the oldest *sensei* still actively teaching, the exchange among the different *dōjō* was not as common as it is today, and students more or less limited their practice to within their own *dōjō.* There were also visiting kendo teachers to Hawai'i, including the prominent masters such as Takano Sasaburō and Mori Torao. Yasuda Masao, another senior *sensei* of Hawai'i, vividly remembers Mori Torao and his style of kendo prior to World War II.

At its peak, the kendo population in Hawai'i was estimated to be approximately 2,500. On May 5, 1940, the Hawai'i Chapter of Dai Nippon Butoku Kai held a kendo and judo tournament at Konpira shrine in the Palama district of Honolulu with 3,500 participants from all over the territory. During the tournament, Wada Takashi *(uchidachi)* and Sugiura Yonematsu *(shidachi)* performed Teikoku Kendo Kata.

The number of kendo practitioners declined drastically at the onset of America's involvement in World War II with the Japanese attack of Pearl Harbor on December 7, 1941. During the war many prominent leaders of the Japanese community, including kendo instructors, were placed in the internment camps, and all things Japanese, especially kendo, as it was considered the embodiment of the samurai spirit as well as a tool of nationalism, became a target of suspicion and hatred for many Americans. Kendo was banned during World War II.

After the release of the Japanese community leaders and kendo practitioners at the conclusion of the war, kendo once again became acceptable in Hawai'i and many small kendo clubs were formed. The Mikami Dōjō was also closed during the war, but reopened in September 1945, soon after the conclusion of the war on August 15, 1945.

In 1947 the Hawai'i Budō Kyokai was established, five years ahead of the Zen Nihon Kendo Renmei. In 1955, the Hawai'i Budō Kyokai was officially renamed the Hawai'i Kendo Federation. The Hawai'i Kendo Federation became affiliated with the Zen Nihon Kendo Federation in 1959. In 1972 the Hawai'i Kendo Federation became independent from the Zen Nihon Kendo Federation, and in 1988 from the International Kendo Federation, in large part due to the effort of Dr. Noboru Akagi. This enabled Hawai'i to send its own kendo practitioners to the World Kendo Championships. However, the entire kendo population in Hawai'i never reached prewar levels. It is good to note that there is an upward trend, and currently there are approximately four hundred kendo practitioners in Hawai'i. More women and younger kendo practitioners are joining the *dōjō* today.

According to the research done by Roxie Kubo, the decline of the kendo population can be attributed not only to World War II but also to the disintegration of plantation communities with their concentration of clubs, to commercialism, and to the advertising of other martial arts that appeal to the younger generation, as well as to a changing sense of values in many of the kendo practitioners in Hawai'i.

Hawai'i Kendo Federation

The Hawai'i Kendo Federation has been active in promoting and recruiting members. Unlike some commercialized martial arts instructors, kendo instructors are all volunteers, who are willing to participate in kendo out of their love for the art. It is particularly impressive to see several senior teachers now over 80 years old. They are truly our mentors in kendo. The kendo practitioners in Hawai'i come from all walks of life, but all share a common interest in kendo.

Kendo and Health

The most important health concern in kendo is the prevention of injury. You should get a preparticipation certificate from your family doctor before starting any vigorous physical activity such as kendo, and you should always check your equipment before practice. Young or large students should refrain from excessive roughness such as *taiatari* or *tsuki waza* (thrusting technique) against children and elderly, lightweight, or inexperienced kendo practitioners. Unfortunately, in spite of all your precautions, accidents can happen and first aid should always be available.

Preparticipation Physical Examination

Everyone, particularly older students, should get permission from their personal physician or family doctor before starting vigorous exercise. The doctor may recommend a physical examination, EKG, and a treadmill stress test to make sure the student's cardiac condition can withstand the vigor of kendo practice. Certain cardiac conditions can precipitate an arrhythmia (irregular heartbeat) and sudden death.

It would be prudent to let the *sensei* know about hypertension, diabetes, seizure disorders, asthma, or any other physical disorders or physical handicaps, or medications. This does not mean that illnesses or handicaps should necessarily prevent you from practicing kendo. Some kendo practitioners have prosthetic legs (Gordon Warner, Sekine Takashi), and we have our own kendo practitioner (Henry Small) who has severe physical handicap. However, acute illness or fatigue can impair concentration. In these cases you should avoid participating in kendo temporarily to prevent injury to yourself and others.

Equipment

It is strongly recommended that equipment be checked frequently. If the *sakigawa* is frayed, it should be replaced with new one. When the *sakigawa* is loose, the tip of the *shinai* can pass through the *mengane* and penetrate the eyes, causing serious injuries or even death. If the *nakayui* (middle strap) is not secure, the *sakigawa* may loosen at the time of impact and cause injury. When the *shinai* is damaged it easily breaks and the sharp broken pieces can cause serious injury. If the *shinai* is worm-infested, the resulting fine powder can cause eye irritation. A faulty *tsukidare* (front apron of the *men*) should be mended promptly.

Properly fitting the *men* and tying it snugly in place can prevent a ruptured eardrum. Using your hands or the tip of the *tsuka* of the *shinai,* lift the sides of the *menbuton* away from your ears so that there is a space between your ears and the *menbuton.* This space will lessen the impact of the *shinai* on the eardrums. It is equally important to avoid striking your opponent over the ears.

Uniforms

The kendo *gi* (*dōgi* and *hakama*) is made of thick cotton or synthetic material for protection. It is important to wear the *dōgi* and *hakama* properly. Being hit on the *dōgi* or *hakama* is not as damaging as being struck directly on exposed skin. I do not recommend rolling up the sleeves of the *dōgi*. It is always important to follow the instructions of the *sensei,* proper etiquette, rules, and techniques of kendo to avoid unnecessary injuries.

Heat Injury and Dehydration

With full *bōgu* on and especially in the summer, the core temperature of the body during exercise may rise tremendously. This may lead to perspiration, dehydration, and in severe cases even heat exhaustion and heat stroke.

The early signs of heat stroke are extreme thirst, cessation of perspiration, dry skin, nausea, headache, ringing in the ears, and dizziness. If left untreated heat stroke can progress to seizures, coma, and even death. It is extremely important to drink adequate amounts of liquids during practice and matches.

Fainting

Fainting is a reversible loss of consciousness and of postural tone. People who faint lose consciousness, become unresponsive, and fall to the ground from a standing or sitting position. Fainting is relatively common and has many causes, ranging from simple to quite complex, and the consequences of fainting can range from the benign to potentially life threatening. Sometimes fainting is preceded by nausea, cold sweats, hearing loss, visual changes, and a feeling of impending doom. At other times there may be no warning symptoms. Fainting with a cardiac cause may lead to a sudden death.

The initial management of fainting is basic life support. The first thing to check is the victim's pulse and respiration. If a person has fallen and hit his head, use extreme caution in removing the *men* so that the neck is not moved. If there is no pulse, start CPR and call 911 (or your local emergency number) immediately. Remove the *men* and *dō* by cutting the *menhimo* and *dohimo* without moving the person.

It is wise to stop a person from participating in further kendo training until the cause of the fainting has been thoroughly evaluated. Causes such as dehydration, illness, anemia, or the side effects of medication may be addressed quite easily, and the person can resume training. Causes that are related to the heart and nervous system may need a thorough work-up and an expert opinion before the person may return to training.

Contusions

To prevent contusions and bruises, you may use extra protective padding under the *men* or *kote*. Eye shields, elbow guards, and special footwear such as *katatabi* (heel guard) are also available. Ask the *sensei* about protective gear.

Other Injuries

Other potentially serious injuries include head trauma, for example from falling backward and hitting the back of the head on a hard floor. The brain will shake and bounce against the skull, causing a concussion. It is important to use properly fitting *men* to avoid the direct impact of the head against the floor. Another potential threat is a hyperextension injury (whiplash, burners, stingers) to the vertebrae of the neck.

In comparison with other sports, kendo tends to have more lower-extremity injuries: fractures, sprains, contusions, torn tendons, lacerations, toenail avulsions, dislocations, torn muscles, fractures, dislocations, and nerve damage. Upper extremity, torso, and head injuries are less common but not rare.

Injuries occur most frequently when a player falls, receives *datotsu,* collides with another player, or is involved with a *hansoku* (illegal move) or some other violent act.

The frequency of injury increases with age (greater after 30 years of age) and amount of exercise. It is interesting to note that between the ages of 16 to 20, the rate of injury in female practitioners exceeds that of males. A similar rate is seen between the ages of 41 and 60. Between the ages of 31 and 40, the rate of injury for men and women is equal. There is no data available for women above the age of 60.

An analysis of activities associated with the injuries indicates the following primary causes: *jigeiko* (match practice), *kakari keiko* (charging practice), and *kihon uchi* (fundamental striking practice). These are followed by *fumikomi* (stepping-in-technique), *taiatari* (body crush), *hiki waza* (withdrawing technique), and *suburi* (empty swing). Presumably those injuries are attributable to a lack of balance while assuming the fundamental stance, sliding movement to the side after *datotsu,* and mental and physical fatigue.

With respect to the seasons, the injuries occur more frequently in the spring and fall. Friday seems to be the most frequent day of injury. It is prudent to pay adequate attention to biorhythms (including time-zone difference).

Management of Injury

It is common to have pain related to a repetitive motion injury. According to an expert in sports medicine, such pain is classified into four classes. Each requires a different method of treatment.

Type I	After the activity	Reduce workload by 25 percent and ice the area of pain after activity. Stretch adequately before the activity and consider physical therapy and rehabilitation exercises.
Type II	During activity but not enough to restrict performance	Reduce workload by 50 percent and ice the area of pain after activity. Stretch adequately before the activity. Seek medical attention for possible physical therapy and rehabilitation exercises with medication.
Type III	During activity restricting the performance	Complete rest. Medical attention for physical therapy, rehabilitation exercises, and medications or injections.
Type IV	Chronic, precluding any activity	All of the above, including conservative therapy. If the pain is intractable, consider surgery as recommended by a physician.

A reduction of the workload means reducing the frequency or intensity of the activity. Also, consider changing or modifying the type of activity. For example, avoid *chōyaku suburi* (jumping empty swing) or *fumikomiashi* (thrusting footwork) when the Achilles tendon is injured. Ask the *sensei* for advice. Incorrect movement will lead to injury and pain. Always ask the *sensei* about form and grip on the *shinai* to reduce injury. At appropriate times, use braces and pads. Ultimately pain should guide activities. Do not expect overnight cures.

Glossary

A

Aichūdan: Both kendo opponents are in *chūdan no kamae.*

Aigedan: Both kendo opponents are in *gedan no kamae.*

Aijōdan: Both kendo opponents are in *jōdan no kamae.*

Aisu Ikōsai (1452–1538): A founder of Kage ryū.

Aiuchi: Both kendo opponents receive *yūkō datotsu* simultaneously.

Ari: As in *men ari, kote ari, shōbu ari,* the *shushin* declares after *yūkō datotsu* and raises the winner's flag diagonally.

Ashisabaki: Footwork, which is an important fundamental skill. Common *ashisabaki* includes *ayumi-ashi, tsugiashi, hirakiashi, okuriashi,* and *fumikomiashi.*

A-un no kokyū: Exhaling and inhaling in synchronization with the opponent.

Ayumiashi: Type of *ashisabaki;* the footsteps in a normal walking pattern, left right alternately in *suriashi.*

B

Bakufu: Military government of Japan.

Bōgu/kendogu: Protective gear. In kendo, refers to the *men, kote, dō,* and *tare.*

Bokken or ***bokutō:*** Wooden sword, often used in Nihon Kendo Kata. Made from oak, loquat, ebony, coconut tree, or other wood.

Budō: Way or study of martial arts such as kendo, *iaido,* aikido, judo, karate, sumo, *jūjutsu, jōjutsu, naginata, bōjutsu, kusarigama, kyujutsu,* and *yabusame.*

Bui: Zone or area; *datotsu bui* refers to an area of a clear strike zone in which *datotsu* count.

Bunbu ryōdō: Duality of academics and martial skills considered an essential ingredient of the good samurai.

Bu or budō: Military arts or martial arts and related matters.

Butoku Kai: Also called Dai Nippon Butoku Kai; Association of All Martial Arts, established in Meiji 28 (1895).

Byōjōshin: Neutral state of mind even in the face of crisis.

C

Chadō: The way of tea, a ritualized ceremony perfected by Sen no Rikyu (1522–1591).

Chakin shibori: Technique of grasping the sword handle with both hands as if wringing the tea ceremony towel.

Chakusō: Manner of wearing a uniform or armor.

Chakuza: Command to sit down.

Chi: Earth, *chi no maki* or "Book of the Earth" in *Gorin no Sho* by Miyamoto Musashi.

Chi: Knowledge and wisdom; an important virtue of samurai.

Chiba Shūsaku (1794–1855): Famous kendo practitioner who lived at the end of the Edo period. The founder of Hokushin Ittō ryū, he was born in Rikuzen (Miyagi prefecture), moved to Edo to learn kendo, and practiced under Asari Matashiro and his teacher Nakaishi Chubei, who were followers of Ito Ittōsai and Onoha Ittō ryū. He opened his own Genbukan Dōjō in Kanda Otamagaike. Sakamoto Ryōma studied under Chiba Shūsaku.

Chichi: Breast.

Chigiri: Small metal piece that fits into a groove at the end of the *shinai* to stabilize the four pieces of bamboo, also called *tomegane*. Approximately 10 mm by 10 mm.

Chikama: Close *ma'ai,* where there can be no hesitation in attacking.

Chokken: Straight sword.

Chonmage: Topknot.

Chōyaku: Jump.

Chūbuto: *Shinai* shape between the *dōbari* and *hosomi.*

Chūdan or chūdan no kamae: Middle or neutral *kamae.* The most useful and adaptable of all *kamae.*

Chūken: Middle player in a team match.

Chūma: Middle *ma'ai* between *tōma* and *chikama.* Also known as *issoku ittō no ma'ai.*

Chūshi: Halt, stop.

D

Dai Nippon Butoku Kai: Association of All Martial Arts, established in Meiji 28 (1895).

Dai Nippon Teikoku Kendo Kata: Established in 1912 and since the end of World War II called Nihon Kendo Kata.

Daitō: Longer *shinai* of Nitō ryū; long sword measuring more than 2 *shaku* (23.8 in.).

Daiwa: Oval base where *tategane* and *yokogane* are fastened.

Dan: Above the rank of *kyu;* used in various martial arts. Indicates degree of training, achievement in the martial arts, and character.

Dan'i: Rank. In kendo there are *shodan* (first degree) to *hachidan* (eighth degree), according to the new Ranking and Honorary Title Examination.

Dantaisen: Team match.

Datotsu: Clean strike or thrust to the *datotsubui* by the *datotsubu* portion of the *shinai,* with correct *hasuji* and full *zanshin.*

Datotsubu: Area of a *shinai* where the *datotsu* will count, approximately one-third from the tip of the *shinai* to the opposite side of *tsuru.*

Datotsubui: Area of the body where the *datotsu* will count: *men, kote, dō,* and *tsuki.*

Debana: Moment of starting the *waza.*

Degashira: Synonymous with *debana.*

Dō: Area covered by the *dō,* a plastron protecting the chest and abdomen.

Dō: Way or discipline. Also, a way of life.

Dōbari: *Shinai* with wide diameter near the *tsuba.*

Dō, dōdai, or taiko: Vest or plastron consisting of 43, 50, 60, or 70 shaved and curved bamboo strips put together using holes at both ends, with *koto* strings. The front is covered by buffalo skin, sharkskin, or turtle shell. Both front and back are lacquered to protect the *dō* from moisture. May be black, red, brown, or other colors with designs. Receives *datotsu* and is very durable. May also be made of synthetic fiber or plastic.

Dōgi: Uniform worn over the torso; jacket used in *keiko.*

Dōgu or bōgu: Equipment or protective gear.

Dōhimo: Straps used to secure the *dō.*

Dōjō: Place for martial arts or worship. Term is derived from the Buddhist word denoting a place of enlightenment. Long ago *dōjō* was made by roping off a square area in an open field, but in the Tokugawa era it was constructed inside a building. A place to train for both physical and mental fortitude; must be kept clean.

Dokgyōdō: Path one takes alone; twenty-one articles of self-discipline written by Miyamoto Musashi on his deathbed.

Dōmune: Chest portion of the *dō.*

Dōsa: Body movement.

E

Edo: Seat of the Tokugawa shōgunate for almost three centuries. Present-day Tokyo.

Edo Jidai (1603–1867): Edo period began with Tokugawa Ieyasu, who conquered all of Japan with his victory at Sekigahara, where Tokugawa's 70,000 and Osaka's 80,000 soldiers clashed twice in 1600.

Enchō: Extension of a match. When there is no winner in a set time, the match is extended by the call of the *shinpan, "Enchō hajime."*

Enchōsen: Match in which the winner is decided by *enchō.*

Enzan no metsuke: "Gazing at a far mountain." Way of focusing the eyes by seeing the entire opponent and not being preoccupied with small details.

F

Fū (kaze): Wind or style.

Fudōchi Shinmyō Roku: Record of Steadfast Wisdom and Divine Mystery, written by Takuan Sōhō for Yagyū Munenori on Zen philosophy.

Fudōshin: Unmovable mind.

Fukuro shinai: Early form of *shinai.* Length of bamboo split at the end and wrapped by a *fukuro* (bag) of leather. Devised by Kamiizumi (Kōzumi) Nobutsuna.

Fukushiki kokyu: Abdominal breathing used to improve concentration.

Fukushin: Subreferee.

Fukushō: Subcaptain. Second to last person to play in a team match.

Fukusō: Attire.

Fumikomiashi: Jumping foot. A type of *okuriashi.* Back foot kicks off the floor and pushes forward foot toward the opponent.

Fū no maki: In his "Book of the Wind" in the *Gorin no Sho,* Musashi points out the differences between his school of Niten Ichi ryū and other schools.

Fureru: To touch gently.

Fusengachi or *fusenshō:* Winning the match without fighting. Winning by default.

Futon: Japanese quilt or cushion.

G

Gawa or *kawa:* Leather.

Gedan/gedan no kamae: Lower stance with the sword tip 5 cm lower than the opponent's knee level.

Gekken: Common name for kendo in the Meiji period.

Gi: Doubt.

Gi: Clothing, especially the jacket.

Gi: Righteousness, virtue, justice, an upright way of life.

Giryoku: Skill or technique.

Go: Five.

Go: Rear, back, hind.

Gōgi: Conference among the judges during a match.

Gogyō no kamae: Five basic stances: *moku, ka, dō, kon,* and *sui* (tree, fire, earth, gold, and water).

Gohonme: The fifth *kata.*

Gokaku: Equal strength.

Gokaku keiko: Keiko between equal partners.

Gokaku shōbu: Match between partners of equal skill.

Gomen: Excuse me.

Go no sen: Anticipating the strike of the opponent and striking back as soon as the opponent strikes.

Gorin no Sho: "Book of Five Rings" by Miyamoto Musashi. It has five "rings" or books: earth, water, fire, wind, and sky.

Gyaku nitō: Reverse *nitō* or double-sword technique, with the long sword in the left hand.

Gyō: Semi-formal.

H
Ha: Blade.

Ha: Group of people with the same belief, opinion, or school.

Ha: Break through.

Hachi: The number eight.

Hachidan: Eighth degree in the martial arts. In kendo, the highest rank.

Hachiku: Type of bamboo used to make *shinai*.

Haitō rei: Ban on wearing swords.

Hajime: Commence, begin.

Hakama: Trouser-like skirts.

Hakama sabaki: Manner of treating *hakama* when kneeling down.

Hamon: Temper line of a Japanese sword.

Hanamusubi (chōmusubi): Bow knot.

Hangan: Partially closed eyes.

Han-men: One side of the head.

Hanmi: Half-body stance. Not squarely facing the opponent, but turning the body to the side at about 45 degrees.

Hanshi: Highest honorary title given to the kendo practitioner.

Hansoku: Illegal move or act; a foul.

Hantei: A judgment. Majority of *shinpan* decide the winner of a match. Used when there is no winner by a clear *datotsu*.

Haori: Formal Japanese man's coat.

Happonme: The eighth *kata*.

Harai* or *harau: Slapping to the side.

Hari: Slap.

Hassō: Eight-faceted or -featured *kamae*, a variation of *jōdan*. Kamae of *bokū (moku)* or tree; also known as *kamae* of *in* (yin).

Hasuji: Direction of the blade.

Hasuji tadashiku: Correct direction of the blade.

Hataku: Slap with a bigger motion.

Haya: Rapid, fast.

Hayashizaki Jinsuke Shigenobu (1545–?). Founder of the Musō shinden ryū of rapid drawing, called *iaido*.

Haya suburi: Rapid or fast *suburi*.

Heian Jidai (794–1185): Period in which Kyoto was the capital and the samurai class fought battles wielding *kotō* from horseback. Long, curved, and lightweight swords were popular. A transitional period in sword-making, from the double-edged to the classic *tachi* form.

Hera: Fastening plate. Spatula-like plastic piece on the *koshiita;* also known as *koshibasami.*

Hi: Fire. Third book of the *Gorin no Sho,* entitled the "Book of Fire" or *"Hi no Maki."* *Hi no kurai* or rank of fire referring to *jōdan.*

Hidari morote jōdan: Jōdan with the left foot forward.

Hidari or sa: Left.

Hidari shizentai: Left natural stance. Natural or basic posture with the left foot forward and body slightly open to the right.

Hikitate: To uplift, to encourage.

Hikitate keiko: Practice in which the teacher encourages the student to do his best.

Hikiwake: To draw in a game or play.

Hikiwaza: Retreating *waza.*

Hikutokoro: One of the three opportunities to strike. As the opponent withdraws, he becomes vulnerable.

Himo: String (not like a *tsuru* or thread) or strap. A woven fabric like a small rope used to secure the *bōgu.*

Hi no kurai: Rank of fire. Another name for *jōdan* and a very aggressive offensive *kamae* or posture also known as *ten no kamae.*

Hirakiashi: Open footwork; a form of *okuriashi.*

Hiraseigan: Old name for a form of *chudan.*

Hitachi: Ibaraki prefecture.

Hitachi: Secret sword.

Hitoemi: One-layer body stance, almost sideways. More than *hanmi,* which is half-body stance or halfway-angled stance.

Hito no kurai: Rank of person. Another name for *chūdan,* as in *ten-chi-jin* or heaven-earth-person.

Hitori keiko: Solitary practice. Practice of kendo without *sensei* or partners.

Hojō (1205–1333): Military government *(bakufu)* established in Kamakura.

Hokushin Ittō ryū: School founded by Chiba Shūsaku at the close of the Edo period. Named after the northern star, which his family worshipped. Became one of the biggest kendo schools in Edo, producing well-known students who played major roles in the Meiji restoration.

Honmusubi: Square knot.

Hōshin: Ideal state of mind for martial arts, open and flexible, not preoccupied by any one thing and able to meet any change in the opponent.

Hosomi: Most slender type of *shinai.*

Hyakuren jitoku: Practice makes perfect. After arduous repetition in training, one will reach perfection. An old teaching for students of martial arts.

Hyōhōka Densho or Hyōhō Kadensho: Book of Swordsmanship for the Posterity, tactics explained in terms of Zen Buddhism by Yagyū Munenori.

Hyōhō Sanjūgo Kajō: The thirty-five articles of martial arts. Written in 1641 by Miyamoto Musashi and the backbone of the *Gorin no Sho.*

I

Iaido: The way of *iai.*

Ichi: The number one.

Ichi gan, ni soku, san tan, shi riki: What the kendo practitioner must focus on, in descending order: first eyes, second feet, third courage, and fourth strength or *waza.*

Ichigo ichie: One lifetime, one meeting. This expression from the tea ceremony means act as if this were your only encounter in a lifetime.

Ichimonji: The number one, written in *kanji.*

Igi: Protest. No one can protest the referees' decisions. However, the contestant's manager may call matters to the attention of the referee director *(shinpan chō)* or presiding referee *(shinpan shunin)* before the end of the match.

Iizasa Chōisai (1387–1488): A priest of the Katori shrine and founder of the Tenshin Shōden Katori Shintō ryū.

Ikkai: Once.

Ikkyodō: Movement in one count.

Ippon: Match point, awarded for a clear *datotsu* on the *datotsubui* with good *zanshin.*

Ippon ari: Point given to a player because of two *hansoku* by the player's opponent.

Ippongachi: To win by *ippon.*

Ipponme: Match for the first *ippon* or *kata* number one.

Irimi: Spirit of offense, ready to close the distance and strike the opponent.

Issoku itō no ma'ai: The one-foot-one-sword distance, between *tōma* and *chikama.*

Ita: Wooden plate.

Itō Ittōsai Kagehisa: Founder of the Ittō ryū.

Itsuita tokoro: Settled. A moment of physical or mental immobility.

Ittchi: State of agreement or harmony.

Ittō ryū: A single-sword school founded by Itō Ittōsai Kagehisa. Contrasted with Nitō ryū or two-sword school.

Iwao no mi: As steady as a rock; immobile, great, and strong-minded, even when facing death.

J

Jigeiko: Practice different techniques among kendo practitioners of equal level.

Jigen ryū: School established by Tōgō Shigetaka (1561–1643) in Satsuma (Kagoshima).

Jihō: Second person to play in a team match, following the *senpō.*

Jinbu: Blade area of the sword or area of the *shinai* where the blade would be located.

Jōdan: Upper stance or stance of fire *(hi no kamae).* A very aggressive, offensive stance.

Jōgai: When a foot or other part of the body is completely outside of the court (not just stepping on the line).

Jōge: Up and down, as in *jōge suburi* or *chōyaku jōge suburi.*

Jūji: The number ten.

Jūmonji: The number ten *(jūji)* written in *kanji.* Looks like a cross.

Junbi taisō: Warm-up exercise.

Jun-kesshō sen: Semifinal match.

Jupponme: Tenth form.

K

Kachinuki: Winner remains until defeated.

Kaeshi waza: Return technique; counterattack technique in which the player blocks first and reverses the *shinai* to strike in one motion.

Kage ryū: School of swordsmen founded in Miye prefecture by Aisuhyūga no Kami Ikōsai.

Kaishi sen: Starting line in a match, comprising a 50-cm white strip 1.4 m from the center cross.

Kakari keiko: Charging practice; the most intense, fundamental practice.

Kakegoe: Used interchangeably with *kiai;* sound expression of the state of mind.

Kamae: A stance; literally means to prepare. *Kanji* character consists of "tree" and "ditch," meaning to prepare for an attack by putting up trees and digging ditches.

Kamae o toku: To disarm oneself by lowering the *shinai* or sword and opening one's stance slightly to the right.

Kamakura period (1185–1333): Period in which the capital was Kamakura (Kanagawa prefecture, near Yokohama). Minamoto Yoritomo established his military government *(bakufu)* in Kamakura. Sword-making reached its peak in quality and beauty.

Kamiizumi (Kōzumi) Ise no Kami Nobutsuna: Founder of the Shinkage ryū.

Kamikaze: Divine wind, typhoon. The Japanese believed that a divine wind helped them defeat the invading Mongols.

Kamiza: Higher seat or upper section reserved for honored guests or the national flag, and located opposite the *shimoza,* where the entrance is. Also refers to the eastern-side seats for instructors.

Kamiza ni mukkate rei: Bow toward the *kamiza.*

Kane (gane, gone, kin, kon): Metal, especially gold.

Kanken no metsuke: To look at the opponent with the mind's eye as well as the physical eye.

Kan kyū: Fast and slow rhythm.

Ka no maki: "Book of Fire," the third book of the *Gorin no Sho* by Miyamoto Musashi. It concerns the tactics of warfare between individuals or between armies. Called the "Book of Fire" because, like the rapidly changing nature of fire, it is about fighting in a changing situation.

Kanyaku imin: Government-contracted immigrants. The first such group arrived in Honolulu on February 8, 1885.

Ka or *hi:* Fire.

Karakasa nigiri: To grip as one would an Oriental umbrella.

Kashima ryū: School of swordsmanship that the priests of the Katori shrine are said to have practiced.

Kata: Prearranged sets of defensive and offensive moves. Important to many disciplines as the fundamental moves and concepts.

Kata: Half. As in *kata tabi, katate uchi,* and *katate tsuki.*

Katana: Japanese sword developed during the middle of the Muromachi period, replacing the older *tachi,* and in use until the end of the Edo period. Unlike the *tachi,* the *katana* was worn in the *obi,* blade up. Generally, *katana* refers to all Japanese swords but, technically, it must be differentiated from the *tachi.*

Katatabi: Half of a *tabi,* leather-soled footwear that protects the ball of the foot.

Katate waza: One-handed technique.

Katori Shinto ryū: Iizasa Chōisai, a priest of the Katori Shrine, is said to have founded this school.

Katsugi waza: Carrying or shouldering technique.

Katsuninken: Life-saving sword.

Kawa **(or** *gawa***):** Leather.

Keiko **or** *geiko:* Training, not only of the martial arts. Derives from a term that means "ponder the ancient."

Keishi ryū: Keishichō (metropolitan police), which formed the first kata, a prototype of present Nihon Kendo Kata.

Keitō: Holding the sword over the left hip, with mind and body alert.

Ken: Sword.

Kendo: Way of the sword. The old Japanese martial art of fencing or swordsmanship, expected of a samurai. Now practiced as a sport all over the world and both a physical and a philosophical discipline.

Kendōgi: Uniform worn in kendo training, consisting of *dōgi* and *hakama.*

Kendo gu: Synonymous with *bōgu;* gear or equipment used in kendo, including *men, dō, kote,* and *tare.*

Kendo no rinen: A precept of kendo.

Kensen **or** *kensaki:* Tip of the sword beyond the *yokote.*

Kenshi: Person who practices or excels in kendo.

Ken shin tai ittchi: Sword, mind, and body in harmony.

Ken tai hyori: Same as *ken tai ittchi.* Offensive and defensive modes are front and back. When the body is in an offensive mode, the mind should be on the defensive.

Ken tai ittchi: Defense and offense in harmony. Important concept of kendo in which attack is defense and defense is attack. The states must coexist.

Ken Zen ittchi: Kendo and Zen are in harmony.

Kera: Wrist portion of the *kote.* Soft and can be bent without difficulty.

Kesshō sen: Final or championship match.

Ki: Opportunity; time to strike.

Ki: Mind, spirit, energy, or air. Force that connects the opponents.

Kiai/kakegoe: Loud cry originating from deep in the abdomen; an expression of the state of mind; to concentrate and encourage oneself and intimidate the opponent.

Kiate: Synonymous with *kuraizume;* to press opponent with superior *ki.*

Kigurai: Loftiness of mind. Superior state of mind that presses the opponent without using *waza.*

Kihin: Dignity, grace, and refinement; bearing or aura. *Kihin* is self-assurance and poise that come from long years of training.

Kihon: Fundamental.

Kihonkeiko: Practice of fundamental skills.

Kihon waza: Fundamental techniques.

Ki ken tai ittchi: Mind, sword, and body in harmony.

Kin: Metal, especially gold.

Kirikaeshi: Cut alternately; the most fundamental practice in kendo.

Kirima: Cutting space.

Kirimusubi: *Yonhonme* features *kirimusubi* as both *shidachi* and *uchidachi* strike each other's *shōmen* (*aiuchi*) and come to *chūdan* in *kirimusubi* as if chafing the *shinogi.*

Kisen o seishite: Seizing the moment the opponent initiates the *waza* to strike; taking the initiative and striking first.

Kissaki: Portion of the sword beyond *yokote.*

Ki o mite: Surmise the right moment. See the opportunity to strike.

Ko: Small.

Koban: Old Japanese gold coin with an elongated, oval shape, or a *shinai* with a *tsuka* shaped like a *koban.*

Kobudō: Old martial arts.

Kōbusho: Tokugawa military academy established in 1855. Toward the end of Tokugawa era, it set the length of the *shinai* at 3 *shaku* 8 *sun.*

Kōchaku jōtai: Stalemate. The *shinpan* calls "*Wakare!*" to separate the players.

Kodachi: Small or short sword, measuring 1–2 *shaku.*

Kōdansha: High-ranking person. Definition differs depending on the circumstances, but generally accepted as fourth *dan* or above. (Kendo Nippon Editorial Board)

Koiguchi: Opening in a scabbard that resembles the mouth of a carp *(koi).*

Koiguchi o kiru: Loosening the sword from the scabbard in preparation for drawing it.

Kōjin no ma: When the tips of the blades at the *yokote* are crossed slightly.

Kojinsen: Individual match.

Kojiri: Butt end of the *saya.*

Kokyu: Breathing, respiration, tempo, timing.

Komono: Small leather strip tied to a *tsuru.*

Kon (gon): Metal, especially gold.

Kon (gon) no kamae: *Kamae* of gold, *wakigamae.*

Koshi: Hip, back, or waist.

Koshibasami: Fastening plate. Small piece of plastic or wood attached to the *koshiita* and inserted into the *obi.*

Koshihimo: Hip strap.

Koshiita: Plate at the back of the *hakama* to help wearer maintain good posture.

Kōtai: Exchange or rotation of referees during a match.

Kōtai: Retreat.

Kotare: Two smaller, inner aprons or pads of the *tare.*

Kote: Forearm as a *datotsubui* (strike zone) or the gauntlet-like glove that protects the hand and forearm.

Kote ari: A *yukōdatotsu* (effective point) to the *kote* area.

Kotebuton: Cylindrical portion of the *kote* above the wrist or *kera.* A *datotsubui* (striking zone).

Kotehimo: String or lace for the *kote.*

Koto: Traditional Japanese stringed instrument. *Koto* strings used to tie bamboo strips of the *dō* together.

Kotō: Ancient sword from the period 900 to 1530. A single-edged and curved blade used for mounted combat.

Kozuka: Small knife stored in the *kōgaibitsu* of the *saya* or scabbard.

Ku: Fear.

Kū (sora, kara): Sky, emptiness, or void.

Kumitachi: Set of prearranged defensive and offensive movements used to learn fundamental forms in *koryū* or the old schools of kendo.

Kumite or kumiuchi: To tackle or wrestle; illegal in modern kendo.

Kumo kazari: Chest portion of the *dō* featuring a cloud-like embroidered design.

Kū no maki: "Book of the Sky" in the *Gorin no Sho,* in which Miyamoto Musashi summarizes his enlightened state of mind as emptiness.

Kurai: Rank, class, or grace.

Kuraizume: To seize with superior poise. Synonymous with *kiate.* Press opponent with superior *ki* or spirit without using actual *waza. Sanbonme* in Nihon Kendo Kata features this technique.

Kyo: Surprise, startle.

Kyodō: Movement.

Kyo, ku, gi, waku: Four forbidden states of mind: surprise, fear, doubt, and hesitation.

Kyōshi: Honorary title, ranked between *renshi* and *Hanshi.* To qualify, the applicant must have a superior knowledge of kendo and an outstanding character, and hold the seventh *dan.*

Kyūhonme: Ninth kata.

Kyu kyō: Fast and strong. Describes tempo and intensity of the *waza.*

M

Ma'ai: Distance between opponents, not only physical but also spiritual and temporal.

Maedare or *tsukidare:* Small plate-like apron under the chin portion of the *men,* backed by the *uchi dare,* that protects the neck. Receives the *tsuki.*

Maehimo: A belt attached to the front portion of *hakama.*

Mage: Topknot.

Maki kaeshi: Coil and return movement.

Maki otosh: Coiling and dropping technique.

Makoto: Truth.

Mei: Inscription on the *tang* portion of the sword giving the name of the swordsmith and the place where the sword was forged on the *omote (omote mei)* and the date it was forged on the *ura (ura mei).*

Meiji Jidai (1868–1912): Meiji restoration transferred seat of power from the Tokugawa shōgun to the Meiji emperor. Wearing of swords was abolished, together with the class system that ranked samurai as highest.

Mejirushi: Red or white cloth strip marker (5 cm by 70 cm, folded in half) tied where the *dō* strings cross in back.

Mekugi: Rivet or peg made of bamboo or animal horn. Goes through the *mekugi ana,* securing the sword/tang to the *tsuka.*

Mekugi ana: Rivet hole.

Men: Face or head. The *men* is one of the *datotsubui.* Also refers to head-gear protecting the face, neck, head, and shoulders.

Men ari: A clear *datotsu* on the *men.*

Menbuchi: Leather strap around the base of a *men* stitched with leather string.

Menbuton or *mendare:* Large, thick, cushioned plate of cloth covering the *men,* which protects the head and shoulders.

Men chichigawa: Looped leather strips attached to the fourth *mengane* for one end of the *menhimo.*

Mengane: Metal grid that covers the face of the *men* consisting of one vertical bar *(nakagane)* and fourteen horizontal bars *(yokogane).*

Menhimo: Two long straps used to secure the *men,* tied in a *hanamusubi* at the back of the head. They measure 40 cm from the knot to the ends when appropriately tied.

Menuki: Small decorative metal carvings under the wrapping of the *tsuka.*

Migi: Right.

Migi shizentai: Shizentai (natural stance) with the right foot forward and the body open slightly to left.

Mimizuri: Pair of leather pieces sewn over either side the *menbuton* at the junction of the *daiwa* and *maedare.*

Minamoto Yoritomo: Founder of a military government *(bakufu)* in Kamakura after the defeat of the Taira clan.

Mine/mune: Side opposite the tempered edge.

Mino: Old province in Japan, now the Gifu prefecture; the town of Seki was the center of the Mino school of sword-making.

Mitori keiko: Method of learning by observation.

Miyamoto Musashi Genshin (1584–1645): Famous kendo practitioner. Musashi was a somewhat eccentric character who developed Nitō ryū or the double-sword technique. In *Dokgyōdō,* which he wrote a week prior to his death, he details twenty-one precepts of self-discipline. Talented in the martial arts, brush painting, literature, and sculpture, he called himself, "Shinmen Musashi no Kami Fujiwara no Genshin" in *Gorin no Sho.*

Mizouchi/suigetsu: Solar plexus.

Mizu no kurai: Rank of water; another name for *chūdan no kamae.*

Mizu no maki: "Book of Water" in the *Gorin no Sho* by Miyamoto Musashi. Longest book of the *Gorin no Sho,* it describes the mental attitudes necessary to achieve victory, including how to hold the sword, different *kamae,* and footwork.

Mochida Moriji (1885–1974): First person to win the title of *Hanshi* tenth dan, Moriji taught kendo at the *dōjō* of the metropolitan police and the imperial police.

Mohan: Example or model.

Moku rei: Bow silently or show respect by lowering the eyes.

Mokusō: Meditation. *Seiza* is used instead of *mokusō* at times.

Monomi/mushamado: Window or viewing space between the eighth and ninth *yokogane* (counted from the bottom), or between the ninth and tenth for children.

Monouchi: Cutting zone of a Japanese sword or the part of the *shinai* between the *nakayui* and *kensaki* (about one-third of the *jinbu*).

Morote: Both hands.

Morote hidari jōdan: *Jōdan no kamae* with both hands up and the left foot forward.

Motodachi: Practice instructor.

Moyai musubi: Bowline knot.

Mugamae: No stance or void stance. Strong spiritual force and confidence without offensive posture.

Mumei: No inscription; absence of inscription over the *tang* does not necessarily lower the value of a sword.

Munamachi: Border between the *tang* and the *mine;* straight line between the *munamachi* and *kensen* (sword tip) is the *nagasa* (length) of the sword.

Mune chichigawa: Pair of leather rings attached to the *mune* portion of the *dō.*

Munehimo: Chest strap of *dōgi* or *dō.*

Munen musō: Detached state of mind.

Mune or mine: Back part of the blade or the opposite side of the tempered edge.

Mushamado: Window or viewing space on the eighth and ninth *yokogane* counted from the bottom, or between the ninth and tenth *yokogane* for children.

Musha shugyō: Martial travel; travel to train with teachers of different schools.

Musōshinden ryū: School of *iaido* founded by Hayashizaki Jinsuke Shigenobu (1545–?).

N

Nagasa: Length of a sword from the *kensen* to the *munamachi* in a straight line.

Nakago: *Tang* portion of a sword. Covered by the *tsuka* or hilt.

Nakagojiri: Butt portion of the *nakago* or *tang*.

Nakayui: Leather strap that fastens the *tsuru* at the first one third of the *shinai*.

Namako: *Kera* or wrist portion of *kote*.

Nanahonme: Seventh form.

Nana or shichi: The number seven.

Nanban tetsu: Top-quality iron imported from Southeast Asia and Europe during the Muromachi and Edo periods.

Nayasu: To weaken or weakening. A technique of fending off the opponent's *kensen* by using the *shinogi* portion of the sword.

Ni: The number two.

Nigiri: To grasp or grip; sometimes the handle or the fist portion of the *kote*.

Nihon: Second time.

Nihon Kendo Kata: Formerly the Dai Nippon Teikoku Kendo Kata, established in 1912 for physical education curriculum.

Nihonme: Second point.

Nihon or Nippon: Japan.

Nihontō: Japanese sword or *katana*.

Nikai: Second.

Nikyodō: In two movements.

Niten Ichi ryū: Two-Heavens, One School. School of swordsmanship established by Miyamoto Musashi.

Nitō ryū: Two-sword technique school.

Nōtō: Action of returning the sword to the scabbard.

Nuketō: Command to draw the sword or *shinai* to prepare for *kamae*.

Nuki (adj) or nuku (v): Technique of dodging the opponent's sword while moving to strike back.

Nuki waza: Dodging technique.

Nusumiashi: Stealthy footwork.

O

Obi: Belt or sash.

Ōji: Counter, respond, or return.

Ōji waza: To parry the opponent's *shinai* and strike back; counterattack.

Okori: Also called *debana*, the beginning of a *waza* (technique).

Okuriashi: Sending footwork.

Omote: Front. Holder's left side of the *shinai* or sword. Also the *tsuka (tang)* portion, showing the *mei* or the name of the swordsmith.

Ō or *dai*: Large.

***Orishiki waza*:** Striking-with-one-knee-on-the-floor technique. A rarely used *waza*. The *shidachi* cuts the *migidō* of the *uchidachi* by placing the right knee and left foot on the floor.

***Osaeru*:** To press on.

***Osametō*:** To put the sword/*shinai* back. Order to sheath the *shinai* at the end of *keiko*.

***Otagai ni rei*:** Bow to each other.

***Ōtare*:** Three of the five pieces of the apron-like protective gear; the three in front part of the *tare*.

R

***Rei*:** Etiquette or bow. Meaning more than just bending the back, it symbolizes respect, humility, and honor. One of the virtues of a good samurai is to know the etiquette for all activities of daily living and even death.

***Reihō*:** Rules pertaining to manners.

***Renshi*:** Honorary title below *Kyōshi* and *Hanshi*.

***Renzoku*:** Technique that uses sequences of *waza*.

***Ri*:** Separate.

***Ritsurei*:** Bow from a standing position.

***Roku*:** The number six.

***Rōnin*:** Literally, "wave person"; a lordless or out-of-work samurai.

***Ropponme*:** Sixth form.

***Ryoku* or *riki*:** Not simply physical strength but skill in kendo.

***Ryū*:** Usually refers to a school of ancient discipline, such as martial arts or flower arrangement.

***Ryūha*:** Division or subdivision within the same school.

S

***Sabaku* or *sabaki*:** Handle or handling.

***Saburoku*:** The number thirty-six; abbreviation for *sanjūroku*.

***Sagetō* or *teitō*:** Holding the sword at rest.

Sakakibara Kenkichi (1830–1894): Kendo master from the Edo to Meiji periods; he called kendo *gekken* and promoted it by performing in public.

***Sakigawa*:** Leather cap that fits over the tip of the *shinai*.

***Sakigomu*:** Small rubber plug that fits on the tip of the *shinai* and protects the *sakigawa* from direct impact.

***Sakki*:** Intention to kill.

***Samurai*:** Originally the guards serving the nobles but eventually came to mean warriors and developed into a dominating force controlling the government.

***San*:** The number three.

***Sanbon*:** Three points.

***Sanbonme*:** Third form.

***Sanbon shōbu*:** Kendo match in which it takes two points to win.

***Sandan*:** Third degree.

***Sandanuchi*:** Three consecutive strikes.

Sanku: The number thirty-nine; abbreviation for *sanjūku.*

Sankyodō: Three-count movements.

Sanpachi/sanhachi: The number thirty-eight; abbreviation for *sanjūhachi.*

Sansappō: Three kill techniques: kill *ki* (spirit), kill *ken* (sword), and kill *waza* (technique).

Sanshi: The number thirty-four; abbreviation of *sanjūshi.*

Sanshichi/san nana: The number thirty-seven; abbreviation of *sanjūshichi.*

Sasamori Junzō: A master of Onoha Ittō ryū and a scholar, Junzō studied in the United States for many years after graduating from Waseda University and received a doctorate from the University of Denver.

Sashiko: Extensive Japanese needlework used in protective gear for the martial arts.

Satori: Enlightenment; to reach the ultimate state of understanding.

Saya: Scabbard.

Sayū: Left and right.

Sa-za u-ki: Left sit and right rise. A sequence of *seiza:* Left knee bends first when you sit down in *seiza* but the right leg rises first when you stand up from *seiza.*

Seichu sen or *seimei sen:* Centerline or lifeline.

Seigan: Chūdan replaced this term. Not used in modern kendo or Nihon Kendo Kata practice.

Seikatanden: Since there are several *tanden, seikatanden* refers to the one below the umbilicus.

Seiza: Formal Japanese sitting stance.

Seiza: To sit in tranquility. Sitting quietly or in silence with the mind at ease and breathing from *tanden* very slowly.

Sekirei-no-o: Wagging tail; describes the movement of the *shinai* vacillating up and down like a wagging tail. Irregular rhythm that the opponent cannot ride.

Seme: Spiritual and physical pressure or force. Important concept in kendo.

Sen: Ahead of time. In kendo meaning ahead of an opponent's *waza.*

Sen: War, match, competition, or battle.

Sen: Line.

Sengoku Jidai (1485–1568): Period marked by constant upheaval; the Age of Wars.

Sen no sen: To strike a split second before the opponent begins a *waza* by detecting the opponent's *sen.*

Sen or *tai no sen:* To sense the physical or spiritual intent of the opponent.

Senpō: Player who goes first in *dantai sen* (team match).

Sensei: Teacher, instructor, or one who has trained more.

Senshu: Participants in athletic events such as the martial arts.

Seppa: Spacer or washer fitted at both ends of the *tsuba* for stability and close fitting.

Setsunintō: Murderous sword.

Shaku: 30.3 cm; 1 *shaku* is 10 *sun*; 1 *sun* is 3.03 cm; old Japanese unit of length.

Shiai: Match.

Shiai-jō: Match court.

Shiai keiko: Practice method similar to a match.

Shidachi: Sword that belongs to the *shikata* (student).

Shikai: Four forbidden states of mind: *kyo, ku, gi,* and *waku.*

Shikake: Work on.

Shikake waza: *Waza* that forces an opponent to make a *suki.*

Shimoza: Lower seat of the *dōjō.*

Shin: Belief, conviction, principle.

Shin: Formal.

Shinai: Bamboo sword; from the word *shinau,* meaning flexible

Shinai bukuro: Carrying case or bag for the *shinai* made of canvas, cotton, silk, leather, or synthetic leather.

Shinkage ryū: School of swordsmanship founded by Kamiizumi (Kōzumi) Ise no Kami Nobutsuna.

Shinken: Real sword as opposed to a *shinai* or *bokken.*

Shin ki ryoku no ittchi: Heart, mind, and power in harmony.

Shinkokyu: Deep breathing.

Shinogi: Ridge line that separates the *shinogiji* (upper surface) and *ha* (lower surface).

Shinogiji: Texture of upper surface above the *shinogi.*

Shinpan: Judging or pertaining to judging.

Shinpancho: Referee responsible for conduct of entire match and procedures for multicourt matches. Referee makes judgments based on rules and regulations, and makes decisions when there is an unexpected event or accident.

Shinpanin: Referees. Three for each court: one *shushin* and two *fukushin.*

Shinpanki: White and red flags measuring 25 cm by 25 cm with a 5 cm handle; used by the *shinpanin* to indicate various decisions.

Shinpan kisoku: Rules of judging.

Shinpan shunin: Presiding referee. Assigned to individual courts for the procedures in multicourt matches.

Shinsa: Examination.

Shinsain: Examiner.

Shinsengumi: Military police force of the Tokugawa *bakufu* headed by Kondō Isami.

Shintō ryū: Abbreviation of Tenshin Shōden Katori Shintō ryū.

Shinzen: Before the altar or deity.

Shisei wo tadashite: Command to straighten posture.

Shishin: Distraction that leads to misjudgment and certain defeat.

Shitsurei shimasu / Goburei shimasu: "Excuse me"/"pardon me" in polite form.

Shi, yon, or yottsu: The number four.

Shizen: Nature or natural.

Shizentai: Natural stance; fundamental and stable stance.

Shōbu: Final match point.

Shōbu ari: When a winner is determined the *shushin* announces, *"Shōbu ari!"*

Shodan: First degree.

Shōdan: Promotion.

Shōgō: Honorary title, such as *Renshi, Kyōshi,* and *Hanshi.*

Shokko: Decoration on part of the *dōmune.*

Shokujin no ma: *Ma'ai* in which the tips of the blades barely touch each other.

Shōmen: Front section of the *dōjō.* Also, center part of the *men.*

Shōmen ni rei: Bowing to the *dōjō shōmen.*

Shōwa period (1925–1988): A period of turmoil in Japanese history. Defeat in World War II changed many traditions. Many fine swords worn by military officers were lost or confiscated.

Shu-ha-ri: Principle of kendo practice. *Shu* means to follow and preserve fundamental rules. *Ha* means to break away from fundamental teachings. *Ri* means to separate to establish a school. Expression describing different stages of learning.

Shumoku ashi: Stance in which the feet are wide apart at almost *ha no ji,* or forming a nearly 90-degree angle, foot stance akin to T-shaped wooden striker of a bell in a Japanese temple.

Shunsoku: Lightning speed.

Shushin: Chief referee for individual match, who makes announcements and has an equal vote with the *fukushin.*

Sō: Informal.

Sonkyo: Squatting on balls of the feet.

Sori: Curvature. Length between *mine* and a line drawn from tip of the sword to hilt *(tsuka)* or *munemachi.*

Sōsai: To cancel each other out; both competitors commit *hansoku* simultaneously and no penalty is given to either competitor after one penalty each.

Suburi: Empty swing; a basic exercise.

Suigetsu: Solar plexus. A weak spot.

Sui no maki: "Book of Water" in the *Gorin no Sho.*

Sui or mizu: Water.

Suki: Fleeting space, mind, *waza,* or time when one is vulnerable to attacks.

Suriage: Fending off opponent's sword by sliding up in a semicircular motion.

Suriashi: Sliding-foot technique. Walking as if gliding across the floor without showing the bottoms of the feet. A very stable and flexible way to walk.

Surikomi: The *shidachi* slides up the *kodachi* over the *tachi* of the *uchidachi* after a strike to the *migidō* is blocked in *kodachi no kata sanbonme.*

Surinagashi: The *shidachi* blocks the sword with a left *shinogi* of the *kodachi* as the *uchidachi* attacks the *migidō* in *kodachi no kata sanbonme*.

Suriotoshi: The *shidachi* blocks the *shōmen* attack with the *suriage* technique, and immediately pushes it down and forward with the *suriotoshi* technique in *kodachi no kata sanbonme*.

T

Tachi: Long sword used in the Heian, Kamakura, and Muromachi periods. Measures over 60 cm in length, has deep curvature *(sori)*, and hangs from hip blade down.

Tachiagari: Standing up from the *seiza* position.

Tachiai: Stand up and meet. Presenting oneself formally in a match.

Taiatari: Body crush.

Taiko: Drum or lacquered portion of the *dō* made of bamboo strips covered by leather.

Tai no sen: Sense the opponent's strikes and strike back so that match will end with *aiuchi*.

Taishō: Captain.

Taitō: Sword in sash *(obi)*. Act of placing sword into the sash.

Takano Sasaburō (1862–1950): Great kendo practitioner through the Meiji, Taisho, and Shōwa periods. A member of the committee that formed the Dai Nippon Teikoku Kendo Kata.

Takuan Sōhō (1573–1645): Zen priest of Rinzai sect who wrote *Fudōchi Shinmyoroku* for Yagū Muenori.

Tamegi: Instrument used to straighten warped bamboo or wood.

Tan: Courage.

Tanden: Three *tanden* are the areas where life energy resides, according to ancient Japanese philosophy.

Tanrenbō: Heavy pole used for training.

Tare: Apron-like protective gear consisting of three *ōtare*, two *kotare*, a *tare obi*, and *wakihimo*.

Tare obi: Sash attached to the *tare*.

Te: Technique.

Teitō or sagetō: Holding the *shinai* or sword at a 45-degree angle with the left hand and gently extending the elbow.

Ten: Heaven. Also the top portion of the *mengane*.

Ten no kamae: The *kamae* of heaven, or another name for *jōdan*. Rank of fire or *hino kurai* and a very aggressive posture or *kamae*.

Tenouchi: General term referring to the use of both hands.

Tenouchigawa: Palm portion of the *kote*. Made of deerskin or other leather.

Tenshin Shōden Katori Shintō ryū: School established by Iizasa Chōisai.

Tōgō Shigetaka (1561–1643): Founder of the Jigen ryū in Satsuma (Kagoshima).

Toku: To do good things to the public; one of the virtues of a samurai.

Tokugawa (1542–1616): After the death of Toyotomi Hideyoshi, Ieyasu won the battle of Sekigahara and became the first shōgun of Tokugawa.

Tokugawa era (1603–1867): Same as the Edo period; named for the ruling Tokugawa family.

Tokui waza: Forte or specialty, or strongest *waza*.

Tōma: Longest distance between opponents.

Torikeshi: After *gōgi,* the *shushin* can revoke *ippon* by waving the flags across the lower front for lack of alertness, a superfluous gesture, or verbalizing boisterously.

Toyotomi Hideyoshi (1536–1598): A general of Oda Nobunaga, who became powerful after killing Akechi Mitsuhide (who assassinated Nobunaga), and who almost conquered Japan.

Tsuba: Hand guard, usually made of plastic or leather for the *shinai,* or metal for the sword. Decorated *tsuba* are collected as artwork.

Tsubadome: *Tsuba* stopper; rubber disc that holds the *tsuba* in place on the *shinai.*

Tsubazeriai or tsubazeri: Hand guard fight. Competing with the *tsuba* or making contact with the *shinai* near the *tsuba* and looking for a *suki* or next move. Similar to *shinogi wo kezuru* (chaffing the ridges) using a real sword.

Tsuchi no kurai: Rank of earth, another name for *gedan no kamae.* Not an aggressive stance.

Tsugiashi: Connecting footwork.

Tsuka: Hilt or handle; handle portion of the *shinai* or sword.

Tsukagashira: Head of the *tsuka* of *shinai* or sword. Butt end of the *tsuka* with a metal cover.

Tsukagawa: Leather sheath for the *tsuka.*

Tsukahara Bokuden: Completed the Kashima ryū.

Tsukahimo: Small leather strap fastened to open end of the *tsukagawa.*

Tsukamaki: Cotton, silk, or leather lace/strap wrapped around the *tsukagawa* for ease of gripping and to prevent slipping.

Tsuki: Thrust, jab, or stab.

Tsukita tokoro: Moment that the *waza* is completed.

Tsuru: String.

Tsutsu or kote tsutsu: Cylinder-like portion of the *kote.*

U

Uchidachi: Sword belonging to the *uchikata* or teacher; striking sword.

Uchidare (yōjin dare or nijūago): Inner *tare.* Inside cover of the *maedare,* which reduces impact of the *tsuki* on the neck.

Uchikomi: Striking in proper form.

Uchikomi-bō: Bamboo stick used for *uchikomi* practice.

Uchiotoshi waza: Strike-down technique.

Uchiwa (hohowa): Inner ring that comes in contact with the face, chin, and forehead. Cotton wrapped with a cloth for comfort.

Uketome: Blocking.

Uketometa tokoro: Moment of blocking a strike.

Ura: Back or reverse.

Uramei: Inscription on reverse side of sword, usually date sword was forged.

W

Wa: Compassion, tranquility, serenity, peace, and harmony.

Wa: Ring of leather sewn on the back of the *dō* between the *mune* and *dōdai*.

Wakare: To separate or break away. Command given by the *shushin* when players are at stalemate *(kōchaku jōtai)*.

Waki: Side, flank, hip, and underarm.

Wakigamae: Hip stance, *kin no kamae* (stance of steel or gold), also known as *yō no kamae* (stance of yang), a variant of *gedan*.

Wakihimo: Hip strap of *tare*.

Wakizashi: Medium sword worn with the *daitō*. Measures from 1 to 2 *shaku*. Commoners were permitted to wear it for protection.

Waku: Doubt, hesitation, and indecision. State of mind prohibited in kendo.

Waza: Technique.

Y

Yagyū Sekishūsai Muneyoshi: Founder of the Yagyū Shinkage ryū. Studied under Kamiizumi (Kōzumi) Ise no Kami Nobutsuna.

Yagyū Tajima no Kami Munenori (1571–1646): Fifth son of Yagyū Sekishūsai Muneyoshi, Munenori was chief kendo instructor and *sōmetsuke* (police chief) for the Tokugawa shōgunate, and author of *Hyōhōka Densho*.

Yakumaru Gyōbuzaemon (1607–1689): Student of Tōgō Shigetaka who further improved the Jigen ryū, known as Yakumaru Jigen ryū.

Yamaoka Tesshū (1836–1888): Son of a Tokugawa retainer and student of Chiba Shūsaku, Tesshū is credited with saving Tokyo from the ruins of war by negotiating with an enemy general.

Yame: Halt.

Yokogane: Horizontal metal bars at the front of *men*, which protect the face.

Yoko ichimonji: The number one, written in *kanji*.

Yokote: Perpendicular line that borders the *kissaki* or one end of the *bōshi*.

Yonhonme: Fourth form.

Yotsukata chichi: Four leather loops at the corners of the *dō* where the *munehimo* and *koshi himo* are attached.

Yū: Courage.

Yūkō datotsu: Strike or hit counted as an *ippon*. Must meet criteria of *ki-ken-tai ittchi* and *zanshin*.

Z

Zangetsu: A *kamae* in Nitō ryū; long *shinai* is diagonal to floor over the *men* in preparation for *ukenagashi.*

Zanshin: Maintaining alertness over the fallen opponent.

Zarei: Bow from the *seiza* position.

Zekken/nafuda: Name tag, located at the center ōtare portion of the *tare.*

Zen: Sect of Buddhism. Has great influence on kendo and permeates Japanese culture in general.

Zen Ken Ren: Abbreviation of Zen Nihon Kendo Renmei.

Zen Nihon Kendo Renmei: All Japan Kendo Federation, sometimes called Zen Ken Ren.

Zen Nihon Kendo Renmei Iai: All Japan Kendo Federation Iai.

Zenshin: Advance.

Zenshin kōtai: Advance and retreat.

References

All Japan Kendo Federation. *Kendo Fundamentals,* Vols. 1 and 2. Tokyo: Satou-Insyokan, 1995.

————. *Nihon Kendo Kata Kaisetsusho.* Tokyo: Zen Nihon Kendo Federation, 1985.

Andou, Kouzou. *Kendo Vocabulary.* Tokyo: Tōshinsha, 1995.

Armstrong, William. *Around the World with a King.* Tokyo: Charles E. Tuttle Company, 1977.

Baba, Kinji. "Kendo: Dentō no Gijyutsu." *Ski Journal,* 1995.

Bisignani, J. D. *Japan Handbook.* California: Moon Publications, 1983.

Chamberlain, Basil Hall, trans. *The Kojiki Records of Ancient Matters.* Tokyo: Charles E. Tuttle Co., 1981.

Ezuchi, Kōkichi, et al. *Kendo Renshūhō Hyakka.* Tokyo: Taishūkan Shoten, 1991.

Fu, Freddie, and David Stone. *Sports Injuries.* Baltimore: Williams & Wilkins, 1994.

Hawaii Kendo Federation. www.hawaiikendo.com.

Hirakawa, Nobuo. "Kendo." *Baseball Magazine,* 1995.

Iho, Kyotsugu. "Shin Kendo Jōtatsu Kōza." *Ski Journal,* 1994.

Ikenami, Shōtaro. *Bokuden Saigo no Tabi.* Tokyo: Kadokawa Bunko, 1980.

————. *Kondo Isami Hakusho.* Tokyo: Kadokawa Shobō, 1972.

————. *Nobunaga to Hideyoshi to Ieyasu.* Tokyo: PHP Kenkyusho, 1993.

Ishibe, Kōji. *Kendo Yōgu Manual*. Saitama, Japan: Fukuda Kikaku, 1994.

Iso, Kiyotsugu. "Kendo Hisshō Kōza." *Ski Journal*, 1987.

Iwasaki, Tamihei, and Jujiro Kawamura. *New English-Japanese Dictionary*. Tokyo: Kenkyusha, 1960.

Japanese-English Dictionary of Kendo. Tokyo: All Japan Kendo Federation, 2000.

Kanazawa, Shozaburō. *Kōjiri*. Tokyo: Sanshōdō, 1935.

Katana to Kendo. Tokyo: Yūzankaku, November 1932.

Kawada, Tokukaku. *Kendo Kyokun Roku*. Ed. Kaga Yoshihiro. Aichi, Japan: Yamada Printing, 1995.

Keishicho Kendo Renmei. *Kendo no Shiori*. 1999.

Kendo Jidai monthly periodical.

"Kendo Nippon." *Ski Journal*.

Kendo Nippon Editorial Board. "Kōdansha e no Michi." *Ski Journal*, 1994.

Kogure, Mikio. *Himo to Rope no Musubikata Hyakka*. Tokyo: Shinsei Shuppansha, 1997.

Kumamoto Ken Kendo Renmei. *Kendo Shodokuhon*.

Lueras, Leonard. *Kanyaku Imin 1885–1985*. Honolulu: Toppan Printing Company, 1985.

Maki, Hidehiko. *Kengi-Kenjutsu*. Tokyo: Shinkigensha, 1999.

Makoto, Sugawa. *Lives of Master Swordsmen*. Tokyo: The East Publications, 1985.

Matsukawa, Budō. *Kendo Iaido Gakkashinsa Mondaishu*. Osaka: Nihonbudo Buka Kai, 1969.

Matsunobu, Ichiji, et al. *Kendo Zukai Coach*. Tokyo: Narumidō, 1987.

Miyamoto, Musashi. *The Book of Five Rings*. Trans. Victor Harris. New York: Overlook Press, 1974.

———. *The Book of Five Rings*. Trans. Steven Kaufman. Boston: Charles E. Tuttle Company, 1994.

———. *The Book of Five Rings*. Trans. Ōkōchi Shōji. Tokyo: Kyoikusha, 1992.

———. *The Book of Five Rings*. Trans. Watanabe Ichiro. Tokyo: Iwanami Shoten, 1985.

———. *The Book of Five Rings*. Trans. Matsumoto Michihiro and William Scott Wilson. Tokyo: Kōdansha, 2001.

Nakamura, Taizaburō. *Iai Kendo*. Tokyo: Santō Sha, 1973.

Nihon Kendo Kata. All Japan Kendo Federation. Videocassette.

———. Andou Kouzou. Videocassette. Produced and published by T & H, 1995.

Nippon Budo Bunkakai. *Kendo/Iaido Gakka Shinsa Mondaishu*. Osaka: Nippon Budō Bunkakai, 1969.

Nitobe, Inazō. *Bushido*. Trans. Naramoto Tatsuya. Tokyo: Mikasa Shobō, 1993.

———. *Bushido: The Soul of Japan*. Tokyo: Tuttle Publishing, 1969.

Nitōsai, Arazeki. *Nitō Ryū no Naraikata*. Tokyo: Sōshinsha, 1994.

Noma, Seiji, ed. *Budo Jikkan: Showa Tenran Shiai Henshūkyoku*. Tokyo: Dai Nippon Yubenkai Kōdansha, 1934.

Ohtsuka, T., et al. *Nobinobi Kendo Gakko*. Tokyo: Sosha, 1969.

Okuyama, Kyōsuke. "Shōnen Kendo Shidō Kōza." *Ski Journal*, 1986.

Otake, Risuke. *Katori Shintō Ryū: The Deity and the Sword*. Tokyo: Minato Research, 1977.

Ozawa, Hiroshi. *Kendo: The Definitive Guide*. Tokyo: Kodansha, 1997.

Sasamori, Junzō. *Ittō Ryū Gokui*. Tokyo: Taiiku to Supōtsu Shuppansha, 1985.

————, and Gordon Warner. *This Is Kendo*. Tokyo: Charles E. Tuttle Co., 1964.

Sato, Nariaki. *Kendo: Seme no Jōseki. Ski Journal*, 1987.

Schwartz, George, et al. *Principle and Practice of Emergency Medicine*. Philadelphia: W. B. Saunders Company, 1986.

Sen, Sōshitsu. *Chado: The Japanese Way of Tea*. Tokyo: Weatherhill, 1990.

————. *Ochano Michishirube*. Tokyo: Shufuno Tomo, 1984.

————. *Urasenke Chado no Oshie*. Tokyo: Nippon Hōso Kyōkai, 1986.

Shaw, George Russell. *Knots*. New York: Bonanza Books, 1933.

Shiba, Ryotaro. *Bakumatsu*. Tokyo: Bungei Shunjū, 1977.

————. *Hokutono Hito*. Tokyo: Kōdansha, 1972.

————. *Saigo no Shōgun*. Tokyo: Bungei Shunjū, 1997.

————. *Shinsetsu Miyamoto Musashi*. Tokyo: Kōdansha Bunko, 1983.

Shizawa, Kunio, and Hakamada Daizō. *Irasuto Kendo*. Tokyo: Satsuki Shobō, 1987.

————, et al. "Kendo." *Baseball Magazine*, 1988.

Suzuki, Monjiro. *Tsukahara Bokuden*. Tokyo: Ōkawaya Shoten, 1911.

Tobe, Shinjūro. *Miyamoto Musashi Kōshō*. Tokyo: PHP Kenkyusha, 1990.

Tokeshi, Jinichi. *Kendo Aiea Taiheiji Kendo Manual*. Honolulu, 1995.

Tsumoto, Yō. *Buno Kokoro*. Tokyo: Bungei Shunjū, 1996.

————. *Chiba Shusaku*. Tokyo: Kōdansha, 1991.

————. *Katsugokui Ikirugokui*. Tokyo: Kōdansha, 1991.

————. *Ken ni Kakeru*. Tokyo: Gentōsha, 1997.

————. *Kikotsu no Hito*. Tokyo: Kadokawa Bunko, 1995.

————. *Miyamoto Musashi*. Tokyo: Bungei Shunjū, 1985.

————. *Nobunaga Shiki*. Tokyo: Shinchōsha, 1991.

————. *Shuzaya Yasubei*. Tokyo: Kōbunsha, 1996.

Ueda, Tadao. *Shin Nihon Rekishi Zukan*. Tokyo: Ikueisha, 1951.

Warshaw, Steven. *Japan Emerges*. Berkeley: Diablo Press, 1990.

Yamatsuta, Shigeyoshi. *Musōshinden Ryū Iaido*. Tokyo: Airyudo.

Yoshikawa, Eiji. *Musashi*. Trans. Charles Terry. New York: Pocket Books, 1989.

Zen Nippon Kendo Renmei. *Kendo Iaido Jōdo Kōdansha Meikan*. Tokyo: Sōken, 1979.

Index

About the Author

Jinichi Tokeshi, M.D., was born and raised in Japan. After completing his medical studies in Hawai'i and Michigan, he opened a private practice in Honolulu and began teaching at the John A. Burns School of Medicine, University of Hawai'i. He has attained a *yondan* in kendo and a *sandan* in *iaido*.

Production Notes for Tokeshi/KENDO: ELEMENTS,
RULES, AND PHILOSOPHY

Cover and interior design, and composition by Argosy.
Text in Bembo with display type in Bembo Bold.

Printing and binding by Versa Press, Inc.

Printed on 60 lb. Starbrite Opaque.